Changing Minds

Mind, Consciousness and Identity
in Patañjali's Yoga-sūtra and
Cognitive Neuroscience

India's Scientific Heritage

Founder Editor : Late Dr L M Singhvi

14

Changing Minds

Mind, Consciousness and Identity in Patañjali's Yoga-sūtra and Cognitive Neuroscience

MICHELE MARIE DESMARAIS

MOTILAL BANARSIDASS PUBLISHERS
PRIVATE LIMITED • DELHI

First Edition: ***2008***

ISBN: 978-81-208-3328-9

MOTILAL BANARSIDASS
41 U.A. Bungalow Road, Jawahar Nagar, Delhi 110 007
8 Mahalaxmi Chamber, 22 Bhulabhai Desai Road, Mumbai 400 026
236, 9th Main III Block, Jayanagar, Bangalore 560 011
203 Royapettah High Road, Mylapore, Chennai 600 004
Sanas Plaza, 1302 Baji Rao Road, Pune 411 002
8 Camac Street, Kolkata 700 017
Ashok Rajpath, Patna 800 004
Chowk, Varanasi 221 001

Printed in India
BY JAINENDRA PRAKASH JAIN AT SHRI JAINENDRA PRESS,
A-45 NARAINA, PHASE-I, NEW DELHI 110 028
AND PUBLISHED BY NARENDRA PRAKASH JAIN FOR
MOTILAL BANARSIDASS PUBLISHERS PRIVATE LIMITED,
BUNGALOW ROAD, DELHI 110 007

Dedication

for my Teacher
Prof. Ashok Aklujkar
with deepest respect and gratitude

Contents

Acknowledgements ix
Foreword xiii
Abbreviations xix
Introduction: Getting Ready for the Show 1

CHAPTERS

1. Entering the Theatre 7
2. Taking the Stage 23
3. All the World's a Stage 83
4. Following the Plot 123
5. The Plot Thickens 177
6. Lights Up 213

References 227
Index 247

Acknowledgements

It was my great privilege as a graduate student at the University of British Columbia, Canada, to study Sanskrit and Indology with Professor Ashok Aklujkar. During my last years studying with him, Prof. Aklujkar and I read the *Yoga-sūtra-bhāṣya* together and this work became the basis of my dissertation. Prof. Aklujkar also encouraged me, throughout my Master's degree and doctorate, to continue developing my knowledge of western psychology and philosophy of mind. Therefore, Prof. Aklujkar's voice and reflections echo in every line of this book. I can honestly say that whatever is of merit in *Changing Minds* is due to Prof. Aklujkar, and whatever errors exist here are entirely my own.

My sincerest thanks to Dr. S. N. Bhavsar in Pune, India for carefully reading and commenting upon the manuscript. His suggestions have strengthened many portions of this book. I am so deeply grateful also for his kindness in writing the preface for *Changing Minds*. Many thanks also to Dr. L. Mahadevan at Śrī Śāradā Āyurvedic hospital in Tamil Nadu for taking time from a busy schedule to review the manuscript and encourage this and future works.

My doctoral dissertation, which examined mind-body concepts in the *Yoga-sūtra* (YS) and western philosophy of mind, was in part inspired by Dr. Gerald James Larson's article "Classical Yoga Philosophy and Some Issues in Philosophy of Mind." Later, Dr. Larson was the external examiner for my dissertation. I thank him, and the doctoral committee, for their comments and encouraging words about that initial research.

The research and writing for *Changing Minds* was largely done during my time as an Assistant Professor at the University of Nebraska at Omaha (UNO). My colleagues in the Philosophy and Religious Studies programs not only encouraged me in this work, but also excused me from service duties in the department, and provided me, sometimes at great cost to themselves, with a protective shield behind which I could complete the book. Professors Bill Blizek, Dale Stover, Paul Williams, Guy Matalon and Rory Conces, along with Kathryn Schwartz, have become friends as well as respected colleagues over these years. I count myself as truly fortunate to have such people in my life. I can never thank them enough for their kindness and support.

My students at UNO inspire me with their questions, enthusiasm and deep commitment to the study of Sanskrit. Here I would particularly like to acknowledge and thank Todd Daganaar, Tammi Owens, Sarah Moulton and Andrea Porter. When I moved to Omaha, Nebraska I was also pleasantly surprised to find several schools of Yoga that pay particular attention to the Classical tradition and practice of Yoga. I had the great pleasure of teaching classes on the YS at the Omaha Yoga School where founder Margaret Hahn and her students inspired me with their dedication and challenged me with their questions. Similarly, it has been a great pleasure to meet and work with Susi Gillespie Amendola, founder and director of Omaha Yoga and Bodywork Center, and her students. These teachers and practitioners remind me of the rich, lived, tradition of Yoga.

Friends have cheered me on and given me every kind of encouragement throughout the years of work on this book. Here I especially thank Tanya Chapman, Anusha Fernando, Dr. Anne E. MacDonald, Dr. Paul Burns, Karen Kempkes, Dr. Beth Ritter, Dr. Judy Boss and Scott Hoffman. Many thanks also to my friend Alan Baker who not only cheered me on but helped me with computer support.

Finally, to my family—Mom, Dad, Brad, Elizabeth, Robert, Brian, Helen, Nancy and John—many many thanks for all your kindnesses and unfailing support. I couldn't have done this without you. And to my husband, Bill, you lived through every line of this book with me and kept me smiling (and fed) throughout. You are beyond my dreams. Thank you.

One last note: when I was a graduate student, I found that I could purchase some of the best books in Indology because Motilal Banarsidass published them and made them available at reasonable prices. My shelves are lined with classic books in the field, such as Dasgupta's *History of Indian Philosophy*, Sinha's *Indian Psychology*, and too many more to mention. I cannot express enough my deep gratitude to Motilal Banarsidass for spreading knowledge of Indological texts and traditions throughout the world. *Changing Minds*, which has been patiently guided to completion by Śrī R. P. Jain at the Delhi branch of Motilal Banarsidass, is my own humble thanks for all that I have been given.

Foreword

This book by Dr. Desmarais is by all means a positive contribution in the field of Yoga, Indology and cognitive neurosciences. It covers Eastern and Western, ancient and modern, religion and metaphysics, psychology and epistemology, as well as the cultural heritage for these.

The book is arranged in six chapters using our common concept of show as a metaphysical stage: getting ready for the show; entering the theatre; taking the stage; all the world as stage; following the plot; thickening of the plot; and finally, the lights come up. This has its source in the Sāṃkhya metaphor of *prakṛti* as analogous to a divine actor, on the world stage and in a cosmic drama. Another symbolic metaphor that comes before our mind is that of Ardhanārīnāṭeśvara of Lord Śiva, depicted as the Cosmic divine Supreme actor endowed with half-female in his person. The reader, the spectator or audience member, symbolizes the Puruṣa of Sāṃkhya and Yoga.

The author, using this structure, provides an excellent exposition of the contents of the Yoga-sūtra (YS) text of Patañjali; serially, with all its major technical terms and concepts. Dr. Desmarais, with utmost care and balance, focuses on mind, consciousness and identity as the central trinity. Within this, the complex issue of mind and its relation to matter is considered from a number of dimensions in the YS.

Accompanying this explanation of mind, consciousness and identity in the YS, is a parallel exposition of these topics from the perspective of the cognitive neurosciences today. The book successfully fulfills the aim of bridging the gap between what belongs culturally to the West, and what belongs to the East. The one side exhibits the material objective character, the other subjective spiritual—the two dimensional profile of man. The task is certainly not an easy one. But Dr. Desmarais remarkably has accomplished this task. With both the traditions, the author displays a very close familiarity. This is due to two strong holds. One is her semantic and etymological approach to technical terms in Sanskrit, the other is her clear integral vision. Dr. Desmarais knows and states that the YS is of an interdisciplinary nature. So also are the cognitive neurosciences. The exposition and the interpretation by her of the important terms are very clear, appropriate and significant. Among the most noteworthy of these terms are: *puruṣa*, *prakṛti*, *manas*, *buddhi*, *ahaṃkāra*, *citta*, *vṛttis*, *nidrā* (*turīya*), *smṛti*, *saṃyoga*, *abhyāsa*, *vairāgya*, and lastly the *kaivalya.* In this march she has taken into account important Sanskrit commentaries and translations, modern authors and their interpretations, and, wherever necessary, provides her own translations and analysis. Dr. Desmarais takes the reader through a brief survey of Yoga tradition before and after Patañjali: through Vedas, Upaniṣads, Gītā, up to Jainism and Buddhism—Yoga being the common internal disciple for all. Similarly she provides an overview of relevant topics in the cognitive neurosciences till to date. Dr. Desmarais' treatment of the subject, so complex and wide, is judicious, positive and constructive in spirit.

The author is well nigh aware of the internal difficulties while paraphrasing and explaining terms, and tries to minimize these by descriptively defining and interpreting the concepts. No less aware is she of the external difficulties that one faces while switching over from one language to another that belongs to a distant family, such as the Sanskrit (ancient India) and English (modern European) languages, subjects and traditions. She declares rightly that exact translation of Sanskrit terms is not possible, very often the words need to be accepted as they are and supplemented with the nearest translation possible or a word approximately synonymous in meaning. Dr. Desmarais' resolution of these difficulties is well acceptable. One of her observations about Yogic research, assessment and evaluation needs to be noted and highlighted. **Yoga is a practice, a field of experience, subjective in nature**. The number of cases for research is very small compared to other fields. The experience is ever changing. As for instruments, they have limited capability, a limited range of applications (confined to part not to whole), and also are subject to interpretation. The results often are not consistent or similar, but sometimes contradictory, or controversial. While analysis based upon research in the neurosciences on Yoga is interesting, under such conditions much of it must necessarily remain hypothetical.

Such limitations come even clearer to light if we consider the issue of bi-laterality. In living beings respiration mechanism is bilateral. Bi-laterality is in fact neglected even in modern medicine. Instead, we treat the body only as a whole. The tests carried about of blood, sugar, cholesterol or the measurements taken of blood pressure, temperature, resistance or other neuro-cognitive responses are not bilateral, nor simultaneous, so experimental results show discrepancies or anomalies here as well.

Thus there is need to understand and develop bilateral anatomy, bilateral physiology, bilateral pathosymptomology and bilateral therapeutics to do justice to not only Yogic practices but to any prescription of medicine, diet and lifestyle (*auṣadha*, *anna*, *vihāra*), to be corroborated by in vivo (clinical, subjective) and in vitro (objective, laboratory) experiments. The total picture and total perspective arising from these developments would be more meaningful.

In this context it has to be noted that there is a deep-seated problem about mind, as a substance/category, its location, function and nature. In fact this is true of all the inner faculties. Modern science does not officially accept them as there is no objective proof for their existence or location, nor does it accept them *a priori* like previous science (classical or ancient), or like Indian sciences or most of the schools of philosophy. How, therefore, can these experiments be made? So the inner faculties are beyond experiments to date. The research is confined only up to the nervous system and structural part of the brain. Inner faculties are functional, but brain, nerves etc. are structural. Only by mutual correspondence and inference can we assert their existence, contents and their meaning. This involves all the fundamentally important issues: structure–function, subjective-objective, experience-experiment, *a priori-a posteriori*.

Modern medicine (life sciences, cognitive neurosciences) follows modern science, therefore it does not accept inner faculties officially, but could not escape them in practice or in clinics. This is the situation in mathematics: AB - BA, whose converse may or may not be true. Yoga and Āyurveda took the positive view, accepting the inner faculties as a priori and also functional in character, yet further assigned material or substantial status to them. Their location has been assigned to the heart, in light of meditation and contemplation (subjective experience and experiment with eyes closed generally), while the brain (head) is accepted as a place of manifestation (*indriya-sthāna*), a field of sensory perceptions; in fact the whole body is an extension of the same.

Once this position is accepted, then it is within the realm of physics and the laws of physics. Functional modification, expansion, extension, mutation, transformation is then possible. *Rasāyana* and *vājīkaraṇa* (revitalization, rejuvenation, stimulant) are the two classes and *cyāvanaprāśa*, *brahma-rasāyana*, *bhallātaka-rasāyana* and all mercurial and sulphur compound products called *Bhasmas*, are the examples in this direction. *Kāyakalpa* i.e. the technique and the procedure to transform the psychosomatic person aimed at this. *Khecharīvati*, and Yogic *Khechārīmudrā* run parallel to achieve levitation, aerial flight etc. Patañjali's Sūtra in which the author has elucidated "*jāty-antara-pariṇāmaḥ prakṛty-āpūrāt*," is noteworthy in this context. Modern genetic engineering would make this claim objectively possible tomorrow. It would be a culmination of cognitive neurosciences, when Quantum Field Theory practically achieves Grand Unification. If modern science positively incorporates observer and inner faculties, in addition to genetic engineering, there certainly would be emergence of Great Grand Unified Theory of modern science.

Yoga subjectively, and Āyurveda, objectively on an individual, and a very small scale, no doubt, have paved the path in this march. They displayed not only a model, not only a method but also a procedure, which would remain a psycho-physiological standard, parallel to the modern scientific achievements.

The technical term plasticity (or neuroplasticity), used by the author, when abstracted would be analogous to fluidity i.e. the field of Fluid Mechanics, that would cover hydrodynamics, thermodynamics, aerodynamics and space dynamics. From this, we can correlate the earth, water, heat, air and ether of ancient sciences, to a great extent. If this is accepted, then the role of air (*pneuma*), the bridge between all the rest of the elements and principles, would become more prominent and pronounced. Then further the role of *vāyu* (*prāṇa*, breath) as a link, a bridge between microcosm (bilateral respiration mechanism in living beings) and macrocosm, would become clear. As Nyāya, Yoga and Āyurveda accept, air accommodates thermal and hydraulic properties as a continuum (heat-cold), and spatial properties also. Operationally then, air appears like a complex conjugate that unifies QM and GR theories harmoniously. This is the message of Yoga and Āyurveda to be precise. Modern science has to elevate itself to that height, which would imply an integral version of it, by accommodating religion, metaphysics, philosophy and epistemology. Dr. Desmarais' book is definitely a step ahead in this progression. Therefore aptly she states that Patañjali's Yoga-sūtras stand for a transformative approach to human resource development.

Changing Minds is the title and aim also of the book.

Pune *Dr. S. N. Bhavsar*

Abbreviations

AV	*Atharva-veda*
BhG	*Bhagavad-Gītā*
CS	*Caraka-saṃhitā*
Kaṭha	*Kaṭha Upaniṣad*
MBh	*Mahābhārata*
MU	*Maitrāyaṇi Upaniṣad*
RV	*Ṛg-veda*
SK	*Sāṃkhya-kārikā*
TV	*Tattva-vaiśāradį*
Up	*Upaniṣad*
YBh	*Yoga-bhāṣya*
YS	*Yoga-sūtra*
YSBhV	*Yoga-sūtra-bhāṣya-vivaraṇa*

Introduction

Getting Ready for the Show

Mind, Consciousness and Identity in the *Yoga-sūtra* and Cognitive Neuroscience

Most of us love to go to the theatre. Whether we are watching a movie or a very good play, going to a show allows us to forget ourselves and to be caught up, affected for better or worse, by the events that play out before us on the stage or movie screen. No matter how riveting the show, however, we are separate and the events on stage or on the screen are in no way directly caused by us. We are at the theatre as witnesses to events and we have no other role. When the show ends, the lights come up, we return to our sense of reality and we leave the theatre.

In the Indian schools of Yoga and Sāṃkhya, *puruṣa* (Self, soul) is the witness of *prakṛti's* (material nature's) workings, particularly the workings of the mind, just as an audience member watches a play. But what does it mean to witness the mind, or to be conscious of awareness, or to be aware of consciousness? What, in fact, do we mean when we use terms such as "mind," or "consciousness," or "identity"?

The *Yoga-sūtra* (YS) of Patañjali is a 2nd or 3rd century C.E. Sanskrit text that is the foundation for the classical Yoga tradition. It influences many later forms of Yoga and modern practitioners of

Yoga still study these *sūtras*. The YS combines elements of psychology, a dualistic metaphysics, epistemology, and categories of practices that are meant to enable a person to attain *kaivalya* (liberation). While the text is well known and many translations exist, there is little consensus regarding how to translate key terms that are roughly synonymous with mind, consciousness, conscious awareness, thought, intellect and cognition. Two major problems arise from this situation. First, the definition and purpose of Pātañjala Yoga rely on our understanding of the phrase "*yogaś citta-vṛtti-nirodhaḥ*" (Yoga is the suppression/cessation of the processes of the mind-field/intellect/cognition) (YS 1.2).[1] A lack of clarity regarding the nature of mind, intellect, and cognition, as well as ambiguity over the translation of *nirodha* (suppression *or* cessation), means that the very definition of Yoga remains unclear. A second problem arises because translation is not explanation, particularly for terms such as 'consciousness.' Furthermore, modern psychology and the neurosciences lead us now to revise or modify what we mean by 'mind,' 'consciousness,' and 'identity.'

The purpose of this study therefore, is to explore, as thoroughly as possible, the transformative psychology and philosophy of mind in the YS, and then to propose, on the basis of this, a definition of Yoga according to YS 1.2. As the YS itself is interdisciplinary, our fullest understanding of the text will only come about if we preserve and respect this interdisciplinary nature. That is, we must not ignore philosophy in favor of spirituality, or psychology in favor of philology, or practice in favor of history.

---

[1] Madras Government Oriental Series, Government Oriental Manuscripts Library, Madras, 1952. This edition contains the *Yoga-sūtra* (YS), *Yoga-bhāṣya* (YBh), and *Yoga-sūtra-bhāṣya-vivaraṇam* (YSBhV). Unless otherwise noted, all translations provided are my own.

Although Grinshpon[2] is correct in noting that the YS does not seem to present in a direct way the results of personal experience or observation, a significant portion of the YS examines practice and the results of practice. We can assume, given the brevity of *sūtra*-style texts, that these, at some point, were considered too important to omit. Close attention must be paid to these sections of the text. Indeed, modern philosophers often use thought experiments in order to support and explore a theory or perspective. In some ways, we can view the practices in the YS as a type of thought experiment. According to this thought experiment, given a certain system of metaphysics and a particular perspective on psychology, various practices will effect changes in a person's mind, consciousness and identity. They may even, according to this tradition, bring about a state of liberation (*kaivalya*). We must therefore explore each element of the YS, and yet be clear from the start that it is difficult to maintain a perspective, as the YS does, that incorporates psychology, philosophy, tradition and practice.

The basis of this book is a traditional philological, philosophical and psychological analysis of terms and concepts as they appear in the YS and, where relevant, in the broader Indian tradition, but this represents only a portion of this study. The YS also describes a transformational psychology that is almost entirely based upon *prakṛti*, material nature. In other words, mind is largely explained in terms of matter.

This perspective on mind as matter has a number of parallels with modern cognitive neuroscience. I do not mean to imply that I equate the YS with current programs of research in the

---

[2] Grinshpon, 1997, 557ff.

neurosciences. Yet both the YS and cognitive neuroscience—along with modern psychology and philosophy of mind—share interests in explaining the relation between mind and matter, and in examining the nature and functions of the mind and consciousness. The YS therefore represents part of the world's heritage of serious explorations on these topics. In turn, modern psychology and cognitive neuroscience can encourage clarity in terminology. These fields can remind us that even when we are satisfied that we have translated a term correctly as "mind," or "consciousness," we must still seek to uncover what these terms mean in the YS, and to be aware of how a reader might currently understand these terms. Beyond this, cognitive neuroscience can help to explain the relationship between mind (consciousness, identity) and matter. Some Indologists have been reluctant to even translate *prakṛti* as matter or material nature because of the concern that matter implies only such things as rocks, houses, bodies, etc. but not minds, emotions, identity, and thoughts. The YS includes all of these under *prakṛti*, and cognitive neuroscience aims to explain these in terms of matter as well, albeit with differences. Finally, to the extent that we regard the practices in the YS *at least* as a thought experiment, and perhaps even as practices that are actually to be performed (as indeed they are still to this day), then cognitive neuroscience and psychology can allow us to push the thought experiment further. *What if*, we may ask, someone actually did these practices? What would happen? Which, if any, studies actually examine these practices and what have they found? Given what we know now about the nature of the mind/brain, what might a person be like who undertook some of the practices that we find in the YS? Can a real world, or scientific, analysis in the end shed any light on the final stages and purposes of Yoga?

In this book, Chapter One gives a brief overview of Yoga history and also provides an introduction to the structure and nature of the YS itself. Chapter Two examines the dualistic metaphysics of the YS and then explores psychology—the nature of mind, consciousness and identity—in the YS. Before moving to the practice and results sections of the YS though, Chapter Three looks briefly at some similar topics—such as mind and matter, consciousness, perception, sleep, memory and so forth—from the perspective of cognitive neuroscience. Chapter Four then explores the three categories of practice in the YS: *abhyāsa-vairāgya* (repeated practice and detachment), *kriyā-yoga* (yoga of activity), and *aṣṭāṅga-yoga* (eightfold yoga). Chapter Five includes an analysis of the effects of some Yoga practices again from the perspective of cognitive neuroscience. In some cases we have studies that help in exploring these topics. Even where these studies are lacking, or are of limited use, reference to physical processes such as neuroplasticity can help us to understand how Yoga practice might affect the mind/brain. Taking all these perspectives into account, Chapter Six explores the final stages or results of Yoga. In the end, just as an actor slips off the stage, or an audience member leaves the theatre, we must allow the YS and tradition to step away from language, concepts, material nature and, consequently, scientific study. Until that point, an interdisciplinary perspective best represents the actual composition of the YS, and cognitive neuroscience provides us with a useful perspective on many facets of this interesting text.

Despite the reference to cognitive neuroscience, the foundation of *Changing Minds* is Indological. The Western chapters are largely separate from the Indian chapters, and the topics are first examined within the context of the YS alone. The YS provides the foundation for later research and theories. I am also cautious and critical about reading modern or Western concepts into the YS. If nothing else, this study serves as a reminder that practices and theories relating to mind, identity and consciousness have a cultural context that informs their usage and meaning.

The poet T.S. Eliot once wrote, "a people without history / Is not redeemed from time." The modern science of mind is fascinating and challenging. It is my hope that this book communicates something of that excitement and challenge, while at the same time serving as a bridge to an equally fascinating, challenging and exciting heritage—an ancient tradition that reached its finest expression in the *Yoga-sūtra* of Patañjali.

One

Entering the Theatre

The History and Structure of the *Yoga-sūtra*

Yoga is likely one of the oldest spiritual practices of humankind that is still practiced. This does not mean though that we have an unbroken or homogenous tradition of Yoga, nor even that we can trace a clear history of Yoga. Instead, we have early suggestions of practices and concepts that grow, emerge clearly in the scriptures of the *Upaniṣads* and the epic *Mahābhārata*, and then are systematized, representing a Classical school of thought and practice, in the *Yoga-sūtra* of Patañjali. Certain practices are also included in heterodox movements such as Buddhism and Jainism. After the systematization of Yoga, a great flourishing of practices takes place, but the Yoga-sūtra is widely recognized as the essential text on Yoga philosophy and practice.

YOGA

The YS provides a definition of the word "yoga,"

yogaś citta-vṛtti-nirodhaḥ.[1]

---

[1] YS 1.2

We may provisionally translate this *sūtra* as "yoga is the suppression/cessation of the processes of the intellect/mind/cognition," but the technical terms within the definition require us to understand the YS as a whole, and specifically the nature of mind, consciousness, identity, and liberation, in order to arrive at an accurate understanding of this crucial definition.

As much as the YS provides us with this definition of "yoga," the word and the tradition are much older than the YS itself. The word "yoga" is derived from the root *yuj*, "to connect or attach, yoke," "to concentrate," or "to use or employ."[2] Each of these meanings applies in some way to Pātañjala Yoga. The YS lists mental exercises that control or yoke the mind and states of concentration that arise from such exercises. These practices and states are then the means—that is, their use is—to attain *kaivalya*, literally "being alone, singularity, independence," which may have the connotation of liberation. Commentaries on the YS, perhaps intent on communicating the essence of Yoga, relate the word more to the second aspect, concentration. For instance, the main commentary on the YS, the Yoga-bhāṣya (YBh) states

> *yogaḥ samādhi*
> "Yoga is the complete stationing [of the mind]."[3]

---

[2] Monier-Williams.

[3] YBh 1.1. *Samādhi* is a problematic word to translate. It is composed from *sam+ā+dhā*, which means "to put together," "to concentrate." The derivation might lead one to translate *samādhi* as "concentration," as Woods does (1914, 3). However, *dhāraṇā* may also be translated as "concentration," since it means "holding the mind on [X]." *Dhyāna* is usually translated as meditation, so "meditation" is not an appropriate translation for *samādhi*. Since scholars offer various translations of this key term, for example *samādhi* as "contemplative calm" (Miller 1995, 34) or "enstasy" (Feuerstein [1979]1989, 40), it seems best to simplify the situation and leave "*samādhi*,"—literally

This technical meaning, however, is likely a later development.[4]

One of the earliest uses of the word "yoga" is in the *Ṛg-veda* (RV) where it designates a union or connection between things, for instance the connection between words of a verse. In the *Athavarva-Veda* (AV), the word clearly relates to the English word "yoking," as it refers to a collection of bullocks and the plough that connects these animals. [5] In later times, this aspect of yoking applies to the person and the senses. For example, in *Kaṭha Upaniṣad*,[6] which is an early middle *Upaniṣad* dating from around the 4th century BCE, the intellect is compared to a charioteer, the body to a chariot, the mind to reins, and the senses to horses. The term "*yuktena*" here gives a strong sense of disciplining the mind (*manas*) and not merely the joining of mind, body and senses. In this manner, an extension of a term that originally may have meant simple joining or yoking takes place whereby it comes to mean a system or method through which the mind and senses can be disciplined or controlled.[7] Finally, the word "*yukti*" ("reasoning" "argument") is also derived from √*yuj*, and even "*yoga*" itself is occasionally used in this sense of "reasoning" in the Nyāya (Logic) and Vaiśeṣika (Atomism, school of ontology) systems of thought.[8]

Thus as we piece together what we know of the history of Yoga, we find Sanskrit *śāstra* composers deriving different technical

---

"full-placing" or "complete stationing"—untranslated. The nature of *samādhi* will become clearer when we consider the practice and results of Pātañjala Yoga.

[4] Joshi, 1965, 53-54.

[5] See, for example RV 10.114.95 and AV 6.91.1. Joshi 1965, 53-54.

[6] *Kaṭha* I.3.3-9.

[7] Joshi 1965, 54.

[8] Halbfass 1988, 278

meanings from the same literal meaning of "yoga," and this is of significance as we seek to understand the nature of mind, body and consciousness in the Yoga tradition. Even a linguistic analysis reveals that while the word "yoga" may primarily mean "yoking" or "concentration" as an action or process noun, the word eventually denotes not only the means of a process, but the entire process toward a result, as well as the result itself. This comprehensive sense of the term "yoga," informs the practice and philosophy of Yoga in the YS.

A BRIEF OVERVIEW OF YOGA HISTORY

Yoga's history may well begin in the ancient Harappan culture of the Indus Valley. Archaeological excavations of this culture have uncovered, among other items, stone seals—dating back perhaps to 2700 BCE—which may have ritualistic as well as economic implications. The most famous of the stone seals is sometimes termed the "proto-Śiva seal." It shows a figure seated on a raised platform. This figure wears a horned headdress, and sits in a meditative-like position with knees pointed to the sides, heels and feet pressed together at the base of the body, and arms quite straight with hands resting on the knees. Most descriptions of the seal do not hesitate in referring to the pose as "yogic-like." Other seals show a similar figure seated with cobras and some scholars view these seals as early depictions of the god Śiva. This association with Śiva is intriguing, as Śiva is later known as "Mahā Yogin," the great or perfect ascetic. Apart from this possible association with Śiva, the seals may well show a form of posture and/or meditation that later becomes common in most forms of yoga.

Early textual references also provide intriguing hints about the possible history of Yoga. RV 10.136, known as the *Keśin* Hymn (*keśin*, "possessing fine or long hair"), appears to describe ascetic practices. In this hymn, the *keśins* have long hair, endure poison and fire, are associated with the wind, and have a vision of heaven or light. The hymn contains highly symbolic language, however it does appear to describe an association of these *keśins* with ascetic practices and remarkable accomplishments. The inclusion of this hymn in the RV, along with the mention of breathing practices in the AV may indicate that, in the Vedic tradition, ritual or sacrificial practices and ascetic practices might have had a close, or at least harmonious, relation.[9] In other words, some acceptance of a diversity of practices and perspectives is present and differences between practices did not necessarily imply disagreements over them.

Over time, yogic practices came to be associated with a dualistic metaphysics known as Sāṃkhya. Precisely when this association took place is not certain, but some of the *Vedas* and the oldest *Upaniṣads* (e.g. *Chāndogya*, *Śvetāśvatara*) contain ideas and motifs that later became assimilated into the Sāṃkhya system.[10]

---

[9] See, for example AV 15.14.15; and 15.15.17 (Werner 1975, 185). Frauwallner maintained that there was a large separation between yogic practices and the Vedic sacrificial cult (1977, 107). Werner's perspective on the development of Yoga is that some independent ascetic practices were gradually incorporated into religious rituals in order to make those rituals more efficacious (Werner 1975, 183). An alternate view would be that the rituals and the practices developed together into the later forms of Yoga (Werner 1975, 185). This is perhaps more likely, since rituals without philosophy are unlikely to have survived. Similarly, rituals without restrictions on the participants are improbable. However the development took place, given that there is no evidence that Brahmins did not respect ascetics *in general*, Werner's view that later on the Brāhmanic culture (from approximately 200 B.C.E. to 200 C.E.) accepted Yoga practices grudgingly (1977, 107) seems overly negative.

[10] The reader is directed to Larson's excellent discussion of Sāṃkhya history in *Classical Sāṃkhya*. Larson (1979, 83-97) notes that there are, for example, passages in

By the time of the *Kaṭha Up*, Sāṃkhya-like speculations are combined with references to Yogic practices.[11] The chariot metaphor referred to earlier is a good example of this combination. Later *Upaniṣads* then begin to refer to a greater number of yogic practices, a sign that these were likely well established, at least in some circles, by that time. For instance, the last five *aṅgas* (limbs) of YS 2.29 along with the practice of meditation on OṂ are mentioned in *Maitrī Up* 6.18. Interestingly enough, by the time of these later *Upaniṣads*, particularly the *Saṃnyāsa* and *Yoga Upaniṣads*, there is more emphasis on postures, breathing exercises and meditation, rather than Sāṃkhya-like theory, although Sāṃkhya-like terminology is still employed.[12]

The *Upaniṣads* are not the only textual source of information on Yoga history. Another main source of information about Yoga practices is found in the *Mahābhārata* (Mbh), particularly the *Mokṣadharma* sections of this huge epic.[13] As in some of the Upaniṣadic texts, passages in the epic speak of withdrawing from sensory experiences; of turning away from the mental hindrances

---

various *Upaniṣads* that may be associated with later Sāṃkhya theories of causation (*Chāndogya Up* 6.2.1-2) and processes of evolution and the later theory of *guṇas* (qualities or strands of primal matter) (*Chāndogya Up* 6.2.3-4 and 6.4.1). There are also enumerations of existents, including seventeen of Classical Sāṃkhya's *tattvas* or twenty-five categories of existence, (*Bṛhadārayaka Up* 4.5.12); the idea that suffering is due to ignorance (*Bṛhadārayaka Up* 4.4.13 ff.); and numerous references to *puruṣa* and *ātman* (soul or Self).

[11] Larson 1979, 96-98.

[12] Larson 1979, 102-103.

[13] Yardi 1987, 309. The *Mokṣadharma* texts or sections are chapters 168-353 in book twelve (critical edition) which is called the *Śāntiparvan*. The *Anugītā*, which is in book fourteen, also offers some information on Yoga, as does the *Bhagavad-Gītā*, which comprises chapters 23-49 of book six (Larson 1979, 108). The texts are dated somewhere in the time period of the fourth or fifth century B.C.E. to the second century C.E. (Larson 1979, 108; Hopkins 1971, 87).

of passion, anger, greed, fear and sleep; and of the emergence of an enhanced state of consciousness. There is also recognition of the importance of moral conduct, specific advice regarding preparation for meditation (for instance, finding a quiet place, and meditating at certain times), and an analysis of meditation objects and progress.[14] Such practices play a significant role in Pātañjala Yoga practice.

The *Bhagavad-Gītā* (BhG) also contains a strong statement regarding the unity of Sāṃkhya and Yoga,

> *ekaṃ sāṃkhyaṃ ca yogaṃ ca*
> *yaḥ paśyati sa paśyati*
> Sāṃkhya and Yoga are one.
> He who sees (this, truly) sees.[15]

This provides further evidence of the coupling of Yoga practice with proto-Sāṃkhya theory. The MBh contains many reference to early Sāṃkhya-like theories. Most notably, there are various enumerations of *tattvas* (existents, principles);[16] references to an ultimate material reality that in classical Sāṃkhya is called *prakṛti*;[17] and many references to *puruṣa*, *ātman*, and *kṣetrajñā* (soul, Self).[18] Such doctrines and theories eventually became the philosophical bases of the classical Yoga school and the classical Sāṃkhya school. Indeed, it was well recognized by MBh times

---

[14] Frauwallner [1973] 1993, 112. In particular, see *Bhagavad-Gītā* 2.53-72.

[15] BhG 5.5.

[16] 12.239.15; 12.267.28.

[17] 12.187.37; 12.298.16.

[18] 12.187.6; 12.291.34; 12.187.1-3. See Larson 1979, 113-115. Larson notes that the Self/soul is referred to in the MBh as an "onlooker" (12.187.1-3) and that it watches or witnesses (*kṣetrajñaḥ paripaśyati*) the *guṇas* (12.187.37, 42) (1979, 115). Such passages indicate that Sāṃkhya-like thinking existed.

that liberation could be achieved through behaviour permeated by conviction generated through logical thought (Sāṃkhya) or through Yoga praxis.[19] The BhG, especially in chapters two and six, discusses these paths in some detail.

Hindu orthodox or *āstika* texts do not exhaust the sources on the historical development of Yoga. Buddhism and Jainism also contain strong strands of Yoga practice. Buddhism in particular, as in *āstika* Yoga, upholds certain moral commandments, stresses the importance of guarding the senses, provides instructions for external preparations for meditation, instructs one to turn the mind away from mental hindrances, and emphasizes liberating insight or knowledge.

Despite correspondences, it may well be impossible to determine if there was a mutual influencing of heterodox (*nāstika*) and orthodox systems, or if one system borrowed the techniques and doctrines of another, or if there was another Yoga tradition from which *āstika* and *nāstika* systems drew. Since biographies of the Buddha record him as having contact with ascetics both prior to and after his enlightenment, it seems likely that there were degrees of borrowing and degrees of independence among individuals, systems of thought, and practice that varied according to time and place.

Thus while we may gain some sense of the development of Yoga practice and Sāṃkhya-Yoga philosophy, the situation is far too complex to trace with any degree of certainty and specificity. Even with the evidence we have, we can conclude that the early historical development of Yoga was unlikely to have been a linear or unitary process. We have, more likely, many strands of thought

---

[19] Frauwallner [1973] 1993, 224.

and practice, some of which are recorded in scriptures and epic texts. Some of these early strands are then found in Patañjali's YS. It is for this reason that many regard Patañjali as a great systematizer in the Yoga tradition, rather than its founder.

PATAÑJALI

The YS is widely acknowledged to be one of the most important texts in the Hindu tradition and is recognized as the essential text for understanding classical Yoga. Nothing is known about Patañjali, who is given as the author of the text, but some sources identify him with the grammarian Patañjali, who wrote the *Vyākaraṇa-mahābhāṣya*. Legends say that Patañjali (yogin and grammarian) was an incarnation of the mythical serpent Śeṣa. The seemingly biographical sources therefore tell us only that Patañjali was highly regarded and there is no unanimity regarding identification of the yogin Patañjali with the grammarian.[20]

---

[20] Dasgupta identifies the two Patañjalis, grammarian and yogin, primarily based on the date of the YS, which he places earlier than most scholars (not earlier than 147 B.C.E., but likely earlier than the 2nd or 3rd century C.E.) ([1922] 1975, 212; 236-238). According to Dasgupta, the author of the *Vyākaraṇa-mahābhāṣya* was familiar with Sāṃkhya-Yoga metaphysics (for example, the *guṇa* theory) and both texts are in agreement regarding *sphoṭa-vāda*, a view not commonly held in other schools of Indian thought (Dasgupta [1922]1975, 232). Briefly, *sphoṭa-vāda* is the view (*vāda*) that the realizations of phonemes enter the ear and vanish, but an ideation of them remains in the mind and enables us to understand what is said or heard. These ideations, language-units, are called *sphoṭa* ("sound," from √*sphuṭ*, "burst open or into view") (Dasgupta [1920] 1989, 161-162). Since Dasgupta therefore finds nothing to warrant the grammarian Patañjali and the yogin Patañjali not being identified, Dasgupta follows tradition and maintains that the two texts were composed by the same author ([1922] 1975, 232).

Unlike Dasgupta, some other scholars do not identify the author of the YS with the author of the *Mahābhāṣya* (Larson 1979; Frauwallner [1973] 1993). One reason for this is that the commentators who hold the view that the two are the same belong to a much later period than the two texts, therefore their position is not necessarily to be accepted (Bhattacharya 1985, 97). Bhattacharya specifically refutes Dasgupta's evidence for identification by pointing to the vast influence of Sāṃkhya-Yoga philosophy in general, and notes that the term "*sphoṭa*" was not used in the YS or its commentary the *Yoga-*

However they may differ on the identification of grammarian and yogin, all scholars are in agreement that Patañjali was not the founder or originator of Yoga. Rather, the author of the YS was a codifier or systematizer, drawing upon many different practices and ideas. Debate also exists regarding whether or not the author of the YS was himself a practicing yogin. A definitive answer to this, given the problem of identifying Patañjali, is unlikely. What is certain is that the YS gained preeminence over any other treatises on Yoga.

The *Yoga-sūtra*

Dates for the YS's composition vary widely, from approximately 500 B.C.E. to the 2nd or 3rd century C.E., with these latter dates being more commonly accepted among scholars.[21] Although the

---

Bhāṣya (YBh). Further, since "Patañjali" is the name of a *gotra* (family, lineage), it is more than likely that the works were authored by two different Patañjalis (Bhattacharya 1985, 95-97).

[21] Bhattacharya, while admitting that nothing in the text helps us determine its date "with a considerable amount of precision," assigns the YS to a period earlier than 500 B.C.E. (1985, 109; 112). Bhattacharya maintains that scholars who assign the text to a later date do so largely on the basis of references in the text to Buddhist views. However, noting that "it is highly improper to hold that a technical word used in different systems bears one and the same meaning," he finds no direct references to Buddhism in the YS (Bhattacharya 1985, 118; 121). According to Bhattacharya, Patañjali, at any rate, would not have mentioned Buddhist views since the Buddhists didn't have the doctrine of the three *guṇas* (strands) and therefore their views on mind have no relevance for Yoga (1985, 118 ff.). Further, Bhattacharya says that the Buddha might not have mentioned the possibly pre-existing YS because it primarily contains topics that he refused to address (1985, 130).

Schweizer (1993) and Raju (1985) also assign early dates to the YS (circa 4th-2nd century B.C.E.). Dasgupta dates the text as not earlier than 147 B.C.E., but does so on the basis of the *inclusion* of Buddhist views and practices such as cultivation of *maitrī* (friendliness), *karuṇā* (compassion), *muditā* (joy) and *upekṣā* (equanimity) in the YS ([1922] 1975, 236-237). Their inclusion, according to Dasgupta, indicates that the text was composed during a time of mutual influence between Hinduism, Buddhism and Jainism. Therefore he places the YS in the second century B.C.E., before later, more insular forms of Buddhism developed (Dasgupta [1922] 1975, 237-238).

YS may well have been composed at an earlier date, given conflicting theories and the paucity of evidence, it seems best to be conservative and assign the YS a possible date of composition in the early centuries of the common era.

Regarding the title "*Yoga-sūtra*," this is not the title of the text assigned by its author, but rather is a description given by its adherents and readers.[22] According to the first *sūtra*, the title of the YS might rather be "*Yogānuśāsana*," "The Teaching On Yoga." This *anuśāsana* (teaching) on Yoga is in the *sūtra* style, whose brevity makes it suitable as a mnemonic device. Traditionally though, some *sūtras* are also viewed as being like *mantras*, inspired utterances by a *ṛṣi* (seer, sage).[23] Such *mantras* were thought to be capable of producing certain this-worldly or other-worldly physical results if uttered in a proper manner by an eligible person. These utterances derived their supposed efficacy not only through their meanings, but also through their sounds.

The brevity of *sūtras* means that each word was perceived as absolutely necessary and would not be there without valid reason.[24] The wording and inclusion of lists, alternative practices, and definitions of terms, are particularly significant for any study of this text. Patañjali uses a number of terms associated with Sāṃkhya (and possibly other systems of thought), but he also provides definitions for many of the key terms. Attention must be

---

The majority of scholars assign later dates to the composition of the YS. Based on textual analysis of common ideas in the YS and other texts from the Hindu, Buddhist and Jain traditions, they consider the probable date of the YS to be around the 2nd or 3rd century C.E. (B. Miller 1995; Feuerstein 1991).

[22] Bhattacharya 1985, 109.

[23] Arya 1986, 6.

[24] Rukmini 1981, 217.

paid to these definitions and the specific ways in which such terms are used in the YS. Furthermore, the order of items on a list is not incidental and particular care must be taken with each list and item. Lists, in other words, are not mere ways to remember concepts or practices, but rather they communicate a host of implicit information due to their organizational properties. In general, items on lists move from the external to the internal, from the most fundamental to the most subtle, and from cause to effect. Finally, despite the brevity of the *sūtra* style, the YS blends psychology, philosophy, mental and physical techniques and spiritual cultivation. Sometimes these are presented as clear definitions or explanations. At certain points, particularly when expressing the higher levels or results of Yoga, the YS employs metaphorical or mystical language. In many places, and this is not surprising, preexisting knowledge or the presence and guidance of a teacher, seems expected. In modern times, when it is so easy to buy a copy of the YS in book form, we may forget that traditionally students of Yoga and the YS would normally have recourse to a guru or teacher who could provide explanations of concepts and techniques.

Structure of the *Yoga-sūtra*

The YS has four *pādas* or chapters: *samādhi* (complete stationing [of the mind]), *sādhana* (means), *vibhūti* (extraordinary powers) and *kaivalya* (aloneness, liberation). Each title indicates, in a general way, the content of that *pāda*. The first, *samādhi-pāda*, contains the most philosophical content and provides the philosophical bases of the highest goals of Yoga. It also contains an explanation of practices, likely for advanced yogins, that fall under the category of *abhyāsa-vairāgya* (repeated practice and detachment). According to the *Yoga-bhāṣya* (YBh), which is the main commentary on the YS, this first *pāda* is meant to explain the forms and results of Yoga attained by a yogin with a concentrated or inward-oriented mind.[25] The *sādhana-pāda* contains definitions of two methods of Yoga: *kriyā-yoga* (Yoga of activity),[26] and *aṣṭāṅga-yoga* (Eight-limbed Yoga).[27] According to the YBh, this *pāda* explains how someone with an externally-oriented or distracted mind (*vyutthita-citta*) can also practice Yoga.[28] The *vibhūti-pāda* details some of the extraordinary powers that the yogin may acquire. The fourth and final *pāda*, *kaivalya-pāda*, explains some additional philosophical concepts and issues.

The division between the first and second *pādas* seems unproblematic. The first *pāda*, containing 51 *sūtras*, ends with a statement about the highest state of consciousness where even the subliminal traces (*saṃskāras*) of *samādhi* have ceased.[29] This is a carefully constructed chapter that begins and ends with the concept of *nirodha* (suppression/cessation).[30]

The division between *pādas* two and three is more problematic. A description of the eight limbs of Yoga begun in 2.28 is interrupted by a *pāda* break after 2.55, when only five of the eight limbs have been discussed. *Pāda* three immediately picks up the discussion, with a definition of the sixth limb, *dhāraṇā*

---

[25] *samāhita-cittasya yogaḥ* YBh 2.1.

[26] YS 2.1.

[27] YS 2.29.

[28] YBh 2.1.

[29] YS 1.51. I use the term "consciousness" here only in its most general, or colloquial, sense.

[30] YS 1.2, 1.51.

(concentration). One possibility for this division between *pādas* two and three is that it represents a separation between the five external or indirect limbs (*bahir-aṅga*), which may be viewed by an external observer, and the three internal or direct limbs (*antar-aṅga*), which are not so observable.[31] Bhattacharya suggests that, alternatively or additionally, the division may be based on a difference in the *siddhis* and *vibhūtis* (extraordinary powers). The *siddhis* in the second *pāda* do not arise from the practice of *saṃyama* (complete control or restraint), while the *siddhis* in the third *pāda* do.[32] Thus such above-normal outcomes, mentioned in the second *pāda*, as the abandoning of enmity (2.35) and knowledge of previous births (2.39) may simply be by-products of the first five limbs. However, the *siddhis* mentioned in the third *pāda* require *saṃyama*, which is defined as the practice of *dhāraṇā*, *dhyāna* (meditation) and *samādhi*—the final three limbs of Yoga—together on a single object (3.4). With this reasoning, the division between *pādas* two and three becomes more understandable.

The separation between *pādas* three and four is clear. The fourth *pāda* clarifies certain concepts from previous *pādas*. It also reinforces some doctrines and returns again to themes of liberation and the final results of Yoga. In many ways, this final *pāda* most clearly blends philosophy, psychology and spiritual cultivation.

Commentarial Sources on the *Yoga-sūtra*

The combination of brevity and complexity means that the YS is short enough to allow a study of the text in its entirety, but also

---

[31] YBh 3.1.

[32] Bhattacharya 1985, 35.

rich enough to allow such a study to be fruitful. However, this same combination can also, at times, obscure the meaning of individual *sūtras*. Thus use of a commentary on the text is necessary at places for additional explanation and clarification. Indeed, the term "Classical Yoga" refers to the YS of Patañjali *and* the commentaries that are attached to it. Of these commentaries, the YBh is the oldest of the extant commentaries and therefore has exerted a strong influence on all later commentaries.[33]

The YBh was composed not later than 650 C.E., and may even date from the 4th century C.E. It is traditionally attributed to Vyāsa, the systematizer of the Veda and the author of the *Mahābhārata*. According to Aklujkar though, it is likely that the name Veda-Vyāsa is a corruption of Vindhya-vāsin—the name of the great Sāṃkhya scholar.[34] This view is plausible, given that the YBh offers detailed analyses of the YS that are based on the dualistic Sāṃkhya system of thought. Although there is some question whether the Bhāṣya author had first-hand knowledge of yogic practices, the commentary is a rich source of information and explains many ambiguous points.

Of the many other commentaries on the YS, Vācaspati Miśra's subcommentary, the *Tattva-Vaiśāradi* (TV) and the *Yoga-Sūtra-Bhāṣya-Vivaraṇa* (YSBhV) are particularly useful additions to the YBh. The latter is a subcommentary that is sometimes attributed to the great philosopher Śaṅkara. His authorship is unlikely though, since the philosopher is credited with the establishment of Kevalādvaita Vedānta, "Absolute Monism," as a distinct

---

[33] Feuerstein 1979, 17, 24.

[34] Ashok Aklujkar, "Vindhyavāsa, author of the Yoga-bhāṣya," in *Excursions into Pre-Bhartṛhari Philosophy* (forthcoming).

philosophical tradition. The YSBhV nevertheless remains a valuable source of information on the YS. It was first published in 1952 as part of the Madras Government Oriental Series.

Two

Taking the Stage

Metaphysics, Mind, Consciousness and Identity in the *Yoga-sūtra*

One of the puzzling aspects about phenomena such as consciousness, mind or identity is that they are simultaneously experiential and abstract. Most people who are of a sound mind have some experience of mind and consciousness, and yet find describing or explaining such phenomena with any degree of precision immensely difficult. This difficulty becomes greater when there is a need to translate terminology or experiences from another language, tradition and worldview into English equivalents or their closest approximations. In addition, cognitive neuroscience constantly clarifies, modifies, and sometimes threatens to render obsolete, some of these English terms. If we ask a neuroscientist, yogin, and lay person the questions, "Do you have a mind?" "Do you have experiences of consciousness?" we will, we hope, receive affirmative answers. What each means by *mind* and *consciousness* though, will vary. In the same manner, a stage manager, director, actor or rigger will speak of "the play." It is only at the most general level though, that each person refers to the same play. Their own *specific* play will be a play of cues, of blocking, of character, or of light. Therefore, in order to understand mind, consciousness and identity in Pātañjala Yoga, we must pay attention to all the elements of a complex staging: metaphysics; psychology; word usages; technical definitions; metaphors and symbolic language. Only then will we gain a sense of a play that is subtle and complex enough to seemingly draw the attention and involvement of a watchful audience.

PURUṢA

The philosophy that underlies the *Yoga-sūtra* (YS) is dualistic and places all existents into one of two categories: *puruṣa* or *prakṛti*. The word '*puruṣa*' may derive from the root *pṝ* meaning 'to fill,' 'to fill with air,' 'nourish,' 'be sated,' or 'make complete.'[1] The Indian tradition also supplies other context-sensitive derivations (*nirukta*), such as from the word *pur* 'citadel,' which leads to the later derivation of *puruṣa* as 'he who lies (*śete*) in the citadel (*pura*)' of the unmanifest.[2] Alternatively, some modern scholars view the word *puruṣa* as a compound of *pu* or *puṃs* and *vṛṣa*, literally meaning 'bull,' but metaphorically meaning 'prominent' or 'foremost' (i.e. human).

Use of the term *puruṣa* stretches back to Vedic times. Its most prominent use in this context is in RV 10.90, a cosmogonic hymn. Here *puruṣa* is a primordial being who becomes the sacrifice that creates *mantras*, living beings, societal systems and the cosmos (moon, sun, wind, earth, atmosphere, etc.). *Puruṣa*, in this hymn, therefore acts as both the material and instrumental cause of the

---

[1] Monier-Williams [1899]1995.

[2] Feuerstein 1980, 16. See *Atharvaveda* 10.2.28,30; *MBh* 12.294.37; *Bṛhadāraṇyaka Upaniṣad* 2.5.18.

universe.[3] While *puruṣa* in Yoga is not a material cause, *puruṣa* could be thought of as an instrumental cause—as a seemingly occasioning entity. Regardless of whether this is historically valid or not, the functional or theoretical role of being the first cause is similar. Returning again to RV 10.90, we find that most of *puruṣa* is also said to be hidden, except, perhaps, from the *ṛṣi* (seer). "Three quarters of Puruṣa went upward, but a quarter of him was here below."[4] This esoteric nature may foreshadow the Sāṃkhya and Yoga understanding that the true nature of *puruṣa* is hidden from everyone except those who have experienced a thorough insight into the true nature of reality.[5]

The word *puruṣa* is also used in the sense of person or individual man (RV 97.4-5), or people in a collective sense. In the earliest *Upaniṣads*, the term refers to both the empirical personality and the ultimate person (*uttama puruṣa*)—the person who has attained the highest level of insight.[6] In the middle *Upaniṣads*, *puruṣa* is conceived of as the Self or soul.[7] Larson notes that the descriptions of *puruṣa* found in these texts begin to combine old Upaniṣadic notions of the self with the beginning of Sāṃkhya ideas of *puruṣa*. For example, in *Kaṭha* 3.10-11, *puruṣa* is placed as the highest in a series of existents.[8] This brings us close then, not only to the usage of *puruṣa* in the Sāṃkhya system, but also to the concept of *puruṣa* in Patañjali's text.

---

[3] Feuerstein 1980.

[4] Mauer 1986, 271.

[5] See, for example, YS 2.20-26, SK 65, and 68-69.

[6] Werner 1996, 100.

[7] For an example, see *Kaṭha Upaniṣad* 2.18-19.

[8] Larson 1979, 97.

One of the key definitions of *puruṣa* in the YS occurs in 2.20. This *sūtra* reads,

> *draṣṭā dṛśi-mātraḥ śuddho'pi*
> *pratyayānupaśyaḥ*
> The seer is only seeing; although
> pure, it is the one who perceives
> cognitive events.

Here we see three aspects of *puruṣa* in the YS. *Puruṣa* is the *draṣṭṛ* (seer), is *śuddha* (pure) at least at some level of experience, thinking or existence, and is the *pratyaya-anupaśya* (perceiver of cognitive events).[9]

"The seer" (*draṣṭṛ, dṛś, dṛśi*, all from the root *dṛś*, 'see') is one of the most commonly used metaphors for *puruṣa* in the YS. It is used once each in the first *pāda* (1.3) and the fourth *pāda* (4.23), four times in the second *pāda* (2.6, 2.17, 2.20, 2.25) where the references all occur before the section on *aṣṭāṅga* yoga, and not at all in the third *pāda* on the *vibhūtis* or *siddhis* (extraordinary cognitive achievements). Some maintain that the concept of *puruṣa* arises from yogic experience of the numinous or Absolute. However, the occurrence of these references to *puruṣa* as seer in the primarily philosophical or psychological portions of the YS suggests that the role of *puruṣa* is not *solely* salvific or ontological. Indeed, other references to *puruṣa*, containing both explanations and different metaphors, follow the same pattern as the seer metaphors, and are confined largely to the first and second *pādas* (up to 2.25) and the fourth *pāda*.

---

[9] For the sake of clarity, I will only provide preliminary explanations and translations of key concepts other than the main one under consideration here.

Sūtra 2.20 is important for it emphasizes that *puruṣa* is not simply the seer as agent or subject in the manner that it seems to be in other *sūtras*.[10] In YS 2.20, *puruṣa* is *dṛṣi-mātra*, pure see-ing, stressing action and function, or verb rather than noun. The YBh explains this *dṛṣi-mātra* as, in part, *dṛk-chaktir eva*, "nothing but the capacity/capability (*śakti*) made up of (or consisting in) seeing."[11] Here then we get a sense of linguistically trying to transcend the difference between actor and action, of straining against the limitations of subject-object based language in order to communicate the nature of this abstract concept. This metaphorical language in 2.20 thus suggests that *puruṣa* has a functional role and is, perhaps, just as much *process* as *thing*. *Sūtra* 2.6 also gives some sense of this, combining the agentive noun *dṛś* (what sees) with *śakti* (capacity).[12] With this meaning of *dṛṣi-mātra* in mind, we may now examine the implications of other references to *puruṣa* as seer.

Puruṣa, the seer, is said to abide in its own nature,[13] alone,[14] implying that *puruṣa* is one of the two basic categories in this

---

[10] For contrast, see YS 1.3, 2.17, 2.25, 4.23.

[11] *Dṛk-chaktir eva* (YBh 2.20) suggests that this capacity is an innate property of *puruṣa*, but is not necessarily identical or synonymous with *puruṣa*. Bhavsar notes that, "By keeping aside soul, self or spirit [from consciousness], one conveniently keeps away the controversies as regards nihilistic, theistic or atheistic schools in the Indian context and such issues in the western context. This is shelving the problem not solving. Such problems are very fundamental." Solutions to the fundamental problem of the relation between consciousness, matter and spirit, will only arise when our knowledge reaches a more advanced stage (Dr. S. N. Bhavsar, correspondence).

[12] *Dṛg-darśana-śak[t]yor ekātmatevāsmitā* "*asmitā* (I-amness) is the apparent identity of the capacity of what sees (i.e. perceives, experiences) with the capacity of what helps in seeing (YS 2.6).

[13] YS 1.3.

[14] YS 2.25.

dualistic metaphysics. The concept that there is a seer necessitates that there is something that is seen (*dṛśya*) and this role is fulfilled by the other basic category, *prakṛti*, which includes everything existent that is not *puruṣa*.[15] To continue in greater depth with the metaphor of seeing, *puruṣa* does not simply see or watch everything, but is specifically the *pratyaya-anupaśya* "the one who perceives cognitive events".[16] *Anupaśya* would literally mean here "one who sees subsequently." Although *puruṣa* is metaphorically the seer, the *buddhi* (mind) that receives perceptions of the world, thoughts and sensations might be regarded, in a metaphorical way, as the first, or first-level, seer. As is obvious from the metaphor, cognition or conscious awareness of things is a kind of 'seeing,' and thus the YBh suggests that *puruṣa* and *buddhi* seem similar in some ways.[17] The YBh also contains an additional metaphor of sight, referring to *puruṣa* as "*buddheḥ pratisaṃvedī*" (the witness of *buddhi*) in 2.20 and 1.29.

If we leave aside the metaphor of seeing, YS 2.20 also presents *puruṣa* as *śuddha* (pure). This further emphasizes the separation or isolation of *puruṣa* from *prakṛti*, as is seen in YS 3.35, which describes the two as *atyantāsaṃkīrṇaya* (completely unmixed). YS 4.18 also stresses this difference between the two categories by

---

[15]Although we shall later discuss this at length, it may be helpful for those unfamiliar with the Yoga system to summarize a few main points here. That there is a seeming connection or conjunction (*saṃyoga*) between *puruṣa* and *prakṛti* that allows *puruṣa* to witness the activites of *prakṛti* in the form of objects and processes of mind (YBh 2.17, 4.18) is viewed as a problem to be avoided or overcome: *draṣṭṛ-dṛśyayoḥ saṃyogo heya-hetuḥ* "the conjunction of seer and seen is the cause of what is to be avoided/abandoned" (YS 2.17). This implies that *saṃyoga* is not ideally welcome. Its remedy is achieved through distinctive knowledge of the difference between the most subtle forms of *prakṛti* and *puruṣa* (YS 2.26).

[16] YS 2.20.

[17] YBh 2.20.

describing *puruṣa* in negative terms as *apariṇāmitva* (being immutable or unchangeable). *Apariṇāmitva* also necessitates that there is something that is its opposite, that is mutable or transformative, and this is the nature of *prakṛti*, and specifically of the *guṇas*, which are the constituents of *prakṛti* or the strands in *prakṛti*. Indeed, most of the references simply to *puruṣa* in the YS occur in *sūtras* where it is contrasted directly or indirectly with the *guṇas*.[18]

Other metaphors for *puruṣa* also highlight the philosophical dualism of *puruṣa* and *prakṛti*. YS 4.18 describes *puruṣa* as the *prabhu* (lord, master) of the activities of the mind, and 2.23 refers to *puruṣa* as the *svāmin* (owner) as opposed to what is owned (*sva*). In a similar way, references to *puruṣa* as *grahītṛ* (grasper) also imply that something else is to be grasped or apprehended, and again this is *prakṛti*.[19] This metaphor of grasping and owning is interesting, for it ties in with the idea that it is the seeming involvement of *puruṣa* and *prakṛti* that causes suffering and rebirth and which must, therefore, be overcome.

Thus the two basic metaphors that we have for *puruṣa* in the YS relate to seeing and grasping.[20] The metaphors of seeing reveal not simply the dualism of *puruṣa* and *prakṛti*, but contain elements relevant to epistemology such as in YS 1.3-4. The metaphors of

---

[18] YS 1.16, 3.35, 3.49, 4.18.

[19] For example, *kṣīṇa-vṛtter abhijātasyeva maṇer grahītṛ-grahaṇa-grāhyeṣu tat-stha-tad-añjanatā samāpattiḥ* "When the mental fluctuations have dwindled (ceased), there occurs a particular state (*samāpatti*, literally 'stepping toward collectively'), in which (the process of mind) is like a jewel, based on and annointed (coloured by) the (process of) grasping and the grasped" (YS 1.41). In other words, like a flawless, perfectly transparent jewel, this particular state of consciousness only takes on, in appearance or reflection only, whatever is near to it, that is, whatever it focuses on, whether this is the perceiver, the process of perception, or the object of perception.

[20] Feuerstein 1980, 18.

grasping also imply a dualism; however, these metaphors are more suggestive of a transformative psychology. In YS 1.15 and 1.16, true knowledge of *puruṣa* is mentioned in connection with the practice of *vairāgya* (detachment, disinterest) and the state of *vaitṛṣṇya* (no thirst, indifference). In other words, a distinctive knowledge of *puruṣa* can overcome the tendency to grasp and own, to make things part of one's identity.

Apart from the above metaphors, the YS also refers to *puruṣa* as "other." YS 4.24 describes the *citta* (mind-field), which is an evolute of *prakṛti*, as *parārtham* "one whose purpose is another (*puruṣa*)". *Prakṛti* always exists for, and operates for, the sake of this other. This differentiation between *puruṣa* and "other-purposed" *prakṛti* is partially based on the internal relationships that exist within the larger theoretical model, namely, that all composites exist for the purpose of another, and therefore, in this case, that other must be *puruṣa*.[21] It expresses logical interdependence in the items the Sāṃkhya-Yoga philosopher puts together to make sense of the world.

The line of reasoning has limitations though, because if *puruṣa* is separate (*kevala*) and unchanging (*apariṇāma*) then it cannot, in reality, have any purpose or any need of something serving its purpose. Indeed, the metaphors of seeing and grasping also have the same implications of need and activity. The response to this is that it only *seems* that *puruṣa* is active, that *puruṣa* experiences or is liberated. In reality, *puruṣa* is always separate and the final goal

[21]According to the *Sāṃkhya-Kārikā* (SK), which is the definitive text of classical Sāṃkhya philosophy, *saṃghāta-parārthatvāt* "(*puruṣa* exists) due to composites having the purpose of another" (SK 17). The examples given for this are of a lamp (SK 13) or a house (YBh 4.24), which are composed of various elements and serve the uses or purposes of another.

of Yoga involves the realization, in some way, of this usually unnoticed state of affairs.[22] We must always, therefore, be sensitive to layers of meaning and use of metaphors in the text. Only in the conventional sense may we think of *puruṣa* as seeing, owning, and grasping. Metaphors have their use and their limit. The implied duality of the metaphors we find in the YS indicates that these are speaking of *puruṣa* in terms of our limited, normal understanding of reality, of *puruṣa* as somehow present and interacting with *prakṛti*. Ultimately, however, *puruṣa* is *kevala* (alone, solo) and unchanging, despite the existence, and potential activities, of *prakṛti*.

On a theoretical level, one can understand why the Yoga and Sāṃkhya systems advance this type of reasoning and defense of the doctrine of *puruṣa*. Unlike the Vaiśeṣikas, whose primary focus was ontology, epistemology and individual liberation are the most important elements of the Yoga and Sāṃkhya systems. Therefore, these systems have a logical need for an epistemological 'first cause' that can both account for conscious awareness and remain pure so that there can be the possibility of individual liberation. If this pure first cause became something worldly and then reverted back to its pure liberated state, this would involve a change and imply, according to these systems, that it is neither eternal nor ultimate. The other option, which these systems chose, is to maintain that there only *seems* to be a change, in reality this *puruṣa* is always liberated. The problem remains though of how something so pure and separate could even *seemingly* have an interaction with *prakṛti*.

---

[22] YS 4.34.

The possibility of individual liberation also leads to the consideration of whether *puruṣa* is singular or multiple—that is, whether *puruṣa* is some type of world soul or multiple individual souls. The YS doesn't address this topic directly, however it seems most logical to assume that if individual liberation exists, then there must be multiple individual *puruṣas*. The SK 18 and YBh 1.24 both speak of a plurality of *puruṣas*. As well, the YS defines *īśvara* (lord) as *puruṣa-viśeṣa*, a particular kind of *puruṣa*.[23] This would also imply that there are multiple *puruṣas*.

Īśvara may represent a theistic element in Yoga,[24] possibly a second tradition as the Yoga system in general does not necessarily require religious belief. Alternatively, it may simply represent the ideal, the highest yogin or *guru*. Occupying one's mind with *īśvara* is one of a number of yogic practices;[25] however, the careful definition in the first *pāda* of the nature of *īśvara* suggests that this practice is different from more popular forms of devotion to a god or gods, and possibly from the type of practice included in the definition of *kriyā-yoga*.[26]

According to the first *pāda* of the YS, *īśvara* is never, unlike other *puruṣas*, even seemingly involved or in bondage with *prakṛti*.[27] The proof for *īśvara's* existence is said to be in the scriptures;[28] however, the scriptures also rely on *īśvara* for their existence because he is the *guru* or teacher even of the earliest

---

[23] YS 1.24.

[24] YBh 2.1.

[25] YS 1.23.

[26] YBh 2.1.

[27] YS 1.24.

[28] YBh 1.25.

gurus and yogins.[29] *Īśvara* is also carefully defined as the highest, most omniscient existent—the existent in which yogic achievement culminates.

> *yad evātiśāyi syāt tad eva tat syāt*
> What very thing is highest, that alone
> would be him.[30]
> *tatra niratiśayaṃ sarva-jña-bījam*
> In that one, the seed of omniscience
> is unsurpassed.[31]

Statements such as these suggest that *īśvara* is primarily a logical, rather than experiential, construct. The YBh does speak of *īśvara* as capable of human-like actions, for instance offering deliverance and teaching.[32] However, even here the function of *īśvara* seems to be more about providing a method for preserving knowledge when the universe goes through periodic dissolutions, than to 'lend a hand' in the manner of most devotional gods.[33]

Puruṣa and *īśvara* have important theoretical roles in the Yoga system. In particular, *puruṣa* as one who is 'only see-ing' plays an important epistemological role. Before we continue examining this topic though, we need to understand the nature and function of

---

[29] YS 1.26.

[30] YBh 1.24.

[31] YS 1.25.

[32] YBh 1.25.

[33] *tasyātmānugrahābhāve'pi bhūtānugrahaḥ prayojanam, jñāna-dharmopadeśena kalpa-pralaya-mahā-pralayeṣu saṃsāriṇaḥ puruṣān uddhariṣyamīti.* "Although there is the absence of he doing something for himself (that is, although he possesses no need of his own) his (*īśvara's*) aim is the assistance of living beings, such as 'I will deliver the worldly *puruṣas* through the instruction of knowledge and *dharma* at the period of dissolution and great dissolution'" (YBh 1.25). Since there is acceptance of the doctrine of the repeated creation and dissolution of the universe, this statement indicates a theoretical need.

other psychological and epistemological elements such as *citta*, *buddhi*, and *saṃyoga*. For now it is sufficient to make use of our metaphors, to conceive of *puruṣa* as the seer or witness who is separate, pure, somehow aware; of *puruṣa* as the grasper or experiencer of the activities of the mind. We conceive of *puruṣa*, in effect, as everything that *prakṛti* is not.

PRAKṚTI

The word *prakṛti* is composed of the prefix '*pra*' (forth) and the root '*kṛ*' (do, make). It is often translated as 'nature' or 'matter,' however these translations may be misleading. *Prakṛti* is a technical term in Vedic ritual theory, Hindu theology, Jainism, Sanskrit grammar, phonetics, medical theory, political theory, and Buddhism.[34] In Yoga and Sāṃkhya thought it denotes the most primary level of *saṃsāric* existence that brings forth all other levels and existents.

Prakṛti, *pradhāna* and *dṛśya* are practically synonymous in the YS. However, perhaps reflecting the epistemological and psychological emphasis of the YS, *dṛśya* is the term used most frequently. We find the definition of *dṛśya* in YS 2.18:

> *prakāśa-kriyā-sthiti-śīlaṃ*
> *bhūtendriyātmakaṃ*
> *bhogāpavargārthaṃ dṛśyam*
> The world of experience is one of the
> following at a given moment:
> brightness (*sattva*), activity (*rajas*) or
> inertia (*tamas*). Its nature is the
> elements and the sense organs. Its

[34] Jacobsen 1993, 75.

> purpose is experience and
> emancipation.[35]

This comprehensive definition indicates that *dṛśya* encompasses existents that are manifest and unmanifest, that are gross and subtle. The characteristics of brightness, activity and inertia refer to the *guṇas*, which are three material qualities or strands in *prakṛti*: *sattva* (brightness, lucidity); *rajas* (activity); and *tamas* (inertia). Since the nature of *dṛśya* is both the elements and the sense organs, this basic category includes both the objective, external world and individual psychological and even subjective realities. Finally, the *sūtra* indicates that *dṛśya* has a teleological purpose. Thus 'nature' or 'matter' may not be adequate translations for this category. On the other hand, advances in cognitive neuroscience and physics lead us to attribute many of the same characteristics, with the notable exception of emancipation, to matter. In our current (scientific) understanding, matter is active, can give rise, somehow, to sentience, and accounts, again *somehow*, for both the objective world and our internal, subjective experiences.

Prakṛti is a basis or field (*kṣetra*) of potentiality. YS 4.2 uses the term *āpūra* (flooding, excess, saturation) to describe its activity and this, in addition to the irrigation metaphor in the following *sūtra*, gives a sense of its generative power:

> *jāty-antara-pariṇāmaḥ prakṛty-*
> *āpūrāt*

---

[35] A more literal translation: "The seen (i.e. the world of experience) is one whose character is brightness, activity or inertia; whose nature is the elements and sense organs; whose purpose is experience and emancipation."

> The transformation into another birth
> (i.e. form of existence, life form) is
> due to the flooding in of *prakṛti*.[36]
> *nimittam aprayojakaṃ prakṛtīnāṃ*
> *varaṇa-bhedas tu tataḥ kṣetrikavat*
> The instrumental cause is not the
> instigator of these material forces,
> but a break in the barrier/rampart
> occurs (and hence the activities of
> transformation take place), as
> happens with a farmer (when he
> irrigates a field).[37]

Prakṛti itself though, is best understood as the material cause of all existents, linked therefore to the doctrine of *sat-kārya-vāda*, that is, the Sāṃkhya theory of causation that all effects pre-exist in the material cause.[38] For it is not specifically *prakṛti* per se that is active, but rather the *guṇas*.

The *guṇas* are not simply qualities of *prakṛti*, they are three elements which form the "composition of all phenomena, mental or physical."[39] Every thing, whether subtle or gross, is composed of the *guṇas*.[40] The names of the three *guṇas—sattva, rajas,* and *tamas*—are better left untranslated, but they primarily have associations with illumination, action and inertia, respectively.

---

[36] YS 4.2.

[37] YS 4.3.

[38] SK 9.

[39] Dasgupta [1920] 1989, 2.

[40] YS 4.13.

The *guṇas* are active,[41] and always act in conjunction, although one strand tends to dominate,[42] leading to various psychological or physical effects.[43] Thus even though the *guṇas* can't be separated physically, they are conceptually and functionally different. We can think of all of *prakṛti* as a rope comprised of a white strand (*sattva*), a red strand (*rajas*) and a black strand (*tamas*) all distinct, yet inseparably twisted around and around each other. The rope, in part, is what it is, because of each of these strands. Again, conceptually and functionally we can separate rope and strands, but in reality they are all linked.

Since the *guṇas* are active, they are possessed of change or transformation (*pariṇāma*).[44] *Pariṇāma* can be change in general, for instance in *sūtras* 3.9-13 the term refers to changes in both states of consciousness and in substances. In the context of the *guṇas* though, *pariṇāma* is a generative process.[45]

The YS gives a description of the basic transformations of the *guṇas* in terms of different levels of evolutes. These four levels (*parvan*) are *viśeṣa* (particularized), *aviśeṣa* (non-particularized), *liṅga-mātra* (having only a distinguishing mark), and *aliṅga* (without a distinguishing mark).[46] YBh 2.19, largely in accordance with Sāṃkhya metaphysics, explains each of the terms. There are sixteen *viśeṣas*, namely: the five *bhūtas* (elements) of *ākāśa* (air or

---

[41] YS 2.15, YBh 3.13.

[42] YBh 2.15, 2.18.

[43] YBh 2.15.

[44] YBh 2.18.

[45] *pariṇāmaikatvād vastu-tattvam* "Because the outcome is one, there is thatness (unity, reality) of a thing" (YS 4.14). That is, because the *guṇas* unite to produce one effect, single individual objects really exist.

[46] YS 2.19.

ether), *vāyu* (wind), *agni* (fire), *udaka* (water), and *bhūmi* (earth); the five *buddhīndriyas* (sense organs) which are ear, skin, eyes, tongue and nose; the five *karmendriyas* (organs of movement) which are voice, hands, feet, anus and sex organs; and *manas* (mind). Dasgupta writes that these are all termed *viśeṣas* because they are too particularized or specialized to "allow the evolution of any other substance of a different grade of existence from themselves."[47] This is in contrast to the levels above the *viśeṣa*, which are generative in a much more non-specific way and which can give rise to different *tattvas* (real substances).

Further analysis reveals the logic underlying this list of *viśeṣas*. The distinction between air or ether and wind is, at least in part, based on the correspondences that exist between the five elements and the functions of the five sense organs. Air or ether possesses, or allows, the quality of audibility, it corresponds, therefore, to the ear. Wind possesses touchability, which corresponds to the skin. Fire possesses the quality of visibility, which corresponds to the eyes. Water possesses the quality of taste, which corresponds to the tongue. The earth—not in the planetary sense, but in the sense of "that which imparts solidity"—possesses the quality of smell, which corresponds to the nose.

We can see from this that the categories represent the way the sense-organs allow us to know and categorize the world. If it were not for the existence of the more abstract categories, however, such as sound, touch, colour, taste and smell, which are the *tanmātras* (subtle elements), we could neither know nor conceive of such particular existents. *Sat-kārya-vāda* is also honored or maintained in the model, for the cause (abstract, unmanifest and subtle when

---

[47] [1924] 1987, 41.

compared to the effect) must at least have something in common with the effect. There is a logical dependence then, between gross object, sense organ and more subtle aspects of material nature.

There are six *aviśeṣas*: the five *tanmātras* (subtle elements) of *śabda* (sound), *sparśa* (touch), *rūpa* (colour), *rasa* (taste), and *gandha* (smell); as well as *asmitā*, which is literally 'I-am-ness,' but not in an individualized or particularized sense. *Asmitā* here is that bare potential or possibility of *individuality itself* existing, rather than the existence of specific individual *things.* Moving to an even more abstract level, the *liṅga-mātra* is said to be *mahat*, that which is copiously, in a big way, existent. Finally, at the most subtle and abstract level,[48] *aliṅga*, there is *pradhāna* which is neither existent nor non-existent.[49] Although in this text *prakṛti* and *pradhāna* sometimes seem synonymous, *pradhāna*, according to the YBh, is the generative stage of *prakṛti*. *Pradhāna* is therefore marked or characterized by the activity of the *guṇas*.[50]

In effect then, we have the following schema:

Levels and Evolutes
Level: *aliṅga* (without a distinguishing mark)
prakṛti (material nature)
pradhāna (when *prakṛti* is about to give rise to something)
Level: *liṅga-mātra* (having only a distinguishing mark)

---

[48] YS 1.45.

[49] YBh 2.19.

[50] YBh 2.18.

mahat (that which is copiously existent)
Level: *aviśeṣa* (non-particularized)
asmitā (I-am-ness, but not in an individualized sense) +
five *tanmātras* (subtle elements): sound; touch; colour; taste; smell
Level: *viśeṣa* (particularized)
manas (mind) +
five *karmendriyas* (organs of movement): voice; hands; feet; anus; sex organs +
five *buddhīndriyas* (sense organs): ear; skin; eyes; tongue; nose; +
five *bhūtas* (elements): air; wind; fire; water; earth

Prakṛti, *pariṇāma* and the evolutes, which are the *guṇas* in their general levels, thus do not represent a cosmology but rather a logical scheme that is both individual (or singular) and general. They represent the epistemological and phenomenological aspects of the individual. At the same time, they also account for the general objects of knowledge and experience. The schema, as depicted above, moves from the most abstract and subtle level to gross matter. Since everything, in reality, is composed of the *guṇas*, and therefore of *prakṛti*, even those things that are as basic as the material elements, the *bhūtas*, contain a number of levels. In YS 3.44, these levels are given as *sthūla* (gross), *sva-rūpa* (nature), *sūkṣma* (subtle), *anvaya* (connection, threading element), and *artha-tattva* (purposiveness). Thus water has its gross level (as water), it nature (liquidity), its subtle element (taste), its *anvaya* (the *guṇas*), and its purpose—which it shares with all *dṛśyas*—to provide a particular kind of experience to *puruṣa* and thereby, at a different level, to become a basis for *puruṣa's* liberation.[51]

Thus what is of greatest significance for understanding mind-body concepts in the YS, is that the body, mind, identity, and sensations of individual humans all fall under the category of *prakṛti*. The nature and action of the *guṇas* thus influence humans at every level of their being. Indeed, there is no separating, except conceptually, human from the *guṇas* and/or *prakṛti*. Consequently, if someone has a preponderance of the *sattva guṇa*, *prakhyā* (comprehension) will be that person's basic characteristic of mind. This results in a peaceful state and the emotion of happiness.[52] In like manner, *rajas* is associated with *pravṛtti* (physical activity), *ghora* states (philosophically frightening or undesirable states) and the emotion of *duḥkha* (sadness, suffering—especially in the form of feeling frustrated or not being content).[53] Finally, the dominance of *tamas* results in *sthiti* (stagnation, inertia), a *mūḍha* (stupefied) inner state, and the experience of *moha* (confusion, indecision).[54] These are, of course, only basic categories. Since the *guṇas* are always active, various combinations and interactions take place at all levels.

The logical scheme of evolutes thus provides the philosophical basis for how and why the Yoga system works. For the yogin, the process of *pariṇāma* is associated with *duḥkha* (dissatisfaction of

---

[51] YBh 3.44.

[52] YBh 2.15.

[53] YBh 2.15.

[54] YBh 2.15.

the world),[55] yet also with serving the purposes of experience and emancipation or liberation.[56] Since outside objects, the body, mind, individuality, emotions, etc. are all part of the same general process or category, and indeed are composed of the same three *guṇas*, then these can all mutually influence each other. That is, a change in the position of the body may, given the logic of this system, have psychological effects. Nutrients in the body could likewise have psychological effects, as well as effects on more abstract activities of the mind, such as meditation. The activities a person engages in, obviously tied to the *guṇas*, would also have multi-leveled effects. In the same way, the perception of a specific object could conceivably lead to psychological changes, and, being a part of the same process, the mind could also change the physical object. This would all be logically possible, even to be expected, according to this interconnected way of understanding the nature of things.

Thus the theory of *prakṛti* and the evolutes is ingenious and influences, as well as accounts for, the practice of Yoga at every level. It can also account for aspects of Yoga, such as the *siddhis* (extraordinary powers), that often seem fantastic. However, and here is the problem that needs much more discussion, this theory, up to this point, does not provide an explanation for conscious awareness or thought. *Dṛśya*, i.e. *prakṛti*, is the opposite of *puruṣa*, and therefore is not self-illuminating (*sva-ābhāsa*).[57] In other words, *dṛśya* alone cannot account for the phenomenon of conscious awareness or sentience. There must, therefore, be some

[55] YS 2.15.

[56] YS 2.21.

[57] YS 4.19.

interaction or influence of *puruṣa* on *prakṛti*, and specifically, on the mind.

Citta, Manas, Buddhi

The YS employs three terms, *citta, manas,* and *buddhi,* that all refer in some way to mind, intellect or ideation. Translations of these terms vary widely. For instance, Arya translates *citta* as mind-field and *buddhi* as the faculty of intelligence, intuitive wisdom, intellection, and discrimination in a sentient being.[58] J. H. Woods translates *citta* as mind-stuff and *buddhi* as thinking-substance.[59] Feuerstein translates *citta* as consciousness and *buddhi* as cognition.[60] Miller translates *citta* and *buddhi* as thought and intelligence, respectively.[61] Most people translate *manas* as mind; however, Woods translates it as central organ.[62]

Variation in translation can result in significantly different readings of sūtras. We may compare, for example, two translations of YS 4.4 *nirmāṇa-cittany-asmitā-mātrāt*: "created mind-stuffs may result from the sense-of-personality and from this alone,"[63] and "individual thoughts are constructed from a measure of egoism."[64] While both translations are plausible, examining how the terms *citta, manas,* and *buddhi* are used in the YS reveals patterns that help to clarify the terms' meanings.

---

[58] 1986.

[59] [1914] 1988.

[60] [1979] 1989.

[61] 1995.

[62] [1914] 1988.

[63] Woods [1914] 1988, 303.

[64] Miller 1995, 76.

Out of the three terms, *citta* appears most frequently in the YS, occurring in over twenty *sūtras*. *Citta* is associated with psychological processes such as valid cognition, erroneous cognition, mental construction, sleep, memory,[65] and particularly the act of knowing.[66] *Citta* functions as a storehouse, as a support for the data it receives either consciously or unconsciously, and as a type of scaffolding for cognitive activities.[67] In the YS, *citta* is therefore the core component of psychology and epistemology and Larson notes that one can accurately consider it as either mind-stuff or brain-stuff.[68] Since it has such an important role and also has a number of specific functions associated with it, it is best to leave the term untranslated, although Arya's translation as "mind-field" gives a sense of the comprehensive nature and processes of *citta*.[69]

The term *manas* is used only three times in the YS.[70] Feuerstein notes that, reflecting pre-classical usage, these *sūtras* always refer to *manas* in conjunction with the senses.[71] More specifically though, *manas* is always mentioned in connection with practice, for instance the practice of stabilizing the *manas* by focusing on an object,[72] or the results of practice—that is, fitness of *manas*,[73] and

---

[65] YS 1.2 and ff.

[66] YS 4.17; 4.23.

[67] Bhavsar, correspondence.

[68] 1995, 47.

[69] Arya 1986, 452.

[70] YS 1.35; 2.5; 3.48.

[71] 1980, 59.

[72] YS 1.35.

[73] YS 2.5.

quickness of *manas*.[74] The term *manas* can therefore be translated as mind in the general, or colloquial sense.

In contrast to both the YBh and the SK, *buddhi* is used less frequently in the YS than the other two terms. In fact, the term appears only twice and in a most specific context. Although there is no definitive translation of the terms in YS 4.21, it is clear at least that the *sūtra* examines how the mind can be conscious or aware of itself:

> *cittāntara-dṛśye buddhi-buddher*
> *atiprasaṅgaḥ smṛti-saṃkaraś ca*
> If (one *citta*) were to be perceived by another *citta*, there would be the logically sticky consequence (i.e. infinite regress) of there being a *buddhi* of *buddhi* and the confusion of memory.

The *sūtra* suggests that one might easily fall into a logically sticky situation if one says that the mind perceives the mind, for, in that case, what perceives the mind perceiving the mind? YS 4.22 posits a solution by referring to an external, *citi* (*puruṣa*) whose presence is necessary for self-knowledge:

> *citer apratisaṃkramāyās tad-*
> *ākārāpattau sva-buddhi-*
> *saṃvedanam*
> When there is conforming to the form of it (*citta*) on the part of the *citi* (pure consciousness), which does not cross over to the other side, there

[74] YS 3.48.

is (complete) awareness of one's own
buddhi.

Therefore, although the exact meaning of *buddhi* is not clear, the term is used only in this one particular philosophical discussion.

Citta is thus the term the YS employs in most discussions of psychology or epistemology. This usage, however, has been clouded by the YBh, which offers useful interpretations and explanations, but employs these terms somewhat differently than the YS.

Feuerstein has noted that the commentators on the YS tend to use the terms *citta* and *buddhi* "rather indiscriminately."[75] There are, however, again some patterns of usage. In general, if a *sūtra* refers to *citta* specifically, then the YBh will also use that term.[76] When the *sūtra* wording does not include the term *citta*, *manas* is sometimes used as mind in a general sense.[77] The commentator does seem to regard both *manas* and *citta* as synonyms since they are each associated with the *vāsanās* (underlying mental traces),[78] and both are *na svābhāsa* (non-self-illuminating).[79]

The YBh also, in general, uses *buddhi* as a synonym for *citta*. For instance, *puruṣa* is the witness of *buddhi*,[80] or the witness of *buddhi's* cognitive events,[81] while the YS refers to *puruṣa* knowing

---

[75] 1980, 58.

[76] For example, YBh 1.2, 2.15, 4.18-19, 4.23, 4.26.

[77] YBh 1.24; 4.11.

[78] YBh 4.11, YS 4.24.

[79] YS, YBh 4.19.

[80] YBh 1.29; 2.17; 2.20.

[81] For "cognitive events or processes" we have the term *pratyaya* in YBh 2.20, or *buddhi-vṛtti* in YBh 4.22.

the *citta-vṛttis* (processes or activities of the mind-field).[82] As well, the YBh calls the activities of *buddhi* collaborative—that is, it brings things together,[83] while the YS refers to the activities of *citta* using the same term.[84]

However, unlike the YS, the YBh uses the term *buddhi* frequently. The YBh of course refers to *buddhi* in its commentary on YS 4.21 and 4.22. It also tends to use *buddhi* in discussions that are closely related to Sāṃkhya philosophy. For instance, the YBh's epistemological discussions of *puruṣa* as witness of the mind's activities usually adopt *buddhi* rather than *citta* or *manas*.[85] Similarly, *buddhi* is described as being composed of the three *guṇas* or material qualities,[86] and is particularly the term of choice in discussions on mental *sattva*,[87] and on the evolutes.[88]

Thus, while *citta*, *buddhi* and *manas* are generally synonymous in the YBh, their pattern of usage first follows the usage in each specific *sūtra* and then tends more to a pattern in line with the SK. The SK shows some preference for the term *buddhi* (especially in the context of enumerating the evolutes), uses *manas* somewhat less frequently and *citta* not at all.[89] There are a few passages in the YBh which use two or three of the terms in the same

---

[82] YS 4.18.

[83] *saṃhatya-kāritva*, YBh 2.20.

[84] YS 4.24.

[85] YBh 1.29; 2.17; 2.20.

[86] YBh 2.15; 2.20.

[87] YBh 1.47; 2.17; 3.35,

[88] YBh 2.19,

[89] The SK may not necessarily be earlier than the YBh. Both the YBh and the SK might be following the terminology of an earlier Sāṃkhya text or teacher.

discussion, however these passages are countering faulty theories or opponents' views and therefore are not as helpful in determining usage as they might otherwise be.[90]

There undoubtedly remain subtle differences in the usages of *citta, buddhi* and *manas* in the YBh, however, for the purposes of this discussion it is enough to note their very specific usages in the YS. It then becomes apparent that an understanding of mind in the YS must focus primarily on the concept of *citta* rather than *manas* or *buddhi*.

Citta

The concept of *citta* in the YS is both multi-layered and dynamic. Although it might be easy to construe some aspects of *citta*, such as *vṛttis* (cognitive processes or activities), *kleśas* (taints), and *saṃskāras* (specific impressions), as structures, the *vṛttis, kleśas,* and *saṃskāras* are processes, particular transformations of *prakṛti* that are of a cognitive and individual nature.

Pātañjala Yoga opposes the philosophical stance of idealism and instead maintains that both object and *citta* are existents, although on different levels:

> *vastu-sāmye citta-bhedāt tayor*
> *viviktaḥ panthāḥ*
> (Even) with respect to the same
> object, a difference (still) exists
> between *cittas*; therefore there is a

[90] See, for example, YBh 2.24, 4.19, or 4.21.

> different path for them (i.e. the
> object and *citta*).[91]

In other words, because different people can cognize the same object—albeit with possible difference with respect to the qualities of that object—we can assume or conclude that the object has an existence, a basic ontological status, that is independent of the *citta.* The YBh also strongly affirms this realist position:

> *bahu-cittālambanī-bhūtam ekaṃ vastu sādhāraṇaṃ, tatkhalu naika-citta-parikalpitaṃ, nāpy aneka-citta-parikalpitaṃ, kiṃ tu svarūpa-pratiṣṭham. katham? vastu-sāmye citta-bhedāt.*
>
> One object (can) become the common support of many *cittas*. That (object) is not dependent on one *citta*, neither is it imagined by many *cittas*, rather it rests in itself (i.e. its own form). How is this so? Since there is a distinction (difference) of *cittas* (even) with respect to the same object.[92]

Thus the *citta* does not create the world, but has an important and necessary role in the formation of one's perceptions of the world. Although separate from the *citta* of a person,

---

[91] YS 4.15. More literally, "Because there is distinction (difference) between *cittas* even when the object remains the same, there is a different path for the two of them."

[92] YBh 4.15.

> *tad-uparāgāpekṣatvāc cittasya vastu jñātājñātam*
> An object is known or unknown due to the requisite colouration of the *citta.*[93]

Uparāga (colouration) of the *citta* represents an epistemological process.[94] An object can only be known, we can only have conscious awareness of it, if it is reflected or represented in *citta.* However, since *citta* is part of the *prakṛtic* category, it can not be self-illuminating, that is, it can not give rise to conscious awareness, even of other objects.[95] Therefore the theory of the colouration of *citta* by an object does not completely account for our awareness, our knowledge, of the object. The epistemological theory is completed by the concept of *saṃyoga*, which will be explained below.

Since the *citta* is *prakṛtic*, it is formed of the three *guṇas*, *sattva, rajas,* and *tamas.* These *guṇas* give *citta* the basic characteristics or power of *prakhyā* (comprehension), *pravṛtti* (activity) and *sthiti* (inertia). They also result in the dynamic nature of *citta*, which is itself the locus of a number of cognitive processes that are also active and changeable.[96] Indeed, the entire Yoga system aims at

---

[93] YS 4.17.

[94] *Uparāga* derives from *upa* + the root *rañj* (influence, affect, dye).

[95] *Na tat-svābhāsaṃ dṛśyatvāt* "There is no self-illumination for it (the *citta*) due to its being an object" (YS 4.19).

[96] See, for example, YS 1.33, 3.10-12. In accordance with the dynamic nature of *citta*, we find a number of other psychological typologies present in the YBh. We have, for instance, five types of *cittas* enumerated in the list of *citta-bhūmis* (generalizations about states of *citta*). These are: *kṣipta* (pathologically distracted or agitated—within unproblematic limits); *mūḍha* (pathologically stupefied or somnolent); *vikṣipta* (distracted or agitated); *ekāgra* (one-pointed); and *niruddha* (restrained or disciplined) (YBh 1.1). While the first two *citta-bhūmis* represent pathological states of *citta*, and

effecting profound changes in the activities of *citta*, as is apparent in the very definition of yoga:

> *yogaś citta-vṛtti-nirodhaḥ*
> Yoga is the cessation/control (literally, 'holding down') of the activities of *citta*.[97]

This definition of yoga leads to definitions of the activities, the *vṛttis* of *citta*. The word '*vṛtti*' derives from the root '*vṛt*' (turn, revolve, proceed). In the YS and YBh it refers to any general process or activity. There is, for example, *vṛtti* of the *guṇas*,[98] of the breath,[99] and of the knowing *buddhi*.[100] *Citta-vṛtti* refers not to just *any* cognitive activity, but to five specific activities: *pramāṇa* (valid cognition); *viparyaya* (erroneous cognition); *vikalpa* (mental/intellectual construction); *nidrā* (sleep); and *smṛti* (memory).[101]

Pramāṇa, valid cognition, arises from *pratyakṣa* (direct perception), *anumāna* (inference), and *āgama*, which is usually translated as 'scriptures,' or 'tradition,' but here refers to any form of inherited knowledge. According to YBh 1.7, *pratyakṣa* takes place when the external object reaches or affects the *citta* through the channel of the sense organs, thereby "colouring" the *citta*. The

---

vikṣipta the normal distracted *citta* that most people experience, Arya (1986) notes that the YS and YBh focus on the latter two *citta-bhūmis*. This, of course, is in direct contrast to Western psychology which traditionally focusses on pathological states of mind and, occasionally, on more normal states (Arya 1986, 83).

[97] YS 1.2. We shall return to consider the implications of this *sūtra* once we have examined possibilities of practice and the transformation of the activities of *citta*.

[98] YS 2.15.

[99] YS 2.50.

[100] YBh 4.22.

[101] YS 1.5, 1.6.

focus of perception is the object's peculiar or particular characteristic(s), rather than *both* the universal and particular nature of the object. The category of *anumāna* (inference) is necessary as a type of valid cognition, for it allows acceptance of concepts such as *puruṣa* that a practitioner might not directly perceive. Furthermore, the logical consideration that things made of parts always exist for the sake of another, and therefore *dṛśya* exists for the sake of another (*puruṣa*),[102] is a type of *anumāna*. Finally, *āgama* (inherited knowledge) would include the valid knowledge gained from scriptures that speak of liberation and *puruṣa*. YBh 1.7, in addition, includes in *āgama* any form of inherited knowledge, for instance the knowledge a person acquires from a trustworthy friend concerning matters that are seen or inferred.

Viparyaya (erroneous cognition), is

> *mithyā-jñānam atad-rūpa-pratiṣṭham*
> false knowledge (false cognizing)
> based on a form that is not its (the
> thing's) own form.[103]

This category includes experiences of misperception, as in the classic example of perceiving a coiled rope to be a snake, or, in the example from the YBh, the seeing of two moons due to eye problems.[104] *Pramāṇa* (valid cognition) can replace, or correct, erroneous cognition.

Vikalpa, mental construction, is

> *śabda-jñānānupātī vastu-śūnyaḥ*

---

[102] YBh 4.24.

[103] YS 1.8.

[104] YBh 1.8.

> devoid of an object, following upon
> (i.e. dependent upon) verbal
> knowledge.[105]

The category of *vikalpa* is necessary to account for our ability to conceptualize and speak of objects such as a sky-flower. The YBh restricts this category to words, and the knowledge that arises from them, that do not refer to a substance or physical correspondent (*vastu-śūnyatva*).[106] An example of this *vikalpa* is the statement "*caitanyaṃ puruṣasya sva-rūpam*" ("consciousness is the nature of *puruṣa*). Now, the commentator asks, since *puruṣa* is consciousness itself, then what, in the previous sentence, is designated by what?[107] In other words, according to this statement *puruṣa* has no attributes, so consciousness is not an attribute of *puruṣa*, it *is* rather *puruṣa*. Our regular usage of language communicates subject and predicate, yet even without this, the phrase "*caitanyaṃ puruṣasya sva-rūpam*" means *something* thanks to the great power of this form of verbal expression and knowledge.

Nidrā (sleep) is

> *abhāva-pratyayālambanā vṛttir*
> the *vṛtti* that depends upon the
> cognizing (cognitive event) of (what
> is) absent.[108]

Since YS 1.38 uses the terms *svapna* and *nidrā* to mean dream sleep and dreamless sleep, respectively, the *vṛtti* the *sūtra* refers to

---

[105] YS 1.9.

[106] YBh 1.9.

[107] *yadā citir eva puruṣaḥ tadā kim atra kena vyapadiśyate*

[108] YS 1.10.

in 1.10 is dreamless sleep. The commentators are in agreement with this reading. The YBh mentions nothing of dreams. Instead, the reflection after sleeping about how well or poorly one slept, rather than the content of dreams, again supports the understanding of *nidrā* as dreamless sleep.[109] Arya rightly notes that the entire mind does not sleep, but only the part that undergoes wakefulness and dream sleep.[110] *Nidrā* is thus a *vṛtti*, a cognitive event or process of absence of objects, identity and conscious awareness. It is valuable, for it can give a glimpse that such a state might exist. However, *nidrā* is not synonymous with liberation, because it is necessary to restrict this *vṛtti* since it reflects, according to Vācaspati Miśra, a state where *tamas* dominates.

Finally, *smṛti*, memory, is the

> *anubhūta-viṣayāsampramoṣaḥ*
> non-robbing (non-loss) of the object
> that was experienced.[111]

The YBh here questions whether we remember the object itself or the experience or process of cognizing that object. It notes that since a *pratyaya* (cognitive event) is formed or coloured both by the sense perception of the object itself and the process of perceiving that object, both object and the process of cognizing that object are remembered.[112]

Regarding the list of *vṛttis* as a whole in YS 1.6, the order of *pramāṇa-viparyaya-vikalpa-nidrā-smṛtayaḥ* may seem counter-

---

[109] YBh 1.10.

[110] 1986, 180.

[111] YS 1.11.

[112] YBh 1.11. The process of storing and retrieving these memories involves the formation and awakening of *saṃskāras* (traces of our experiences), which will be explained in further detail later in this chapter.

intuitive, as in the placing of sleep before memory, which is a more conscious act. However, this five-fold division is based on the awareness or non-awareness of an external object. The order of the *vṛttis* thus represents a gradation: in *pramāṇa* the object is present and perceived as it is; in *viparyaya* the object is present but perceived incorrectly; in *vikalpa* there is no external object, but it is perceived as if it is, as if with severed relationship with the world; in *nidrā* there is no external object and no necessary dependence on prior experience; and finally, in *smṛti* there is no external object, but there could be dependence on a certain experience. Thus, since *nidrā* is not necessarily dependent upon a specific experience of an external object, it seems closer to *vikalpa* and *viparyaya* than does *smṛti*. In addition, *smṛti* can capture a trace of each one of the previous *vṛttis*.

The five *vṛttis* represent basic categories of cognitive processes or activities. It would be unmanageable, indeed impossible, to try to account for all our specific mental capacities, processes and experiences, so the five *vṛttis* are the basic headings, as it were, under which more specific cognitive events can be grouped. As the five *vṛttis* are also part of *prakṛti*, they too are active and changeable. Although there are only five *vṛttis*, the specific instances of *vṛttis* are practically countless. The *vṛttis* may be increased or slowed down, and the Yoga system aims at controlling and then reducing both the specific occurrences of *vṛttis*—such as the memory of a red dress, the perception of a leaf, or a daydream about vacationing on a tropical island—as well as the general categories themselves.[113] Just as importantly though, the YS may not intend to classify *all* cognitive processes under the

---

[113] YS 1.2, 1.41, 1.43.

citta-vṛttis. If this had been the intention, YS 1.2 could simply have read "yoga is the restriction/cessation of the *citta.*"

Kleśas

The *vṛttis* are not the only cognitive activities that take place in the *citta.* The YS categorizes the five *vṛttis* as *kliṣṭākliṣṭāḥ* (defiled or undefiled).[114] Here the YS is not speaking of defiled or dirty thoughts, but rather dynamic cognitive elements that are philosophically distorted or that are soteriologically unhelpful. These elements that cause significant distortions and disruption—that trouble or afflict (*kliś*) the *vṛttis*—are called the *kleśas* (defilements). The YS lists five such *kleśas.* However, even before examining the list of specific *kleśas,* we must understand the general nature of the *kleśas.*

The YBh describes the *kleśas* as "*pañca viparyayaḥ*" (five erroneous cognitions).[115] This is problematic though, for *viparyayas* are one of the five types of *citta-vṛttis.* It is not likely that the commentator is suggesting that *kleśas* are a type of *vṛtti,* because some *vṛttis* are undefiled, that is, not affected by the *kleśas.* According to the YSBhV, the *kleśas* are not *vṛttis* (*kleśānām avṛttitvāt*), because the *kleśas* are not merely *pratyayas* (cognitive events), unlike the *vṛttis.*[116] *Pratyayas* are a general class of cognitive events or processes, of which the *vṛttis* are specific types.[117]

---

[114] YS 1.5.

[115] YBh 2.3.

[116] YSBhV 2.3.

[117] The noun '*pratyaya*' derives from *prati* + *i/ay* (to go toward) (either the object or the subject). This gives a sense of the active nature of these cognitive events or processes.

Therefore there is some difference between *kleśas* and at least some *vṛttis*. There is, however, interdependence between the *kleśas* and, specifically, the class of *viparyaya vṛttis*. The absence of *viparyaya*, which is both a *pratyaya* and a *vṛtti*, leads to separation from the taint of the *kleśas* (*kleśa-mala*). If these two categories were completely separate, then it would be possible to destroy the *kleśas* but still have the *viparyayas*, false knowledge based on an untrue form. The YSBhV strongly states, however, that yogins who destroy the *kleśas* do not possess such error.[118] Thus there must be some strong relation or even interdependence between the *viparyayas* and the *kleśas*, even though *kleśas* are not *vṛttis*.

Descriptions of the nature or functions of the *kleśas* reveal further reasons why the *kleśas* are not identical to the *vṛttis*. The *kleśas* are more like psychological drives or motivators rather than basic types of cognitive processes. According to the YBh,

> *te spandamānā guṇādhikāraṃ*
> *draḍhayanti, pariṇāmam*
> *avasthāpayanti, kārya-karaṇa-srota*
> *unnamayanti, parasparānugraha-*
> *tantrī-bhūtvā karma-*
> *vipākañcābhinirharantīti*
> (The *kleśas*) move, strengthen (one's)
> engagement with the *guṇas*, cause
> change, add to the stream of cause
> and effect, and having become a
> source of reinforcement (lit. thread

---

[118] YSBhV 2.3.

> of mutual assistance), bring about the
> ripening of karma.[119]

The *kleśas* are active motivating drives that can affect cognitive events both in the present moment and in the future. They are not merely the effects or consequences of past *vṛttis*, although a connection with the past, almost a training effect or a strengthening thanks to repetition, does exist.

As with the *vṛttis*, the YS lists five specific *kleśas* and offers definitions of each. The five *kleśas* are: *avidyā* (ignorance); *asmitā* (sense of I-amness); *rāga* (attachment); *dveṣa* (aversion); and *abhiniveśa* (clinging to life).[120]

Avidyā (ignorance) occupies the primary place on the list of *kleśas*, and this is not an incidental placing, for *avidyā* is the *kṣetra* (field) of the others.[121] The term *kṣetra* here is philosophically significant, for in Sāṃkhya philosophy, the Gītā, and of course in the YS, the field, or material world, is differentiated from *puruṣa*, who is the field-knower. Describing *avidyā* as the 'field' of the others may indicate that *avidyā* is a source of our mundane, or normal, experiencing of self and the world. The other *kleśas* thus all depend for their existence or activities on *avidyā*, which is defined as

> *anitya-śuci-duḥkhānātmasu nitya-*
> *śuci-sukhātma-khyātir avidyā*
> the knowledge of the
> permanent/eternal in the
> impermanent, the pure in the impure,

---

[119] YBh 2.3.

[120] YS 2.3.

[121] YS 2.4.

> the pleasant in (what is ultimately)
> painful, and the self in what is
> (ultimately) not the self.[122]

In other words, *avidyā* is the opposite of knowing or understanding. It is a pervasive misunderstanding of the nature of things, and this misunderstanding stretches from the profane to the profound and sacred.

The sequence of items in the definition of *avidyā* further reveals the breadth of such basic misunderstanding, for each item shows an increase in philosophical thought. The YBh on 2.5 explains that the predication or seeing of the permanent in the impermanent encompasses views such as that the earth is eternal, or that the sky is eternal, as well as the moon, stars, and gods. Although this may seem true from the perspective of an individual's lifespan, even elementary analysis reveals that these objects are not eternal. Indeed, as the YSBhV notes, all the sacred texts (*śruti*) maintain that there was a time when neither heaven, nor earth, nor the intermediate space existed.[123] Therefore, these are not eternal.

In a similar manner, but on a slightly more analytical level, the *sūtra* speaks of *avidyā* as seeing the pure in the impure. This involves the inaccurate idea that the body, as it is naturally in the case of most human beings, is pure. While it may seem contrary to modern affirmations of the body, the YBh maintains that the correct view is to regard the body as impure and highly disgusting due to its origin, seed, sustenance, excretions, destruction and need for constant care.[124] The idea here is not simply that the body is a

---

[122] YS 2.5.

[123] YSBhV 2.5,

[124] YBh 2.5.

bad thing, but rather that a person must attain purity; it is not a given. Thus purity here may represent an ideal, the highest spiritual achievement for which a person can strive. Modern readers must also keep in mind that viewing the body as impure is a common method of detachment, a form of practice. Finally, the system stresses a comprehensive understanding of non-violence.[125] Therefore, the body's need for constant care violates this ethic, as its maintenance always inflicts some form of suffering and violence on some other life-form. Thus, to regard the body as pure is inaccurate. This view is not as easy to grasp as the previous item on the list.

The third level of the list, *avidyā* as the experience of the pleasant in the painful, might at first seem as though it is discussing masochism or sadism. Instead, this refers to the perspective that we find in YS 2.15, that

> *pariṇāma-tāpa-saṃskāra-duḥkhair*
> *guṇa-vṛtti-virodhāc ca duḥkham eva*
> *sarvaṃ vivekinaḥ*
> due to the pains of (a) material
> transformation, (b) philosophical
> anguish, and (c) the *saṃskāras*, and
> because of the opposition of the
> fluctuation of the *guṇas*, for the wise,
> all is only suffering.

This recognizes that pleasure is never lasting, that suffering, on some level, is a fact of existence, and therefore that a philosophical

---

[125] YS 2.30, 2.31.

awareness of suffering is, or should be, constant for any person who can think deeply enough or take a long-term view of life.[126]

Finally, the last item on the list specifies that *avidyā* is knowledge of the self in what is not self. Here the YBh on 2.5 offers some important commentary on the topic, for it describes this type of ignorance as identification of the self (*ātman*) with external things that are sentient or insentient—for example, with one's job, offspring, or wealth—or with the body as the basis of experience. Most importantly though, if a person identifies self with the mind, and views this combination as an instrument of *puruṣa*, this is also a form of *avidyā*, for the mind is also *anātman* (not the self).[127] Here again, the commentary makes clear the notion that the mind is part of *prakṛti*, and therefore, most definitely is not the self.

Thus the definition of *avidyā* in YS 2.5 reveals ever increasing subtlety in philosophical analysis. And again, from this a reader will note that the order of items on the list is anything but incidental. Yoga praxis will aim to remedy this pervasive influence of *avidyā* in the external, social, physical and mental spheres of an individual's existence.

Since *avidyā* is so powerful, pervasive, and subtle, we can understand better now the earlier statement that it is the root of the other *kleśas*.[128] For *avidyā* is not merely the absence of knowledge or insight, but rather the presence of a radical misunderstanding of the true nature of things. *Avidyā* is an existent, just as a "non-friend" or enemy is not simply the absence of a friend, but rather

---

[126] Although some may identify this view of suffering as originating with Buddhist sects (most obviously in the four noble truths), the Hindu tradition clearly has it as well. It therefore represents a common foundation in the *śramaṇa* (ascetic) tradition.

[127] YBh 2.5.

[128] YS 2.4

the existence of a malicious being.[129] Along the same lines, we could consider psychosis to be not just the absence of sanity, but an active, pervasive mental disorder. *Avidyā* is an active counter-force—it is not a *pramāṇa* (valid state of cognition), nor merely the absence of such a state, but rather some type of perverted knowledge that is contrary to spiritually or philosophically desirable knowledge.[130] Consequently, a yogin must not only aim to attain an accurate and appropriate form of knowledge, but also must eradicate the counteractive force of *avidyā* and its associated *kleśas.*[131]

Returning now to the remaining four *kleśas* (*asmitā, rāga, dveṣa,* and *abhiniveśa*) in the list from YS 2.3, we can observe the dependence of *asmitā* on *avidyā* in YS 2.6. This *sūtra* defines *asmitā*, literally a sense of I-amness, as

> *dṛg-darśana-śaktyor*
> *ekātmatevāsmitā*
> the apparent (*iva*) identity of the
> capacity of what sees (i.e. perceives,
> experiences) with the capacity of
> what helps in seeing.

While we will need to address the concept of *saṃyoga* to fully understand this *sūtra*, we can at least see that the *sūtra* develops a concept found in YS 2.5, that our sense of identity, or I-amness, arises from misidentification of the mind as the self, or vice versa. The commentary clarifies this misidentification even further,

---

[129] YBh 2.5.

[130] YBh 2.5.

[131] YS 2.2.

> *puruṣo dṛg-śaktiḥ, buddhir darśana-śaktiḥ, ityetayor eka-svarūpāpattir ivāsmitā kleśa ucyate*
> *puruṣa* is the power of the seer, *buddhi* is the power through which one sees. The *kleśa* called *asmitā* is an apparent change in which these appear to have a single nature—as if forming a unity.[132]

Since *puruṣa* is separate from *prakṛti*, and *buddhi* "what helps in seeing," is an evolute of *prakṛti*, *buddhi* or mind alone must be the basis for *asmitā*. The mind, when experienced through the distorting lens of *avidyā*, becomes the basis for identity. Although it may seem that *puruṣa* and *buddhi* are identical, in reality they are not.

The reason that humans tend to identify mind as self, or the source of identity, rather than material nature, is easily apparent. One might lose a leg and still retain a sense of personality and identity. However, the issue of identity for a person suffering the latter stages of a disease such as Alzheimer's, or for a person who has experienced severe brain trauma, is more complex and largely remains unaddressed by the Yoga system, which seems predicated, at least in part, on good mental and physical health.[133]

Despite the common identification of mind and identity or sense of self, the YS maintains that to base one's sense of self solely on the mind is a profound mistake that arises from ignorance of the basic duality of *puruṣa* and *prakṛti*. For if the sense of I-amness

---

[132] YBh 2.6,

[133] YS 1.31.

arises from the mind, then any sense of identity or self is not eternal, but rather is part of the material world. It is therefore subject to change and suffering, as well as the experience of the latter three *kleśas*. This would, perhaps, be an acceptable state of affairs provided that no other options existed, such as *puruṣa*. The Yoga system, however, maintains that there are more preferable options.

Having some sense of I-amness, *rāga* (attachment, attraction) and *dveṣa* (aversion, dislike) are the two principle movements of this identity. *Rāga* arises from the experience of pleasure,[134] while *dveṣa* is born from the experience of misery or suffering.[135] These *kleśas* are thus not merely emotions, but the fundamental responses to emotions, thoughts, or any positively or negatively tinged events.

The final *kleśa* on the list is *abhiniveśa*, the will to live. This will to live is instinctive, is produced in the same manner as the previous *kleśas*, and is present even in the wise.[136] The YBh states

---

[134] YS 2.7.

[135] YS 2.8.

[136] YS 2.9 reads "*sva-rasa-vāhi viduṣo'pi tathā rūḍho'bhiniveśaḥ*" "Even for the wise, the will-to-live is instinctive, (and) is produced in the same manner (as the other *kleśas*)." Chapple, in an effort to minimize a dualistic reading of the YS, cites YS 2.9:

> In asserting the "absolute separateness of *puruṣa* and *prakṛti*," Feuerstein has rendered Yoga a disservice, continuing a tradition based on a misreading of the texts. The absolute separation of *prakṛti* and *puruṣa* can only be interpreted as death. Yet, the *Sāṃkhya Kārikā* acknowledges that the potter's wheel continues to turn (SK 67) and the *Yoga Sūtra* states that "even the wise possess the will-to-live" (YS II.9). Although the practice of yoga is certainly a fine preparation for death, yoga is a way of life, emphasizing continuity as opposed to the

that this will to live must be a result of the experience of death in previous lives, for the innate fear of death could not be due to direct perception (in this life), inference, or inherited traditional knowledge, since it exists even in the case of a newborn insect.[137]

Abhiniveśa is the most basic attachment that each living creature will form. Each creature will also develop a natural aversion to anything that threatens its existence. These basic attachments and aversions would be impossible without some rudimentary sense of identity or I-amness. According to the Yoga school, all of these depend on the basic misidentification of self with material nature. The order of the *kleśas* therefore indicates their interrelated, even interdependent, nature.

This order allows us to deepen our understanding of why the YBh classifies the *kleśas* as *viparyayas*. All the *kleśas* depend on a pervasive mistaken view of self and the world, they are thus related to the category of *viparyaya-vṛttis*. However, unlike the *vṛttis*, the *kleśas* are not only cognitive events or sets thereof. As Balslev indicates, a soteriological rather than strictly epistemological analysis reveals that the *kleśas* "drive the mind towards all that is of this world', *saṃsāra*, and block discriminative knowledge,

---

discontinuity inherent in the *citta-vṛtti* schematic (1981, 112).

However, from *abhiniveśa's* inclusion as a *kleśa*, and the concomitant injunction that the *kleśas* are to be removed (YS 2.10), it seems clear that the will-to-live is a defilement that should be overcome. Further, SK 67 states that the body, in association with *puruṣa*, like a potter's wheel, continues to turn because of the force of *saṃskāras* (past impressions). In the end though, both (*puruṣa* and *prakṛti*) attain *kaivalya* (separation, isolation) which is absolute and endless (SK 68). The idea then that yoga, in the final analysis, emphasizes continuity, in terms of the unity of *puruṣa* and *prakṛti*, rather than continuity of the two categories as separate, seems mistaken.

[137] YBh 2.9.

which is essential for salvation or *kaivalya*."[138] Further, the term *vṛtti* implies some active process, while the *kleśas* may be dormant, attenuated (feeble), or intermittent, as well as fully active.[139] Therefore, while they are certainly related to active, erroneous cognition, the *kleśas* may also be subtle, unconscious motivators that for a time lie inactive. Given the right context though, they can influence current and future cognitive events. This process occurs through the functioning of *saṃskāras*.

Saṃskāras, Vāsanās, Karmāśaya

The mind is not a *tabula rasa*, nor a straightforward storage and retrieval system, and a concept of memory alone cannot account for the temporal relations between mental phenomena such as cognition, dreams, actions, and emotions, to name only a few. In the Yoga system, the functioning of *saṃskāras, vṛttis, vāsanās* (traits or tendencies) and the *karmāśaya* (reservoir of karma) give the mind, both conscious and unconscious, its cyclical, dynamic nature.

Unlike some other psychological concepts in the YS, Patañjali does not provide a specific definition of the term '*saṃskāra*,' despite repeated usage in the *sūtras*.[140] According to Kuppuswamy, explicit definitions of the term seem not to exist, although it is used in a technical way in both ancient and medieval Indian thought.[141]

---

[138] 1991, 79.

[139] YS 2.4.

[140] We find the term in *sūtras* 1.18, 1.50, 2.15, 3.9-10, 3.18, 4.9-11, 4.27.

[141] 1990, 180.

Saṃskāra is a difficult term to translate. Literally it means 'to put or form (*kṛ*) together or fully (*saṃ-s*).' In a psychological context, Monier-Williams translates the term as "the faculty of memory, mental impression or recollection, impression on the mind of acts done in a former state of existence."[142]

In the YS, the use of the term *saṃskāra* suggests that it does indeed "put together" by linking the past and present, the conscious and the unconscious. *Vṛttis* produce *saṃskāras* (traces or impressions) of their activities,[143] as do cognitive events in higher states of consciousness.[144] Therefore, the *saṃskāras* are characteristics of *citta*:

> *vyutthāna-saṃskāraś citta-dharmo,*
> *na sa pratyayātmaka iti*
> The emergent (extroverted)
> *saṃskāra* is an aspect (characteristic)
> of *citta*. It does not consist of the
> same nature as cognitive events.[145]

Here then the *citta* along with its cognitive processes or events (*pratyayas*) is seen as a substance, something that possesses (*dharmin*) aspects or characteristics (*dharmas*) such as *saṃskāras*. Thus, even if the workings or fluctuations of the *citta* are completely restrained, there may still exist a residuum of *saṃskāras* that can exert some influence over that *citta*.[146]

---

[142] [1899] 1995, 1120.

[143] YBh 1.5.

[144] YS 1.50.

[145] YBh 3.9.

[146] For example, *virāma-pratyayābhyāsa-pūrvaḥ saṃskāra-śeṣo'nyaḥ* "The other (*asaṃprajñāta-samādhi*) which (only) has *saṃskāras* remaining, is preceded by the repeated practice of the cognitive experience of cessation" (YS 1.18). Or, *tac-chidreṣu*

Since *saṃskāras* are a result of the workings of the *citta*, they represent a history of cognitive events and therefore the tendencies of the *citta* to function in a particular way. If a *citta* has a tendency to become involved with the world, then the *saṃskāras* it generates will be extroverted. For this reason, the YS states that *saṃskāras* should be eliminated since they are associated, consequently, with suffering.[147]

All *saṃskāras* are not completely negative, though. Higher, or more positive, states of consciousness produce their own *saṃskāras* that are opposed to the formation of extroverted *saṃskāras*.[148] Thus the *saṃskāras* produced by states of consciousness leading to *citta-vṛtti-nirodha* block the rise of other, more outwardly-oriented *saṃskāras*.[149]

Since *saṃskāras* form a residuum of cognitive acts and experiences, they also provide a link with memory.[150] For this to occur, it is necessary that there exist uniformity between the *saṃskāras* and *smṛti*.[151] Knowledge of the past, even past lives,

---

pratyayāntarāṇi saṃskārebhyaḥ "In the holes (weak points in the mind borne toward *viveka*) there exist other cognitive events that arise because of the *saṃskāras* (YS 4.27).

147 YS 2.15.

148 YS 1.50.

149 *vyutthana-nirodha-saṃskārayor abhibhava-prādur bhāvau nirodha-kṣaṇa-cittānvayo nirodha-pariṇāmaḥ* | *tasya praśānta-vāhitā saṃskārāt* "The transformative process leading to control/cessation consists of a succession of moments of control/cessation in the *citta*, when the externally-oriented *saṃskāras* are subjugated and when the *saṃskāras* of control/cessation are manifested. As a result of this *saṃskāra*, the *citta* comes to possess a calm flow" (YS 3.9-10).

150 In other words, *saṃskāras* form a residuum, a record, of the cognitive processes that have occurred. They also form a record of the experiences—the external and internal experienced life—of the person. It is possible, within this system, that some of these cognitive processes are subconscious, or not consciously experienced by the person.

151 YS 4.9.

then becomes possible through direct perception of the *saṃskāras*.[152]

The connection of *saṃskāras* with the past also relies on the functions of two other entities: the *vāsanās* (underlying or generalized psychological traits) and the *karmāśaya* (reservoir of karma). While *saṃskāras* are specific impressions of specific experiences (ouch! This stove is hot!), *vāsanās* are the general propensities or tendencies that arise from those experiences and impressions (don't touch hot things; don't do things you find painful). There are clear connections here with these experiences, *saṃskāras*, *vāsanās*, and our fundamental *kleśas* of *rāga* (attraction) and *dveṣa* (aversion). The YBh states that *vāsanās* are preceded by more than one existence, and explicitly mentions their connection with memory and with *saṃskāras*.[153] A later discussion in the YBh emphasizes the interrelationship of *saṃskāras, vāsanās* and memory:

> *yathā'nubhavās tathā saṃskārāḥ. te ca vāsanānurūpāḥ. yathā vāsanāḥ smṛtayaḥ iti jāti-deśa-kāla-vyavahitebhyaḥ saṃskārebhyaḥ smṛtayaḥ. smṛtibhyaś ca punaḥ saṃskārā*
>
> Just as the experiences, so also the *saṃskāras*. And these (*saṃskāras*) correspond to the *vāsanās*. Just as the *vāsanās* (so also) the memories,

---

[152] YS 3.18.

[153] *ye saṃskārāḥ smṛti-hetavas tā vāsanāḥ* "Those *saṃskāras* that are the causes of memory (*smṛti* in a general sense) are *vāsanās*" (YBh 2.13). It is worth noting that at this point in the YBh, there is a fairly long and rare discussion of karma and its fruition.

> as memories are from the *saṃskāras*
> which are separated (from them) by
> birth, place and time. And from
> memories again there are
> *saṃskāras.*[154]

Unlike the *vāsanās*, the *karmāśaya* is confined to a single existence.[155] This complex or reservoir of karma forms when acts of merit or demerit are committed. Additionally, this reservoir forms when these actions originate in the powerful emotional states of *kāma* (desire), *lobha* (avarice), *moha* (confusion/delusion), and *krodha* (anger).[156] These emotions, in turn, have their origination in some of the deeper, underlying, *kleśas.* While *avidyā* certainly underlies all of these states, there are obvious connections between the *rāga kleśa* and *kāma* and *lobha*, between the *dveṣa kleśa* and *krodha*, and finally between the *avidya kleśa* and *moha.*

The *kleśas* thus ensure the continued existence of the *karmāśaya.*[157] In turn, the *karmāśaya* reaches its fruition in the (next new) birth, life and worldly experience.[158] Although there is no one-to-one relationship, the *karmāśaya* of the previous life will lead to a new life dominated by certain psychological traits and tendencies. Thus the *karmāśaya* is also said to be the root of the

---

[154] YBh 4.9.

[155] YBh 2.13.

[156] YBh 2.12.

[157] YBh 2.13.

[158] YS 2.13.

kleśas.[159] With these concepts, the religio-ethical dimensions of this system are firmly linked with the psychological.

At this point, it is also worth noting the interrelationship between the unconscious and conscious mind that is implicit in these concepts. The concept of mind here is cyclical and dynamic. While there are elements that would be conscious or unconscious, the focus seems primarily on the integrated functioning of the two, rather than on thinking of the two as compartments that have some traffic or exchange between them. This integrated view also applies to the inner or psychological versus the external world. While Western psychology has frequently limited itself to either what happened to a person (external events), *or* the psychological makeup of the person—this forms the very basis of the nature versus nurture controversies—the Yoga system acknowledges the influence of both, much as modern cognitive neuroscience does, although explanations of this, of course, differ enormously. In Yoga, experiences result in certain psychological traits and tendencies that in turn will influence the way a person cognizes the world and interacts with it. Given that the underlying philosophy maintains a dualism between *puruṣa* and *prakṛti*, rather than between the individual and the world, the body and the mind, or nature and nurture, this integration is not unexpected.

One question that may arise though is when this cyclical, integrated process began. It is not enough to say that certain tainted (*kliṣṭa*) traits or tendencies that direct the mind to engagement with the world were inherited from a previous life. If that is the case, then what started the process for that life? This question of first cause is basically unanswerable in any theory

[159] YS 2.12.

dealing with similar or larger philosophical, in the broad sense, concerns. The YS states that this process is beginningless, because of the permanence, or continued presence at some deeper level, of desire.[160] This *sūtra* suggests a philosophical-psychological reasoning for why Yoga practice can lead to liberation. Desire leads to karma, and to the accumulation of tainted cognitive tendencies. If this process is halted and the accumulated negative elements are cleared out, then the yogin will be freed from typical psychological patterns and involvements with the world.[161] Further, since all desire is rooted in ignorance,[162] the yogin must attain insight into the nature of reality—which for Yoga means the essential difference between *puruṣa* and *prakṛti*. From these considerations, it is apparent why Yoga practice includes ethical, intellectual, psychological and physical dimensions.

Apart from the question of this first cause of the *citta's* involvement with the world, a fundamental epistemological issue remains. Although the concept of *asmitā* might explain part of the phenomenon of self-awareness, the crucial topic of how conscious awareness in general arises must still be addressed.

Saṃyoga

The key elements in Pātañjala psychology, such as *citta, manas, buddhi, vṛttis, kleśas* etc., are all evolutes of *prakṛti*, and, as such share the same basic principles of *prakṛti*. However, this

---

[160] YS 4.10, *tāsām anāditvaṃ cā'śiṣo nityatvāt* "These (*saṃskāras*) are beginningless because of the permanency of desire."

[161] See, for example, YS 4.11.

[162] YS 2.4.

fundamental *prakṛtic* category can not account, in and of itself, for conscious awareness. YS 4.19 states that

> *na tat svābhāsaṃ dṛśyatvāt*
> It (the *citta*) does not have self-illumination because it is an object.

As clear as this directive is, the term '*svābhāsaṃ*,' which derives from *sva* (self) and *ābhās* (shine, appear), complicates the situation. Is self-illumination synonymous with consciousness, conscious awareness, awareness, self-awareness, sentience in general, or all (or none) of the above? It is of some use here to examine the YBh, the sub-commentaries, and further *sūtras* for clarification.

On YS 4.19, the YBh states

> *yathetarāṇīndriyāṇi śabdādayaś ca dṛśyatvān na svābhāsāni, tathā mano'pi pratyetavyam*
> Just as other objects such as the sense organs and sound are not self-illuminating, so the mind (*manas*) also should be recognized (as non-self-illuminating).

Although the problem of *svābhāsa* remains, the YBh emphasizes that the mind is no different than any other sense organ in this respect [163]

---

[163] The YBh also adds a fairly semantic-based proof at this point:

> *kiṃ ca svābhāsaṃ cittam ity agrāhyam eva cittaṃ syād iti śabdārthaḥ. tadyathā svātma-pratiṣṭham ākāśam apratiṣṭham ity arthaḥ. sva-buddhi-pracāra-pratisaṃvedanāt sattvānāṃ pravṛttir dṛśyate—kruddho'ham, bhīto'ham,*

However '*svābhāsam*' is meant, it is clear that the *citta* shares the same basic nature as other objects, and the YS continues this argument in the next *sūtra*:

> *eka-samaye cobhayānavadhāraṇam*
> There can be no ascertainment of
> both (*citta* and object)
> simultaneously.[164]

Therefore, while the function of *citta* is to cognize objects, it is unable to cognize itself without turning itself into yet another object. The subjective aspect of cognitive awareness is lost in this process. A completely different conceptual category is thus required to avoid infinite regress,[165] and to explain conscious awareness fully.

A different line of argument is found in YS 4.24:

> *tad asaṅkhyeya-vāsanā-citram api*
> *parārthaṃ saṃhatya-kāritvāt*

> *amutra me rāgo'mutra me krodha iti. etat sva-buddher agrahaṇe na yuktam iti.*
>
> Moreover, (a statement like) 'the mind is self-illuminating' would only mean that no one can grasp it. To explain (to give an analogy, the sentence) 'the sky is self-based' means that it is not established on anything else. The activity of living beings is seen to come after taking a note of how their mind (*buddhi*) moved (acted—as in reflections, thoughts, introspections, like the following)—'I am angry,' 'I am frightened,' 'my desire is for that one,' 'my anger (is against) that one.' This (the evidence furnished by such thoughts) would not fit if one's mind (*buddhi*) were not to be grasped (4.19).

[164] YS 4.20.

[165] YS 4.21.

> That (*citta*), although variegated with uncountable *vāsanās* (i.e. although it has much in itself that can make it an experiencer of the world), exists for the sake of another due to the composite (collaborative) nature of its activity.

According to this perspective, anything that is a composite, exists to serve another's purpose. For example, a house, which is made up of many different parts, does not exist for its own sake, but rather exists to benefit the people who live within it.[166] This position reinforces the idea that the *citta* is an object like any other, and that it can not account, in and of itself, for conscious awareness.

The concept of *saṃyoga* (conjunction) offers a solution to the problem of conscious awareness. *Puruṣa*, as "pure see-ing," witnesses the *pratyayas* (cognitive events).[167] Specifically, *puruṣa*, in the cases in which the person is not in the state of liberation, has some sense of identity with the *vṛttis*.[168] Without this seeing and identification, the *citta-vṛttis* could not be known:

> *sadā jñātāś citta-vṛttayas tat-*
> *prabhoḥ puruṣasyāpariṇāmitvāt*
> Due to the immutability of *puruṣa*, who is the master of them, the

---

[166] YBh 4.24.

[167] YS 2.20.

[168] YS 1.4, *vṛtti-sārūpyam itaratra*.

> fluctuations of *citta* are always
> known.[169]

In effect then, without *puruṣa* and *saṃyoga*, the human mind would be a black box—unknowable both to other minds and one's own.

Furthermore, with *saṃyoga*, a better possibility of understanding the nature of the mind and *puruṣa* arises:

> *sva-svāmi-śaktyoḥ sva-*
> *rūpopalabdhi-hetuḥ saṃyogaḥ*
> *Saṃyoga* is the cause of
> understanding the nature of the two
> capabilities of owner (i.e. *puruṣa*)
> and owned (i.e. *prakṛti*).[170]

In effect, material nature and *saṃyoga* allow one to understand, or begin to understand, the true nature of *puruṣa* and reality. However, this holds true only up to a point, because ultimately *saṃyoga*, its cause, and, we must assume, normal conscious awareness must be overcome in order to achieve liberation.

YS 2.24 identifies *avidyā* as the cause of *saṃyoga*. This *avidyā*, as discussed previously, is not some individual piece of inaccurate knowledge, but rather a basic distortion that underlies one's view and experience of the world. Because of this distortion, there is a sense of identity, of I-amness (*asmitā*).[171] Again though, without some influence from *puruṣa*, awareness of this identity, or self, and its thoughts would not be possible.

---

[169] YS 4.18.

[170] YS 2.23.

[171] YS 2.6.

The fourth *pāda* of the YS presents a consecutive series of *sūtras* that discuss, in a more detailed way than any of the previous *sūtras*, Yoga's dualistic epistemology.[172] The topics of each *sūtra* follow a logical order: knowledge of an existent or "thing"; awareness; the impossibility of the mind alone being sufficient for awareness; and being aware of knowing some "thing." Reading all the *sūtras* together then, we have:

> *tad-uparāgāpekṣatvāc cittasya vastu jñātājñātam (17).*
> *sadā jñātāś citta-vṛttayas tat-prabhoḥ puruṣasyāpariṇāmitvāt (18).*
> *na tat-svābhāsaṃ dṛśyatvāt (19).*
> *eka-samaye cobhayānavadhāraṇam (20).*
> *cittāntara-dṛśye buddhi-buddher atiprasaṅgaḥ smṛti-saṃkaraś ca (21).*
> *citer apratisaṃkramāyās tad-ākārāpattau sva-buddhi-saṃvedanam (22).*
> *draṣṭṛ-dṛśyoparaktaṃ cittaṃ sarvārtham (23).*
> A thing is known or unknown because the *citta* expects (i.e. depends on) colouration by it (17). The fluctuations (i.e. modes, states or activities) of *citta* are always known

[172] YS 4.17-23.

because of the immutability of
puruṣa, who is the master of them
(18).
The *citta* (on its own) can't be self-
illuminating because it is an object
(19).
And there can be no ascertainment of
both (the *citta* and an object)
simultaneously (20).
If (one *citta*) were to be perceived by
another *citta* (i.e. if one *citta* were to
be the object of the other *citta*), there
would be the logically sticky
consequence (i.e. infinite regress) of
there being a *buddhi* of *buddhi* and
the confusion of memory (21).
When there is the conforming to the
form of it (*citta*) on the part of *citi*
(i.e. *puruṣa*)—which does not (in
actuality) cross over to the side (of
prakṛti)—there is (complete)
awareness of one's own *buddhi* (22).
The *citta*, coloured by (both) worldly
objects and the seer (*puruṣa*), can
know all manner of things (23).

There are two important epistemological elements in these series of *sūtras*: *uparāga* (colouration) and *ākārāpatti* (conforming to the form, assuming the shape).

In order for something to be known, and for someone to be aware that it is known, the *citta* must be "coloured" by both the object and *puruṣa*. The exact nature of this colouration, figurative language being necessary at this stage of discussion, is unexplained in the text, but it seems that an object must somehow register itself on the *citta* without physically moving into it or occupying the *citta* forever. Otherwise, the *citta* would either know all things or no things. Further, because the *citta* is insentient (we can not, at least, deny Yoga the freedom to take this position), it must also be coloured by sentient *puruṣa*. Colouration by *puruṣa* thus seems to be functionally identical with *sārūpya-vṛtti* (identity with the *vṛttis*)[173] and *ākārāpatti* (conforming to the form).[174]

The obvious problem with this theory though, is that *puruṣa* must somehow be completely separate from the *prakṛtic citta* and world, but still have some type of influence—colouration—that allows the *citta* to be aware and possess knowledge. The YS does not address this problem directly.[175] The *sūtras* describe *puruṣa* in two states: transcendental, in which *puruṣa* is essentially isolated from *prakṛti*; and empirical, in which *puruṣa* exists associated with functions of mind and worldly personality that are falsely attributed to it.[176] However, beyond whatever meaning one may read in *uparāga*, the exact nature of the connection, *saṃyoga*, between the empirical *puruṣa* and the person remains somewhat ambiguous, particularly given that *saṃyoga* in Sanskrit usually

---

[173] YS 1.4.

[174] YS 4.22.

[175] This is a clear indication that the concerns or purposes were other than solely providing a theory of consciousness or epistemology. The thinkers of this time were certainly not incapable of logical thinking or rational criticism. To the composer of the YS, the situation must have seemed evident or applicable to every philosopher who accepted a Self or soul behind the operational mind. Those who did not accept such a Self, such as the Buddhists, are refuted in the YBh.

[176] Kumar 1984, 1-2.

refers to physical contact. The general intention behind 4.22 contradicts this, for it notes that no physical transformation or transfer of *puruṣa* occurs.

Despite ambiguity, Patañjali's epistemological theory offers an interesting perspective on the problem of consciousness, while retaining the ideas of soul and liberation. The *citta*, as insentient matter that constantly changes, is obviously not any type of ultimate. Since the Yoga school maintains a belief in liberation, there needs to be some type of soul as ultimate.[177] The soul, which is eternal and unchanging, must therefore be separate from changing matter. And although it is not directly associated with regular conscious thought of any kind, the soul's very presence allows for conscious awareness, self-awareness, cognition and so forth. The exact nature of this consciousness-spawning relationship between soul and matter can not be explained beyond delineating the perimeters within which it must be discussed. In Yoga's defense though, the relationship between consciousness and matter is still problematic and the hard problem remains unsolved—even minus the concept of a soul.

We have, in the final analysis then, a *conceptual* dependency between *puruṣa* and *prakṛti*. This dependency allows for a complex psychology and also a path to liberation that is based on the experience of various yogic practices. With this approach, Pātañjala Yoga emphasizes that worldly experience, including our ordinary experiences of conscious awareness, self-awareness,

---

[177] Liberation and soul, in this context, do not necessarily have "religious" overtones. In Yoga philosophy, liberation is a logical necessity or another way of admitting the insolubility of problems of human existence. In Yoga practice, it represents the highest goal—a goal which is difficult to express, but is specific nonetheless. Finally, it is worth noting that acceptance of the possibility of liberation does not necessarily turn Sanskrit works with philosophical content into religious or theological works.

rational thought, etc., is not the highest achievement possible. Instead, worldly experience is due to a profound cognitive distortion or misunderstanding of the nature of things.[178] *Saṃyoga* must therefore be abandoned,[179] and this, of course, requires the discipline of the body-mind.

Lastly, if we wish to find an equivalent to what we *normally* mean by our English terms 'consciousness' or 'conscious awareness,' it will be in this combination of *puruṣa* and *saṃyoga*. When we normally use the term consciousness, we are not speaking of consciousness as some type of abstract, pure see-ing, lacking in intentionality (which would be similar to *puruṣa* alone), but rather *regulàr* conscious awareness, with its subjective and intentional nature preserved. In the Yoga system then, this is a type of conjunct consciousness, a consciousness made up of various interconnected parts or processes, such as *puruṣa, saṃyoga, citta* and *prakṛti* in general. This is precisely the type of consciousness, with its basis in world, identity, and ignorance, that must be modified, restricted, and eventually overcome.

---

[178] YS 3.35.

[179] YS 2.17.

Three

All the World's a Stage

Some Perspectives from Cognitive Neuroscience on the Mind/Brain

In Sāṃkhya-yoga thought, *prakṛti* (material nature) moves, it is active. We encounter a similar situation when we consider the mind/brain. Myriad material structures and activities allow us to look at a tree, imagine sky-flowers, or remember what we had for breakfast this morning. Although scientists and philosophers are still unable to explain the precise relationship between brain, mind, consciousness and identity, we might provisionally think of the brain as providing the stage for the mind's play in which one's conscious self is the star actor. The play itself needs all these elements and more. There can be no star without a play and no play without a stage.

The YS contains a view of mind, consciousness and identity based on a particular metaphysics, practice and tradition. In contrast, an entire neuroscience text might address itself to only one of the many topics found in the YS. Furthermore, a scientist might explore any aspect of these topics at a molecular, cellular, anatomical, or behavioural level. Given the enormous range of subject matter and current approaches to the mind/brain, an attempt to find one to one correspondences between particular details in the

YS, such as *vāsanās* (underlying psychological traces), and cognitive neuroscience is impossible. Nevertheless, we can consider, in a general way, some of the key topics common to both the Yoga tradition and the cognitive sciences, such as perception; misperception; abstract thought; sleep; memory; and emotion in order to gain a deeper understanding of how these might relate to the nature of mind, consciousness and identity—the very things that Yoga aims to change. As with classical Yoga, cognitive neuroscientists explain, so far as they can, mind in terms of material nature.

MIND MATTERS: SOME BASIC NEUROANATOMY

One of the central figures in the genesis of modern cognitive neuroscience was not a scientist, but rather an American railway worker. The unfortunate Phineas Gage was setting a charge on September 13, 1848 when an accidental explosion blew his tamping iron through his head. This event, however, is only part of the reason that people refer to Gage as "unfortunate." Gage somehow survived the accident, but in the words of his friends and doctor, Gage was "no longer Gage." Before the accident, Gage was a conscientious, intelligent foreman. After the accident, Gage was no longer employable. This was not due to any physical disability, nor even to changes in Gage's intelligence, memory or language abilities. It was rather Gage's personality that had changed for the worse. Gage was now foul-mouthed, impatient, obstinate, impulsive and lazy. Gage's personality, mind and behaviour could be transformed so dramatically by a physical cause because these things have their basis in matter.

Gage is thus an example, albeit extreme, of mind's material nature and the potential of material nature to change the mind. No matter what connection people conceive of between mind and brain, it is a rare person who still clings to a separation of the two. For neuroscientists and philosophers, mind, however we understand and define it today, does not exist without the brain. Mind and brain are conceptually separable, but not separable in reality. Therefore, in order to consider perception, consciousness and the many other topics of interest in the YS, we must first understand some basic neuroanatomy.

The cells of the brain are of two types: neurons, which can process information or produce behaviour; and glia, or neuroglial cells, which in various ways support and maintain the functioning of neurons. The most common way that neurons communicate, or pass information to each other, is through an electro-chemical process. When a cell receives a strong enough level of stimulation, it fires and passes an electrical charge down its axon. Each neuron generally has only one axon; however, axons can be very long, even reaching to several feet, and can have a number of branches. When vesicles on the terminal of the axon receive this electrical charge or message, they translate it into a chemical message by releasing a neurotransmitter. The neurotransmitter floats across the junction between cells, where it is then taken up by dendrites, the receiver channels of neurons. Dendrites are the usual inputs to the neuron that is receiving the message. Once the message arrives at the dendrites, another act of message translation occurs and an electrical charge begins in the receiving cell. This receiving cell then may, or may not, fire (pass the message on to other cells) depending on the strength of the message. As microscopic as this process is, our sense of identity or self, our thoughts, our decisions to move or to stay still, and most of the other things that we think of as taking place under the category of mind or cognition, all rely on this basic communication between cells.[1]

If we now change from a cellular to an external perspective, the brain appears to be a rather homely organ. The cerebral hemispheres are wrinkled and, in places, deeply grooved. Underneath and behind the hemispheres lies another clearly visible part of the brain, the cerebellum. Along with this, the brain has a long stalk, the brainstem, which stretches between the higher portions of the brain and the spinal cord. To the eye, this entire organ is an unlikely locus for dreams, visions and hopes.

On its way to producing dreams and thoughts though, basic matter undergoes a remarkable transformation. The brain gives rise to genius and is genius in its organization. In an embryo, the central nervous system, or CNS, develops from a tube of tissue, the neural tube.[2] One end of this tube becomes the brain and the other

---

[1] Interestingly enough, the name of the vital communication junction between neurons is *synapse*, a word that derives from the Greek *sunapsis* 'to clasp, connect or join' (LeDoux 2002). Perhaps then, given that the word *yoga* derives from the root *yuj* 'connect, join,' we might say that these activities in the brain are yogic!

[2] The nervous system has two major divisions: central and peripheral. The central nervous system (CNS) consists of the brain and the spinal cord. The peripheral nervous system (PNS) consists of all the nervous structures that are outside of the CNS. The PNS has two subdivisions, namely the somatic division and the autonomic nervous system (ANS). The somatic division transmits information from the sense organs to the CNS. The brain can then send responses back through the PNS to muscles. The ANS is responsible for the functioning of various glands and internal organs. It again has two subdivisions or branches: the sympathetic branch and the parasympathetic branch. The sympathetic branch of the ANS activates the body's systems in order to prepare for an expenditure of energy either toward something that is desired or away from something that is a threat. This arousal state includes pupil dilation, secretion of tears, muscle dilation, a rise in blood pressure, secretion of adrenaline, sweating and an increase in heart rate (Martin 2003). The parasympathetic branch conserves energies and has activities that are antagonistic to the sympathetic system. Some of its functions include pupil constriction, digestion and reduction of heart rate.

end of the tube becomes the spinal cord. Even at three weeks, this embryonic development shows signs of three divisions: the hindbrain, the midbrain and the forebrain.

Hindbrain

The hindbrain is the lowest part of the brainstem and has two main divisions, the medulla and the metencephalon. The medulla links the higher regions of the brain with the spinal cord and controls critical bodily processes such as heartbeat and respiration. Damage to this area can result in death due to disruption of breathing and heart function. The medulla therefore provides the critical foundation upon which existence, identity and all other cognitive functions depend. The lower extension of the reticular formation is also found in the medulla. The reticular formation is a network of neurons or brain cells that plays a key role in motor activation and inhibition, maintenance of posture, arousal, attention and sleep.

The metencephalon includes the pons and the cerebellum. The pons contains several nuclei—large groups of neurons having generally similar functions—and fibers with connections to the cortex and cerebellum. The nuclei include those for audition, head position and motion (vestibular functions), as well as sensory and motor nuclei for parts of the face.[3] The cerebellum is involved with balance, movement and maintenance of muscle tone. Brain imaging shows that this area is also active, perhaps taking a fine-tuning or supportive role, in sensory processes such as pattern

---

[3] Rains 2002.

detection, pitch discrimination, awareness of body movement, and recall of lists.[4]

Midbrain

Moving upward from the hindbrain, we have the midbrain, or mesencephalon, which is like a particularly important stretch of freeway connecting two cities. It has axons that ascend to the forebrain and that descend to the hindbrain. The midbrain also contains its section of the reticular formation, as well as the superior and inferior colliculi, which are sensory integrating areas for vision and hearing. The colliculi are vital in our semi-reflexive orienting responses, such as eye and head movements, to visual and auditory stimuli. The midbrain also correlates information related to equilibrium. Thus if the midbrain sustains significant damage, heart rate and respiration may be preserved, but sensory input will not reach the forebrain. If the reticular formation sustains damage in this area, then a comatose state, a loss of forebrain arousal, may result. The substantia nigra, which contains dopamine rich neurons, is also in the midbrain. Damage to this, with the resulting loss of dopamine, causes rigidity in muscles, as is seen in Parkinson's disease.

Even from such a cursory examination of the hindbrain and midbrain, we gain a sense that brain functions are *both* localized and distributed. Areas of the brain have specific functions, but they also receive projections from and, in turn project to, other areas. In addition, although we think of mind, consciousness and identity as having their basis in our higher functions and regions of the brain, the reality is that we could not be alive, stand upright,

---

[4] Bower and Parsons 2003.

respond to our environment or have a sense of self without the hindbrain and midbrain. These lower and medial sections therefore provide a basic "on-off" switch for all other cognitive activities. Damage to the lower brainstem may result in death, but damage to areas between the medulla and the midbrain can illustrate how levels of conscious awareness are dependent upon these regions. For example, a persistent vegetative state can occur if the reticular formation is preserved and damage is in the upper brainstem, above the medulla but not reaching the midbrain. This state resembles coma, except that the patient shows cycles of apparent wakefulness and sleep. During the wakefulness cycles, the patient may also open his/her eyes in response to stimuli, but there is no evidence of emotion, attention, or purposeful behaviour.[5] In short, these wakefulness cycles do not mean that conscious awareness has returned. However, if the damage spares the medulla and occurs in the front of the brainstem below the midbrain, then "locked-in" syndrome may occur. Here the person is alert, conscious awareness is unimpaired, but the person is paralyzed and has no volitional control over anything other than vertical eye movements.[6]

From these examples, we see support for the physicalist approach to the mind-body or mind-brain. Apart from this, these types of conditions indicate that conscious awareness does not occur in isolation, nor does it occur as some type of unitary existent. As much as the brainstem, especially the lower portions, can function as an "on-off," life or death switch, we find that, with respect to conscious awareness, both "on" and "off" have their gradations, as

---

[5] Damasio 1999.

[6] Ibid.

is evinced by the distinctions between a comatose, vegetative or locked-in state. Terms such as 'consciousness' 'awareness' and 'mind' therefore mask the involvement of complex biological structures and processes. This holds true even before we take into account the forebrain, which many consider the seat of conscious awareness.

Forebrain

The human embryo at five weeks is remarkably similar to the embryos of frogs, birds, rabbits and reptiles. In humans though, over time there is notable growth and enlargement of the forebrain. The hindbrain may be the foundation for life functions, but the forebrain is like the floorboards upon which is erected the *character* of that life—who we are as humans and individuals.

The forebrain has two main divisions, the telencephalon and the diencephalon. The cerebral cortex is part of the telencephalon and is thought to represent the pinnacle of the human brain. Not surprisingly, this cortex comprises 90% of the cerebrum, or main portion of the brain of humans.[7] If, as some do, I picture a little person in my head who runs the body and watches out of the windshield of the eyes, this person—a Captain Kirk of the brain—would undoubtedly sit in the cerebral cortex.

The word *cortex* means 'bark' in Latin, and the cerebral cortex covers the hemispheres of the brain in much the same way that bark covers the outside of a tree. Most of the cerebral cortex is neocortex, consisting of six thin layers of densely packed and interconnected cells. These cells have a gray appearance due to a lack of myelination. A myelin sheath along axons, which aids in

---

[7] Beatty 2001.

the transmission of information, gives the tracts of other neurons a white appearance. Without such myelination, the tightly packed grayish neurons in the neocortex are capable of complex interactions such as correlating sensory information, initiating voluntary motor movement, and maintaining and supporting many cognitive functions such as thought, language and reasoning.

There are regions of specialization within the neocortex. These consist of primary sensory projection areas, which receive sensory inputs, motor projection areas, which are involved in the planning and execution of movements (as opposed to reflexive actions), and association areas. The association areas account for the majority of the cortex. The functions of the association areas fall under the general term 'cognition,' which is "the ability to attend to external stimuli or internal motivation [parietal association cortex], to identify the significance of such stimuli [temporal association cortex], and to plan meaningful responses to them [frontal association cortex]."[8] Association cortices therefore receive projections from many areas of the brain and, in turn, output to many other areas.[9]

Even an untrained eye can discern that the cortex, the outer bark, covers two halves, the left and the right cerebral hemispheres. The left hemisphere processes information from the right visual field and the right hemisphere from the left visual field. As well, the right hemisphere controls the left hand, and the left hemisphere controls the right hand. Both hemispheres can dictate upper arm

---

[8] Purves et. al. 2001, 565.

[9] Specifically, association areas of the cortex receive inputs from the sensory and motor cortices, the thalamus and the brainstem. The association areas output to other association areas, the hippocampus, thalamus, basal ganglia and the cerebellum (Purves et. al. 2001, 565). Association areas in the occipital lobe are primarily involved with vision.

movement.[10] Specialization or lateralization of the hemispheres is not generally problematic since the hemispheres are joined by a thick collection of nerve fibers, the corpus callosum, and the anterior commissure, which is a smaller nerve bundle. However, in some cases of people with severe, intractable epilepsy, the corpus callosum is split. These split-brain patients, as they are known, provide us with some intriguing insights into the workings of the hemispheres, as each hemisphere retains its own abilities and functions, but is not generally able to communicate with the other hemisphere.

In a classic experiment with split-brain patients, each hemisphere of a patient was shown a number of pictures on cards. One of each sets of these cards had an image related to one of two larger images. Each hemisphere only received one of the two large images. The patient was then asked to choose the card whose image best related to the larger image. Each hemisphere processes information from the opposite visual field, and each hemisphere has dominance over the opposite hand, so the right hand could correctly pick out a card that related to the image presented to the left hemisphere. The left hand, in turn, could pick out the card that related to the image presented to the right hemisphere. However, since the ability to talk is almost always a left hemisphere function, when asked why the left hand (right hemisphere) was pointing at an image, the right hemisphere was unable to answer or to pass the information over to the left hemisphere. The patient could still answer, but only from the left hemisphere. Since that left hemisphere didn't have access to the right hemisphere's image and information, the patient made up a story or theory about why the

---

[10] Gazzaniga 2000, 1298.

left hand was pointing at the image.[11] This is a literal case of the left hand not knowing what the right hand is doing. No matter though, the left hemisphere can still formulate a narrative so that the person can maintain a sense of a meaningful reality.

The left hemisphere tends to look for and find meanings or order, even when these are not present. Episodic memory, however, is more accurate in the right hemisphere than the left.[12] Perhaps this is, in part, due to the left hemisphere's tendency to interpret experience and to construct theories. Finally, both hemispheres are capable of facial recognition, but even here there is lateralization. The right hemisphere shows a bias for facial recognition of familiar others, while the left hemisphere shows a bias for self-recognition.[13]

For most people then, the left hemisphere elaborates and draws inferences in order to turn perceived information into a meaningful whole. According to Gazzaniga, the left hemisphere is the place of our autobiography, our sense of a self who has a narrative of dreams, memories, actions and experiences. The right hemisphere meanwhile retains a semantically limited but more accurate perspective of reality.[14]

Along with the main division of the hemispheres, the cortex also has many folds, which allow for greater numbers of cells to be packed into the area. The bumps or hills of the folds are called gyri, and the grooves or valleys are the sulci. These sulci and gyri also divide the cortex into four main lobes.

---

[11] Gazzaniga 2000.

[12] Ibid.

[13] Turk et. al. 2002, 842

[14] Gazzaniga 2000.

Briefly, the frontal lobe, which makes up fifty percent of each cerebral hemisphere volume in humans, is involved in the initiation of motor activity. Its anterior portions, the prefrontal lobes, integrate personality, emotion, and thought. The prefrontal cortex is active in planning, sustaining attention, reasoning, problem solving, impulse control and empathy. The unfortunate Phineas Gage sustained damage to this very area when the tamping iron struck his head. This is why Gage was "no longer Gage." The iron took away attention, impulse control, empathy and other essential aspects of his pre-accident personality. For our purposes, Gage is significant because he shows how a brain-based change can lead to a fundamental change in personality and identity that is recognizable by others. This change can be so far-reaching that it no longer seems accurate to refer to the person by their former name. We might consider the mirror image of this type of change to be the *sannyāsin*, who sets out to change many, if not every, aspect of personality, identity and behaviour, and who signals this by renouncing name as well as class and family.

Posterior to the frontal lobes are the parietal lobes. The parietal lobes are involved in perception and integration of sensory stimuli related to touch, pain, pressure and temperature, as this area of the brain houses the primary cortices and association areas for somatosensation. Each of the parietal lobes receives sensory information from the opposite side of the body. The left parietal cortex mediates attention only to the right side of the body, but the right parietal cortex directs attention to both the left and right sides. If there is a lesion in the left parietal cortex, the right can compensate for it. Damage to the right parietal cortex, however, can result in a person being unaware of objects, including their own limbs, on the left side of the body. In its more extreme forms, this contralateral neglect can include a person denying the ownership or existence of their left arm or leg.[15]

Contralateral neglect thus raises some issues concerning self, awareness and identity. Certainly the people who suffer from this disturbance experience all three. In these cases though, the perception of what is self versus what is not self is altered. Awareness of objects and one's own limbs in the left visual field can cease. Identity remains, perhaps compensating by constructing theories and stories about why a stranger's leg is in bed with them in the middle of the night.[16]

The functions of perception and recognition of auditory stimuli, as well as language comprehension, are found in the temporal lobes since the primary auditory cortex and the auditory association areas are located here. The temporal lobes are also involved in memory, due to the hippocampus, which lies along the bottom of the temporal cortex. Just as the case of Phineas Gage ushered in new ways to consider the mind-brain, another person, known only as H.M., began the modern era in studying the neurobiology of consciousness and memory.

H.M., born in 1953, received brain surgery to relieve severe epilepsy when he was 27. The brain surgery involved lesions to the hippocampus and other adjacent areas of the medial temporal lobe. This surgery resulted in severe memory impairment regarding day-to-day events. H.M.'s intellect remained intact, as did his memory of pre-surgery events, his ability to recite back a list of numbers immediately, and his basic personality. However,

---

[15] Purves et. al. 2001, 571.

[16] *Phantoms in the Brain* (1998) by V. S. Ramachandran and S. Blakeslee, is a fascinating introduction to disorders such as this.

H.M.'s ability to form new permanent memories was severely disrupted. H.M. is so profoundly forgetful that he does not recognize the doctors who have worked with him for years. In addition, he cannot now recognize a picture of himself since he has been unable to retain the knowledge of changes about his appearance over the years.[17]

H.M.'s case shows that memory is not a monolithic structure or something with a singular function. Even the traditional separation of memory into short-term and long-term is no longer accurate. Furthermore, although H.M. possesses conscious awareness of what we colloquially call a sense of self or identity, the damage to this region of his brain affects not only his perception of self, but also his experience of self. H.M., and others like him, may have access to some autobiographical memories, but without the ability to continue the narration of self, we might say that they remain largely in the immediate present and distant past tenses. We shall consider in greater detail the implications of this for the Yoga system, which seeks to control and restrict *smṛti* (memory), in the discussion on cognitive neuroscience and the five *vṛttis* (cognitive processes).

Returning again to the temporal lobe, this region received recent attention in newspapers and magazines as the locus of the "god module," an area of the brain which, when stimulated in a minority of people either by epileptic seizure or, more weakly, with a magnetic field, might give rise to experiences of awe, dread, oneness, and even the sense of divine presence.[18] We should not

---

[17] Squire 1998, 56-58.

[18] For further discussion of this, see Ramachandran and Blakeslee, *Phantoms in the Brain* (1998); Michael Persinger (1987), *Neuropsychological Bases of God Beliefs* (New York: Praeger); and Akira Ogata and Taihei Miyakawa, "Religious experiences in

take this to mean, however, that neuroscientists have just reduced, in Hinduism's case, 330 million gods to a portion of the temporal lobe. If we can track activity in the brain when we feel an emotion, recall what we had for breakfast, decide to move our left foot, or add a list of numbers, then the finding that religiously-tinged events have a corresponding place in the brain comes as no surprise. When someone looks at a tree, the activation of that person's occipital cortex does not negate the existence of the tree. On the other hand, it is clear that spiritual experiences do not occur in a vacuum, physically or culturally. The temporal lobe has connections to structures that play a role in generating emotions such as fear and joy, and drives such as hunger, sex and thirst. Hyperactivation of these regions may give rise to strong and anomalous feelings and emotions that are ineffable.[19] Given the left hemisphere's tendency to look for meaning, we might then draw on memories and ideas from religious education or enculturation in order to explain the experience to ourselves and to others. Even in this case though, the findings are intriguing for helping us begin to understand some possible elements of mystical or spiritual experiences and their connection to culture and the brain.[20]

Finally, the occipital lobe processes stimuli related to visual perception. Both the primary visual cortex and the visual association cortex are located in this lobe. Even here, in a lobe

---

epileptic patients with a focus on ictus-related episodes" (1998) in *Psychiatry and Clinical Neurosciences* 52:321-325.

[19] Churchland 2002, 386.

[20] Patricia Smith Churchland's *Brain-wise: Studies in Neurophilosophy* contains a valuable chapter on the issues surrounding religion and the brain. Churchland's discussion is particularly interesting if read in conjunction with Steven Katz's work on mysticism and culture.

dedicated primarily to visual processing, we find issues that challenge our common understandings of identity and conscious awareness. For example, the condition of blindsight occurs when there is damage to the primary visual (or striate) cortex, which lies in the occipital lobe. A person with this type of damage has a blindspot that is small or large depending on the extent of the damage. Within this region, the person is totally blind. What is interesting is that patients with this type of brain damage can locate and point to visual targets within their blindspot, even though they report that they cannot "see" the target.[21] In such cases, introspection or self-awareness proves to be fallible for something as basic as whether a person sees something or not. One could maintain that the person in these cases really doesn't *see* the object—that is, doesn't have the conscious experience of seeing the object—but in that case, who or what points to the spot where the object is? Thus it seems that even visual perception has implications for considerations of conscious awareness and identity.

While the cerebral cortex dominates the telencephalon portion of the forebrain, there are several other important structures in the diencephalon, the interior region of the forebrain. Any information leaving or entering the telencephalon must first pass through the diencephalon.[22] Of particular interest in the diencephalon, is the thalamus, which transmits sensory and motor information to the cortex, and the hypothalamus, which is part of the limbic system.

---

[21] In tests, patients with blindspots are asked to imagine where a target, such as a spot, might be that falls within their blindspot. The patients can then point to the actual target more often than would be expected by chance (Stein et. al. 1995, 123).

[22] Beatty 2001.

The thalamus is a type of brain relay station, transmitting sensory and motor information to the cerebral cortex. Axons from every sensory system except for smell synapse in the thalamus. Beyond this, the thalamus also integrates the information that it receives. Our awareness or experiences of sensations such as pain, pressure, temperature, touch, taste, sight and sound are all results of the thalamus receiving, processing and then transmitting information to the cortex. The thalamus does not pass all information on, however. It also has a gating or filtering function. When the thalamus allows less input through to the cortex, the person becomes drowsy. If the thalamus closes off even more input, the person falls asleep. Conversely, recent studies have shown that schizophrenia may be linked, in part, to faulty thalamocortical functioning. In these cases, the problem may be that the gating mechanism is faulty, allowing too many inputs to the cortex. The cortex is then flooded with faulty, useless or irrelevant information.[23]

The limbic system is sometimes referred to as the "fifth lobe," although there is also discussion regarding whether it is a proper system or simply a catch-all term that refers to a group of structures that play important roles in emotional behaviour and basic drives. The limbic system structures form a border (L. *limbus*) around the brainstem and corpus callosum. This system includes not only a portion of the thalamus and hypothalamus, but

---

[23] Results are still preliminary, although the theory of thalamic involvement is quite old. Many studies focus on dopamine's role in schizophrenia. However, for some recent studies examining thalamocortical functioning, see: Norra et. al. (2004) High-Frequency Somatosensory Thalamocortical Oscillations and Psychopathology in Schizophrenia; Danos et. al. (2001); or the review by Lahuis et. al. (2003). James Austin's *Zen and the Brain* contains an interesting chapter on the thalamus and meditation.

also parts of the prefrontal cortex, basal ganglia, cingulate gyrus, hippocampus and amygdala.

The primary role of the hypothalamus is the maintenance of homeostasis, the small window within which the body and life can exist. In order to keep life processes functioning, it senses the internal environment. The hypothalamus receives inputs from various parts of the body and can initiate compensatory activities if something disrupts homeostasis. It receives signals about blood pressure, skin temperature and fluid level, and regulates drives such as hunger and sexual behaviour. Through connections with the ANS, the hypothalamus can control heart rate, vasoconstriction, digestion and sweating. Moreover, the hypothalamus, through its connections with the pituitary gland, orchestrates the production of hormones involved in growth, metabolism, and defense. Finally, the hypothalamus also plays a role in the circadian cycle. It receives projections from cells in the retina that permit it to establish sleep and wakefulness cycles in conjunction with levels of external light and darkness. In short, many of our fundamental drives connected to what the Yoga tradition refers to as the *dvandvas* (opposites) such as hunger and thirst, heat and cold, sleep and wakefulness, and, in addition, sexual behaviour, are linked to an evolutionarily old part of the brain and one which is generally thought to be outside of conscious control. This is the most likely reason why modification and control of these drives is difficult, although not always impossible.[24]

Since other structures in the limbic system are associated with the experience and expression of emotion (amygdala) or memory

[24] Austin 1999, 191

(hippocampus), we shall consider them in connection with some of the general topics that the YS includes under the category of *citta-vṛttis* (cognitive processes).

THE FIVE *VṚTTIS* IN LIGHT OF COGNITIVE NEUROSCIENCE

In her book *Brain-wise*, Patricia S. Churchland identifies what things might count, at least provisionally, as "*unproblematic* definitions of consciousness."[25] Her list includes the awareness of, and capacity to be aware of: (external) sensory perceptions as well as somatic sensory experiences such as touch, limb position, pressure, etc.; remembering; knowing; imagining; attending to; wondering; emotional states; drive states; and some sleep states. Churchland's list bears some similarity to the five *citta-vṛttis* and their sub-categories in the YS: *pramāṇa* (valid cognition); *viparyaya* (erroneous cognition); *vikalpa* (mental construction); *nidrā* (sleep); and *smṛti* (memory). We might correlate these with some of the items on Churchland's list: *pramāṇa* may include sensory perceptions and some types of knowing; *viparyaya* may correspond to certain inaccurate types of wondering and imagining; *vikalpa* includes a very specific type of knowing, imagining or wondering; *nidrā* includes sleep states; and *smṛti* includes memory. Along with these five, which shall be our focus, we might also think of the *kleśas* (defilements), *vāsanās* (traits), and *saṃskāras* as accounting, at least in part, for some emotional states, drive states and aspects of memory. Finally, in the YS the collaborative activity of *citta*, along with *buddhi* and the seeming

[25] 2002, 133.

contact (i.e. *saṃyoga*) with *puruṣa*, accounts for awareness, attending to, and our general understanding of consciousness.

It is worth reflecting here on the nature of the *citta-vṛttis*, particularly in light of Churchland's list. Our modern sample of the fluctuations of the mind, or cognitive processes, aims to elucidate the unproblematic elements of consciousness. In the context of Yoga, we would say the list describes normal, *vikṣipta* (distracted) consciousness. It is the activities of normal consciousness that Yoga strives to modify, restrict, or cease, depending on the translation of *nirodha*.[26] For this reason, although it is difficult to avoid the use of terms such as consciousness, or conscious awareness, we must always be aware that our Western understanding of consciousness, as illustrated in this case by Churchland's list, is something quite different from the final stages of what many translate as 'consciousness' in Yoga. Thus, we can examine, in a general way, some topics regarding cognitive processes in the YS and cognitive neuroscience in order to deepen our understanding of these processes within each tradition or perspective, but Yoga, being concerned ultimately with *kaivalya* (liberation), will stretch and move beyond the limits of science.

---

[26] YS I.2.

Pramāṇa (Valid Cognition)

In the YS, the first *vṛtti*, *pramāṇa*, includes *pratyakṣa* (direct perception), *anumāna* (inference), and *āgama* (inherited knowledge, tradition). As the latter two relate more to accepting the reality of *puruṣa*, we shall not consider them here.

The process of *pratyakṣa* has two aspects, physiological and epistemological. Regarding the first, the YBh states that the external object affects or reaches the *citta* through the channel of the sense organs.[27] To gain the epistemological or knowing aspect of perception requires the concept of *uparāga* (colouration). The *citta* can know because it is coloured by both worldly objects and *puruṣa*. Although there is only seeming contact (*saṃyoga*) between *citta* and *puruṣa*, even this seeming contact allows for knowledge and sentience.[28] This epistemological process holds true for the other four *vṛttis* as well.[29] Finally, the focus of perception is on the particulars of an object rather than its universal aspects.[30]

The ultimate purpose of the YS is not to offer a theory of perception, but rather to elucidate a metaphysics, psychology and practice that may enable one to attain *kaivalya*. In order to do this it is necessary, according to the YS, to restrict, even cease, the *citta-vṛttis*, including perception. While perception is an enormous topic in cognitive neuroscience, for our purposes it is best to focus on the links between perception and identity or sense of self.

---

[27] YBh 1.7.

[28] YBh 1.7; YS 4.17-23.

[29] YS 4.18.

[30] YBh 1.7.

A great deal is known about the mechanics of perception, particularly vision. Our ability to walk upright enhances visual perception and tends to make it our dominant sense.[31] This may be one reason why restricting the gaze or closing the eyes is common in forms of meditation.[32]

In visual perception, the eyes "channel" various aspects of perceivable objects to areas of the brain. The first distinctions in visual perception are made long before conscious awareness—at the moment when the eye receives light reflected from objects. This reflected light is the source of our visual information.[33] The retina receives light that passes through the eye. Within the retina are rods, photoreceptors that respond to low levels of stimulation (that is, darkness or low levels of light), and cones, which respond to more intense light levels.[34] Further discriminations take place as some cells in the retina respond to movement—even movement in particular directions—or changes in light intensity, while others respond to detail, colour, or size.[35]

The optic nerve channels visual information from the retina to the brain. Before it enters the brain, the optic nerve from each eye splits into two pathways. One pathway, the temporal branch, proceeds through the same hemisphere, while the other, the nasal or medial branch, crosses to the opposite hemisphere. This crossing over allows the brain to process all the visual information from both eyes.

---

[31] Martin 2003, 85.

[32] BhG 6.12-13.

[33] Gazzaniga et. al. 2002, 150.

[34] Gazzaniga et. al. 2002, 151.

[35] Carpenter 1996, 137.

There are two pathways again once the optic nerve enters the brain. A small, but important, pathway receives about ten percent of visual input from the retina. Some of this input goes to the pulvinar nucleus of the thalamus and the superior colliculus. This pathway is sometimes thought of as a primitive visual system. It is important for orienting the head and eyes, as well as visual attention.

In contrast, approximately ninety percent of visual information passes along the retino-geniculate pathway. This stretches from the retina to the lateral geniculate nucleus (LGN) of the thalamus. From here the information passes to the primary visual (or striate) cortex (PVC) in the occipital lobe. Cells in the PVC respond to light of a particular direction, lines of a particular angle or length, and motion.

The PVC also connects with other areas of the visual system. Some axons project back to the LGN of the thalamus. Others project to the superior colliculus. Still others project to extrastriate or secondary visual areas. One pathway, the ventral pathway or stream, projects from the PVC to the inferior (lower portion) temporal cortex. This area processes high-resolution forms—the *what* aspects of visual perception such as shape, texture, or colour. These aspects allow us to distinguish between, for example, an apple, a volleyball and a bottle cap. Another pathway, the dorsal, connects the PVC to the posterior parietal cortex. This area allows us to locate objects in visual space and in relation to other objects. It enables us to know *where* the apple is.[36]

As with the visual system, other sensory systems such as audition and sensation employ various structures and pathways. The

[36] See Ungerleider and Mishkin, 1982.

systems utilize redundancy and specialization, feedforward and feedback loops. Most, if not all, of these processes take place outside of conscious awareness. The final result of all of this activity, interconnectivity and specialization is our sensory percept—the conscious awareness of a representation, of a sense object.

Although our experience is that we perceive a whole or unified sense object, such as a green apple, our example of the workings of the visual system shows that activities in various areas of the brain, as many as thirty in the visual cortex alone, are necessary to create that representation of an object.[37] Our sense then of a unified object is puzzling, especially since certain object features such as colour, motion, depth, orientation, faces, and facial expressions, are processed and perceived at different rates of speed. How such distributed and variable activities somehow manage to bind together to create a single representation of an object is known as the binding problem.

The concept of binding includes: binding features to an object, such as red and round to *tomato*; binding a number of objects together to form a scene, such as grass, tree and garden to *backyard*; and binding features of objects together across time, so that we can perceive the same object over time or identify change in an object without losing the sense of it being the same object.[38]

Current research on the binding problem suggests that binding may depend on a number of factors. Synchronous activity among neurons, even in different parts of the brain, seems to indicate that items and features form a whole, or belong together. Activity in

---

[37] Engel et. al. 2003, 127.

[38] Robertson 2003, 95.

various regions may account for the richness of our perceptions, while temporal synchronization can explain the grouping or identification of all of this richness with a single object.[39]

Precise synchronous activity alone, however, may not be all that is needed for binding. The parietal lobe, specifically the superior parietal cortex, is active when there are conjunctions occurring such as colour *and* motion rather than just colour *or* motion.[40] Activation of this area, along with the intraparietal sulcus, is connected with spatial attention. Furthermore, this attentional activity must be sustained to allow for visual awareness of the bound features of objects to occur.[41]

In effect, attention is a central factor for visual awareness and binding. Attention allows us to perceive features of an object and to distinguish one object from among many. Without attention, we might look at an object, but not see it. Attention is also necessary for perception of change. Once attention is removed, perception of visual change vanishes.[42]

Since attention can only be directed at a few things at any one time, what accounts for our expansive, detailed and changing visual sense perceptions of the world? The key here seems to be that attention can shift rapidly and is, under normal circumstances, drawn to any part or change of a scene that seems most relevant to the person. As a result, "the subjective impression of an observer will generally be of a richly detailed environment, with accurate

[39] Engel et. al. 2003, 140.

[40] In this latter case, the *what* or ventral stream and temporal cortex are sufficient. Parietal lobe activity is necessary however when spatially binding features of an object to the object, or when binding different objects to each other (Robertson 2003).

[41] Robertson 2003, 98.

[42] Rensink et. al. 2003.

representation of those aspects of greatest importance."[43] From this we gain a sense that a shift in attention, a shift in what the person considers to be "important," might result in an extremely different experience of objects in the world and possibly even sense of self.

Why Restrict Perception?

The YS, and indeed many traditions that use meditation, call for restriction of perception. We have considered perception only in the case of vision and yet even analysis of the workings of one sense modality reveals crucial links between perception and identity. We do not have a Captain Kirk peering inside the brain at an exact representation of objects on our retinal screen. Our *what* and especially our *where* pathways however can reinforce the experience of a self who watches at the center of things. Our representations of objects are viewer-centered.[44] Every moment of perception then reinforces this experience of self-and-world. Furthermore, the phenomenon of binding presents this self with a unified, but ultimately composed, picture of objects in the world. As we have seen, part of this composition is attention and interest driven. While this situation presents no problems under normal circumstances, Pātañjala Yoga is not much concerned with 'normal.' If the goal of this Yoga is to achieve a fundamental shift in identity and the experience of the world or reality, then a process such as perception that builds up and reinforces subject-object experiences and extravertive interest-driven constructions of the world would need to be restricted. Finally, given that *prakṛti* is

---

[43] Rensink et. al. 2003, 259-260.

[44] Austin 2000, 244.

characterized by *pariṇāma* (transformation)—and we see this characteristic clearly demonstrated in our example of visual perception—the finding that attention is crucial for the perception of visual change is significant. It could mean that under conditions of the restriction of perception and the cultivation of *ekāgratā* (one-pointedness, as opposed to extravertive shifting attention) much of the perception or experience of *pariṇāma* would naturally drop out. Perhaps, given enough time, the representations of self as center of the world would also fade and cease.

Viparyaya (Erroneous Cognition)

The second *vṛtti* is *viparyaya* (erroneous cognition), which is false knowledge based on an incorrect form.[45] If we restrict ourselves to the *sūtra* definition, then this category would include hallucination. According to the YBh though, *pramāṇa* (valid cognition) can remove or refute *viparyaya*, such as when the correct sight of one moon refutes the seeing of two moons.[46] As hallucinations due to organic disorders such as schizophrenia are not removable through a *pramāṇa*, we can safely omit these types of hallucinations from inclusion in this category. Indeed, the process of change described in the YS requires some degree of physical and mental health,[47] and, although some practices can perhaps be beneficial to health cultivation, such an aim, at least in the conventional sense, is not the central concern of Pātañjala Yoga.

---

[45] YS 1.8.

[46] YBh 1.8.

[47] YS 1.30-31.

According to the YS and YBh, *viparyaya* occurs when a real, as opposed to imaginary, object is misperceived. Further examination or correction by those whose senses are working properly can then remove this false cognition.[48] The example in the YBh is of moons, but the example of misperceiving a rope as a snake is also an example of *viparyaya.* In this old Indian philosophical puzzle, a person walks down a path in the dark and sees something curled up ahead of him. He jumps and prepares to run from a snake, but after a second look he sees that the object is, in fact, a rope rather than a snake. In the context of philosophy, there is question regarding the ontological status of the snake. If we say that the snake does not exist, then why did the man have a reaction to it? On the other hand, if we say the man was reacting to a rope, then what type of a person reacts with fright to the sight of a mere rope?

For our purposes, the snake-rope case provides us with an example of *viparyaya* and a partial illustration of how this activity can combine with emotion. To begin with, there is the perception and knowledge "That's a snake!" which is incorrect since it is based on an untrue form (snake instead of rope). Closer examination, or correction by another person, then leads to valid cognition or knowledge, "Oh yes, it's just a rope." The perception of snake is thus clearly a case of *viparyaya.*

Philosophical issues aside, there are good evolutionary reasons behind this type of misperception. If we examine the snake-rope events in sequence, we have: perception; a fearful emotional response; more perception (or a second perception); and then conscious correction. Connections between the thalamus, amygdala, and cortex, in part, allow us to have such a sequence of

---

[48] Arya 1986, 163-164.

events. The amygdala, buried in the temporal lobe, is part of the limbic system, the set of brain structures involved in emotions. The amygdala, in particular, has a role in integrating sensory stimuli with emotional significance thanks to connections with the prefrontal cortex. Furthermore, the amygdala has a role in the expression of emotional behaviour through its projections to the brainstem and hypothalamus.[49] In his book, *The Emotional Brain* (1996), Joseph LeDoux notes that the sight of a curved snake-like shape on the path goes straight to the amygdala from the thalamus. The thalamus also passes the stimuli to the cortex, but cells that project to the amygdala are more responsive. As a result, the amygdala can trigger an emotional response or defense against the snake. The cortex, however, is slower but able, especially with more information, to allow us to realize that the curved, slender object is, in fact, a stick. It can then prevent the inappropriate response of fight or flight. As LeDoux observes, the quicker reaction time of the amygdala has survival value for us, as "it is better to respond to potentially dangerous events as if they were in fact the real thing than to fail to respond. The cost of treating a stick [or a rope] as a snake is less, in the long run, than the cost of treating a snake as a stick."[50]

Misperception can thus occur as a result of our perceptual, cognitive and emotional wiring. The ability to correct and learn allows us to function normally—the curled-up shape in the corner that scared us yesterday (until we realized that it was a rope), is still a rope today. At a deeper level though, according to the Yoga system, it is not merely mundane misperception that we need to

---

[49] Purves et. al. 2001, 634-635.

[50] 1996, 165.

correct, but the fundamental misperception of reality. While this end is outside the realm of cognitive neuroscience, the key role the amygdala plays in contributing an element of primal emotion to our perception and behaviour is noteworthy.[51] Overcoming misperception will mean controlling fundamental emotional reactions, or *kleśas* such as *rāga* (attraction, attachment) and *dveṣa* (aversion), something that the YBh notes in its commentary on this *sūtra*. It is towards this end that all erroneous cognition must diminish and then cease.

Vikalpa

According to the YS's definition, *vikalpa*, mental construction, is devoid of an object and dependent upon verbal knowledge.[52] The category of *vikalpa* refers to abstract knowledge or communication deriving from the most subtle use of language available to us as humans. Open most books on cognitive neuroscience and you will find a chapter, or many chapters, on language and cognition. As one neuropsychologist notes, language is referential, it refers to "things and events in the world or to aspects of our subjective experience. As such, the use of language for expression and comprehension is intimately linked with our knowledge of the

---

[51] In *Zen and the Brain*, Austin, considering the amygdala's effects, observes that "Our amygdala enters early into a vital 'loop' of incoming signals. It comes instantly to conclusions about their survival or reinforcement value. It then relays its biased affective valences on to other circuits. They, in turn, will orchestrate the appropriate behavioural responses, both instinctual and learned, somatic and visceral. In addition, the amygdala is a nodal point for many circuits linked to our primary [conscious] experience of fear" (1999, 179).

[52] YS 1.9.

world and of ourselves and thus with the whole fabric of our cognitive and emotional being."[53]

The YS, on the other hand, seems to be talking about some use of language that is not referential, and that lacks an object, or at least the subject-predicate type of formation that most of our sentences have. Since this is a very particular definition of language use, it is difficult to address from the perspective of cognitive neuroscience. Perhaps it is enough to note that the YS recommends restricting even the most abstract, one might even say highest, use of language. If all language is referential though—including statements such as *puruṣa* is consciousness—then we can see why this restriction is necessary. *Kaivalya*, aloneness or liberation, is *not* referential. Our language and abstract concepts eventually must fall away in order to experience this.[54]

Nidrā (Sleep)

As with *vikalpa*, the YS supplies us with a clear definition of sleep. Here, perhaps not surprisingly since we all sleep, there is at least a parallel with modern science. *Nidrā-vṛtti* refers to dreamless sleep. The broadest understanding of this, in modern terms, would be any type of sleep apart from REM, or dream sleep. However, if we take the commentaries into account, then *nidrā* would most likely correspond to stage four sleep, deep sleep.

The changes to brain waves as we move from wakefulness through deepening levels of sleep to REM sleep are well documented by EEG studies. Wakefulness and heightened mental activity correspond usually with beta-activity, with high frequency,

---

[53] Rains 2002, 130.

[54] The results of Yoga will be discussed in the final chapters.

low amplitude activity. As a person relaxes, especially with eyes closed, beta-activity reduces and alpha activity, with waves of medium frequency and amplitude, dominates. Drowsiness, called stage one sleep, has waves with low frequency and amplitude. This eventually leads into light, or stage two sleep, whose waves have even lower frequency and an increase in amplitude, along with some high-frequency bursts. In stage three sleep, these bursts decrease, and the amplitude of the low frequency waves increases. Stage four represents the deepest level of sleep. Delta waves, which are extremely low frequency and high amplitude, dominate stage four sleep. This stage of sleep takes, generally, an hour to reach. Following this period of sleep, REM, or dream sleep occurs. The brain waves that occur during REM sleep are very similar to those while we are awake. The stages of sleep then repeat, with cycles of varying duration, throughout the night.

If we consider stage four sleep in particular, this seems to be the stage that is most similar to what the commentary describes. It displays the least activity, and a person in this stage is difficult to wake up and is oblivious to the environment around them. Heart rate, breathing, blood pressure, muscle tone, and metabolism are all at their lowest during this stage. It does therefore, seem the most similar to the *tamas*-dominated sleep mentioned in the commentaries on the YS. Unfortunately, the purposes of this sleep, and even dream sleep, remain unclear. There seems to be some restorative function associated with sleep and dreaming, and cognitive deficits can occur with sleep deprivation. Some current research is investigating possible links between sleep, including both REM and slow-wave, and memory, but as yet there is no consensus.

Regardless of purpose, our fundamental cycles of sleep and wakefulness are tied to our circadian clock, which is controlled by two small areas, the suprachiasmatic nuclei, in the hypothalamus.[55] When the neurons in these nuclei are inactive, we sleep, when they are active, we are awake. Exposure to daylight seems to regulate the activity of the circadian clock. Lesions to these nuclei may abolish the internal rhythm of sleep and wakefulness, but both are still possible. The reticular formation, however, is even more central to sleep and wakefulness. It is an evolutionarily old network of cells in the brainstem extending from the midbrain to the medulla. Certain groups of these reticular nuclei are active during wakefulness or during sleep. This activating system receives inputs from all over the brain, and through ascending fibers and the thalamus, it influences cycles of sleep or wakefulness by altering levels of activity or information flow to the cortex. Thus whatever the purposes of sleep and dreaming might be, they are experiences that connect us to phylogenetically old structures of the brain and to fundamental biological cycles.

Smṛti (Memory)

It takes only a moment's reflection to realize that we have many types of memory. I might remember being a little girl and riding my bicycle with its banana seat around the neighbourhood. Or I could remember the hair colour of a woman I just saw who was parking a truck. My memory of bike riding might last until the end of my life, providing me with one episode in a life narrative. On the other hand, I won't likely remember the hair colour of the woman unless I rehearse it, but why would I want to do that? What

---

[55] Martin 2003, 245.

we term 'memory' is, in reality, a variety or collection of cognitive activities. Memory involves at least three basic stages, receiving input, retaining input and possibly retrieving input (i.e. remembering). We can analyze memory temporally, that is, in terms of how long items are remembered, or qualitatively, in terms of the types of things that are remembered. Given all these variables, it is not surprising that there is more than one area of the brain that is responsible for 'memory.'

Memory connects us to time, from the distant past—as in my bicycle example—to the present that has just barely passed. The division of memory into short term and long term is no longer detailed enough to cover what is known about the workings of memory. Terminology varies, but many now speak of working memory (WM), which can store and manipulate a limited amount of information for a short time, and long term memory (LTM), which can include, at least conceptually, an unlimited number of items for the length of one's life. LTM also has divisions, primarily according to the type of material that one remembers, and whether one can normally speak of it or not.

The shortest of all the types of memory is buffering or immediate memory, which many include under working memory. Buffers are temporary stores that receive input from sensory or perceptual systems, such as auditory-verbal or visuo-spatial. Since the buffers are associated so closely with perceptual systems, these short-short-term memory systems are located in various regions correlated with forms of perception. For example, from lesion studies it appears that auditory verbal buffering takes place in the left parietal lobe, while visual-verbal buffering occurs in the left occipital lobe.[56] Buffering allows us to hold a perceptual experience from a few milliseconds to a few seconds, long enough to give us a sense of the present moment. Without attention, the sense traces rapidly degrade.[57]

The second component of working memory is short term memory (STM). As with buffering, short term memory (STM), that is memory that lasts for a few seconds to a few minutes, also depends on multiple systems. Hence, auditory-verbal STM deficits, such as the inability to hold a string of words in memory, occur after left parietal lesions.[58] Damage to the parieto-occipital region, especially to the right hemisphere, can result in deficits in visuospatial STM.[59] From such lesion studies we learn that there are *multiple* STM systems linked to various sensory-information processing areas of the brain.

Another key component for WM is the prefrontal cortex (PFC). This area of the brain may not store memories, but it is active during memory tasks. Thus memory is not only about storage, but also about *maintaining* and *remembering*. Sustained activity in the prefrontal cortex appears necessary for remembering the temporal context of an event (*when*). For example, patients with frontal lobe lesions may perform as well as a control group on recognition tasks—have you seen this before?—but display significant deficits when trying to identify whether an item was seen more recently than another.[60] Furthermore, the PFC is active when focusing

---

[56] Rains 2002, 285.

[57] Dehaene and Naccache, 2001.

[58] More specifically, this occurs when there is a lesion to Brodmann's area 40, the left supramarginal gyrus (Gazzaniga, 2002).

[59] Gazzaniga 2002, 313.

[60] Buckner and Wheeler, 2001.

attention on relevant information and inhibiting extraneous information.[61] Attention and memory are therefore intimately related. We are more likely to remember those things to which we pay attention, and conversely memory can also guide attention.[62]

The case of H.M. provides us with an illustration of differences between short term and long term memory. For H.M., surgery to relieve his epilepsy involved lesions to the hippocampus and adjacent temporal lobe. These lesions resulted in the inability to form long term memories. H.M.'s short term and working memory, however, remained intact.[63] From this and other lesion studies, it seems that the hippocampus is crucial in memory consolidation, that is in the formation, strengthening and stabilization of new long term memories. There is some idea now though that the hippocampus is the coordinator for this consolidation process, but that long term memories themselves are stored in the neocortex. Here it seems that the areas of the brain associated with specific cognitive functions store information related to those functions. Thus the association cortex of the superior temporal lobe, for example, has a role in the memory of word meanings.[64] Indeed, the pioneering studies by Wilder Penfield, despite problems in specificity, still reveal this link between various areas of the brain and memory. Penfield electrically stimulated areas of the exposed cortex of awake patients. Stimulation of some of these areas resulted in the vivid experiencing of memories. For example, Penfield found that

[61] Smith and Jonides, 1999.

[62] Rains 2002, 287.

[63] Gazzaniga et. al. 2002.

[64] Purves et. al., 2001.

auditory memories (e.g. the sound of a familiar song) was associated with stimulation of the superior and middle temporal lobes, while stimulation of the posterior temporal and occipital lobes was associated with visual memories.[65]

Apart from analyzing LTM according to activity in regions of the brain, we can also divide LTM into types or categories of memories. The case of H.M. is also significant for this. Despite his amnesia and his problems forming new long term memories, H.M. was still able to learn, that is form new memories, of some semantic knowledge. Amnesiacs like H.M. can also learn, and show improvement, on new procedural tasks, despite the fact that they will state that they have never learned the task before.[66] Thus we have a number of different types of long term memory (LTM).

Although terminology varies somewhat, distinctions in LTM are made between non-declarative or procedural memory, and declarative (or explicit) memory, which includes both semantic and episodic forms of memory. Non-declarative memory is the type of memory that we use constantly, even though we cannot consciously recall the knowledge involved. For example, procedural memory—a type of non-declarative memory—includes our ability to learn, and remember, how to perform motor skills, such as riding a bike or walking. The learning that results from classical conditioning, where one neutral stimulus is paired with another, also falls under non-declarative memory, as do habituation and sensitization. In all of these examples, we draw on our learning, on our memories in order to act, but we are not

---

[65] Buckner and Wheeler 2001, 627.

[66] Gazzaniga et. al. 2002.

necessarily aware of the memory processes or knowledge that underlie our actions.

Declarative, or explicit, memory is semantic or episodic. Semantic memory draws upon the meaning of words and concepts. The types of memory here relate to facts and information about the world, instructions on how to perform tasks, and other types of information that a person can talk about or express, but that don't relate to personal experience. Even within this one class of memory, we store memories for different types of things in different parts of the brain. For example, PET scans done as people identify objects in pictures (semantic memory), show an increase in activity of the lower temporal cortex, an area important for the perception of complex objects, when people are identifying animals or tools. There is also activation of the left premotor area, an area activated when we imagine hand movements, when the person only identifies pictures of tools.[67]

If I now ask you to begin remembering and listing the name of every animal that starts with the letter *d*, you will be drawing upon semantic memory. If, in the process of doing this, you remember the *dog* you had as a child, and the good times you shared with your dog, then you are beginning to draw upon episodic memory. Episodic memory, so severely affected in H.M.'s case, is memory related to our personal history. It supplies us with the material of our personal narrative or autobiography. Some studies suggest that different pathways of the brain are involved in episodic memory retrieval as opposed to semantic memory retrieval.[68]

---

[67] Rains 2002; Martin et. al., 1996.

[68] Wiggs et. al. 1999; Tulving 2002.

Out of all the forms of memory, it is episodic memory that seems most closely related to our identity. It is clear, then, why a system such as Yoga recommends the restriction of this type of memory. Yet we have seen, even from a cursory examination, that there are many types of memory, and it seems likely, although it is not directly stated, that Yoga would restrict many of these. If we consider our shortest of short term memory systems, buffering, we can see that these systems are closely tied to perception. Any restriction of perception would also restrict buffering. Other forms of working memory are likely to be affected by manipulation of attention, in fact, it is likely that shifts in attentional focus would affect all forms of memory storage, consolidation and retrieval. Restriction of language and conceptual thought, finally, would affect semantic memory. In the end, whether we are bringing something to mind and working with it, remembering a fact, or narrating an episode from our past, our sense of self is intimately connected to memory. If Yoga seeks to shift our identity with this self, then restriction of most types of memory is necessary. The exception, however, might be procedural memory, which would likely have to be preserved as we need to know or remember, largely unconsciously, how to walk, eat, and perform other basic skills. These procedural memories are least tied to a sense of identity or overtly autobiographical memories.

Finally, even this brief examination of memory shows how deceptive a term can be. The word 'memory' now stands for many different types of cognitive functions that are located in many areas of the brain. Should one word represent all the various activities in these regions? Are words such as 'memory,' 'consciousness' and 'identity' not deceiving in their simplicity, and in what they mask? We commonly experience ourselves as a conscious self watching, examining, and manipulating the content of our senses and our mind. Cognitive neuroscience indicates that the brain is not merely the stage for the mind and consciousness, but actually *is*, through its matter and functions, somehow what we call self, mind, identity and consciousness. On an intellectual level, we may recognize or agree with this, but our experiences, including language and culturally embedded concepts, tend to ignore or distort this situation. Neuroscience and psychology may, through progress in research, offer a method to correct such distortions and misperceptions, at least at a cognitive level.

Four

Following the Plot

Yoga Practice and the Mind-body

The yogin overcomes *saṃyoga* and achieves *citta-vṛtti-nirodhaḥ* through practice. Practice, as well as being the means (*upāya, sādhana*) to achieve the goals of Yoga, also helps us to understand the nature of the mind-body, identity, and consciousness. In the *sūtras* that describe practice, metaphysical and psychological theories combine with the actual (or hypothesized) mind-body complex. There exists in the YS a theory-practice continuum where theory provides a direction and rationale for practice, and practice, according to the text, leads to a confirmation of theory.

CATEGORIES OF PRACTICE

There are three main categories of practice in the YS: *abhyāsa-vairāgya* (repeated practice and detachment); *kriyā-yoga* (the yoga of activity); and *aṣṭāṅga-yoga* (eightfold or eightpart yoga). Differences of opinion exist regarding the relationship between these categories, particularly since some practices are mentioned in more than one category.[1] For example, the practices of *kriyā-yoga*

---

[1] Many modern scholars agree that the YS divides the basic categories of practices according to the abilities of the yogins. Beyond this, however, there is disagreement over

the relation between practices. For example, Dasgupta takes perhaps the most conservative view, emphasising that the practices of *kriyā-yoga* are "also called *yogāṅgas* [that is, part of the eight limbs of yoga category] as they help the maturity of the yogic process by gradually increasing the lustre of knowledge" ([1920]1989, 114). He further adds that *abhyāsa* and *vairāgya* are by their very nature included within the *yogāṅga* category of practices, and "are not to be considered as independent means different from them" ([1920]1989, 118). According to Dasgupta then, some practices (*abhyāsa* and *vairāgya*) may be suitable for yogins with focused minds, but all practices work together, are basically subsumed under the category of the *yogāṅgas*, and should not be considered in isolation from the others.

Deshpande also sees the three categories of practices as intertwined (1978, 110). Examining the initial *sūtras* of the first and second *pādas*, he notes a corresponding structure between YS 1.2 (*yogaś citta-vṛtti-nirodhaḥ*) and 2.1 (*tapas-svādhyāyeśvara-praṇidhānāni kriyā-yogaḥ*, the yoga of activity is comprised of asceticism, study and devotion to *īśvara*). In this way,

> *tapas* is related to purification of *citta*;
> *svadhyaya* is related to purification of the *vṛttis*;
> and *isvarapranidhana* is related to *nirodha*.
> *Kriya Yoga* is thus a process or action integrally associated with what is signified by Yoga. It is action born of Yoga. Hence the phrase *Kriya Yoga* (1978, 76).

Abhyāsa and *vairāgya* are also associated with *nirodha*, for persistence in *abhyāsa* brings about a state of "disentanglement" or *vairāgya* from the *vṛttis* (1978, 33). However, Deshpande's later statement that *abhyāsa* itself is a state devoid of *vṛttis* and that it is "born of *nirodha*" seems counter to even his own interpretation of *abhyāsa* and *vairāgya* as means to slow down and eventually stop the *vṛttis* (1978, 32, 76). In summary then, Deshpande strongly associates the *kriyā-yoga* of the second *pāda* with the practices mentioned in the first *pāda*. Under this interpretation, there does seem to be some confusion between means and resulting states.

Feuerstein views the *aṣṭāṅga-yoga* section as a possible interpolation, or at least a quotation from an earlier Yoga text or tradition (1979, 86). These limbs of yoga, according to Feuerstein, form a subcategory of *tapas* (asceticism) that is found in the *kriyā-yoga* section (YS 2.1) (1991, 90-91). *Tapas*, in turn, is a form of *abhyāsa* (practice) (1991, 91). Feuerstein considers all forms of yogic practice as *abhyāsa* or *vairāgya*, but also emphasizes that *kriyā-yoga* is the principal means of Pātañjala Yoga: "Kriyā-yoga is not a mere preliminary ritual to the practice of the so-called 'eightfold Yoga,' but it forms a full-fledged tradition of its own which, moreover, must be understood as "Patañjali's teaching proper" ([1979] 1989, 59). However, it becomes evident that all practices only make sense if they are philosophically grounded. The final three limbs of *aṣṭāṅga-yoga* (concentration, meditation and *samādhi*), as well as the (unstated) goal of the *aṣṭāṅga-yoga* section on practice, all suggest some basis in philosophy. Further, unless there was some underlying philosophy of mind-body concepts and liberation, there would be little point in undertaking such practices.

in 2.1 are included under the *aṣṭāṅga-yoga* category of the *niyamas* (observances). However, examining these categories of practices within the overall context of the YS and YBh can help to clarify the relations between them.

The YBh contains an early attempt to clarify the relation between the categories of practice found in *pādas* one and two, and many commentators and scholars tend to follow this explanation. According to this, the first *pāda*, containing the *abhyāsa-vairāgya* practices mentioned in 1.12 and following, is meant for yogins with a focused or concentrated mind (*samāhita-citta*). More specifically, the *abhyāsa-vairāgya* practices occur after the discussion on the nature of the *citta-vṛttis* and are proposed as remedies to these *vṛttis*.[2] The second *pāda* and its practices are meant for those who possess a normal, extroverted mind (*vyutthita-citta*)[3] or who, perhaps, are beginners. The *Tattva-Vaiśāradī* (TV) and the YSBhV follow this view as well, although the latter is more concerned with clarifying the relation between *sūtra* 2.1 and 2.32. The section on *kriyā-yoga*, which begins the second *pāda*, is really a prelude to the exploration of the nature of a mind held under the sway of *avidyā*. Finally, the *aṣṭāṅga-yoga* section

---

Miller takes an opposite view to Feuerstein's on the relation of *kriyā-yoga* to the *aṣṭāṅga-yoga* practices. According to Miller, the three practices of *kriyā-yoga* merely constitute a "subset of the second limb" of *aṣṭāṅga-yoga*, namely *niyama* (observances) (1995, 44). The reason that *kriyā-yoga's* practices are highlighted specifically at the beginning of the second *pāda*, is that the author wishes to emphasize "their particular efficacy in preparing the novice yogi for the arduous discipline that leads to pure contemplation by diminishing the forces that obstruct the path (Miller 1995, 44).

While some lack of clarity does exist between these categories of practice, the division found in the YBh nevertheless seems valid in the general sense.

[2] YS 1.5-11.

[3] YBh 2.

midway through the second *pāda* provides a holistic overview of the entire yogic process—moving from fundamental ethical practices to some of the more advanced states of consciousness. Thus the first *pāda*, by elucidating the goal and practices of elite yogins, provides a standard. The second *pāda* then allows those who are not as accomplished at Yoga to understand the practices and the nature of an extraverted mind. In this way, those practitioners could also aspire to achieve the higher states of Yoga.

ABHYĀSA AND *VAIRĀGYA*

The term '*abhyāsa*' does not occur in the earliest strata of Brahmanical texts, but rather appears in later texts, perhaps most notably in the *Bhagavad-Gītā*,[4] along with *vairāgya*, which is also a post-Vedic term.[5] *Abhyāsa* (repeated practice) and *vairāgya* (detachment) do not share the same nature. However, the two are mutually reinforcing and are useful, perhaps even necessary, for proper practice. They therefore form one main category of yogic practice, although many of the individual practices listed under the category of *abhyāsa-vairāgya* seem primarily to relate to *abhyāsa*. *Vairāgya* is difficult to cultivate directly and external antidotes are unlikely. Other than recommending frequent consideration of the non-attractive, not much can be done.

YS 1.12 states that the control/cessation of the five *vṛttis* is through repeated practice and detachment.[6] *Abhyāsa* and *vairāgya* are thus the primary means to achieve *citta-vṛtti-nirodha*. Leaving

---

[4] BhG 6.35

[5] Feuerstein 1980, 79.

[6] *Abhyāsa-vairāgyābhyāṃ tan-nirodhaḥ* "The control/cessation of these is through repeated practice and detachment" (YS 1.12).

aside *vairāgya* for a moment, the definition of *abhyāsa* is found in YS 1.13,

> *tatra sthitau yatno'bhyāsaḥ*
> repeated practice is the effort to remain in that (state of *citta-vṛtti-nirodha*)

This repeated practice may consist of any number of individual practices described in the *sūtras* following 1.13. Regardless of the individual practices,

> *[sa tu] dīrgha-kāla-nairantarya-satkārāsevito dṛḍha-bhūmiḥ*
> It (*abhyāsa*) moreover, practiced assiduously for a long time, uninterruptedly, and with reverence, becomes a firm foundation.[7]

We gain a sense from this that the repeated effort to achieve or remain in a state of *citta-vṛtti-nirodha* involves a long, demanding and gradual process. The term *satkāra*, with reverence—that is, with awareness of its importance or value—here allows a somewhat emotional side to what is otherwise a fairly rationalistic undertaking. The YBh states that *satkāra* is manifested or indicated by the effort and attitude seen in the pursuit of *tapas* (asceticism), *brahmacarya* (continence), *vidyā* (knowing) and *śraddhā* (faith, particularly faith in the efficacy of Yogic practice).[8] Repetition of such demanding practices will not likely be undertaken unless one values the path and its results.

---

[7] YS 1.14.

[8] YBh 1.14

In this gradual process, there are five aspects that are necessary in order to proceed, in order for the *citta-vṛttis* to cease with only the *saṃskāras*, underlying traces remaining, a state which is termed *asaṃprajñāta samādhi*. These five are: *śraddhā* (faith in efficacy); *vīrya* (energetic effort); *smṛti* (mindfulness, attentiveness); *samādhi*; and *prajñā* (wisdom).[9] Although these five are often termed *upāyas* (means), they represent psychological states and cultivated personality styles as well as techniques. This list of the five *upāyas* that partly comprise *abhyāsa-vairāgya* therefore collapses the distinction that is often made between method and resulting state. Or, more specifically, it acknowledges that psychological states have effects on a person and that repeated practice at developing and holding such states is, in fact, a method.

Further, the list of five *upāyas* also presents a stage theory of psychological progression or psychological changes. The logical order of the list, along with the YBh, supports such a view. *Śraddhā* (faith) according to the YBh, is *cetasaḥ samprasādaḥ* (clarity or serenity of mind).[10] If a person has faith in something, in this case the path the yogin adopts, there is less likelihood that external events will be upsetting. *Śraddhā* is, therefore, not simply faith, but the removal or non-entertaining of doubt. This is why *śraddhā* is also linked with *vairāgya* and not simply *abhyāsa*, for *vairāgya* is only the "negative aspect of this *śraddhā*."[11]

Since *śraddhā* helps to increase desirelessness and also can help cushion a person from the blows of life, the YBh likens it to a

---

[9] YS 1.20.

[10] YBh 1.20.

[11] Dasgupta [1920]1989, 110.

protective parent.[12] This sustaining action that protects one from doubt, from falling from the right path, and from unwelcome or unwholesome things, results in *vīrya*, increased energy to follow. the path. *Vīrya*, in turn, will increase one's ability to concentrate and to practice mindfulness (*smṛti*). Here we must translate *smṛti* as mindfulness or attentiveness rather than as memory as in YS 1.6 and 1.11. Since the practices that comprise *abhyāsa-vairāgya* aim at controlling the *citta-vṛttis*, it is unlikely that the *smṛti-vṛtti* could be the cause, or the instrumental means, in bringing about a state of control/cessation. Instead, it is more likely that *smṛti*, in this *sūtra*, means mindfulness, as it often does in the Buddhist tradition.[13] A link, however, does exist between memory and mindfulness. Remembering past experiences, whether one's own or of others, makes one become aware of what can go wrong. This may lead to cautiousness and watchfulness and, in ascetic traditions, to mindfulness. Mindfulness may, over time, lead to *samādhi*, and repeated *samādhi*, in turn, may lead to *prajñāta-viveka* (discerning or distinctive wisdom).[14]

Yogins who follow the type of practices listed in YS 1.20, or who progress through these stages, will do so at varying speeds. The YS notes that the intensity or ardor (*saṃvega*) among yogins is responsible for such variation.[15] Interpretations of these *sūtras*,

---

[12] YBh 1.20.

[13] Arya 1986, 268.

[14] Here YBh 1.20 reads, *samāhita-cittasya prajñā-viveka upāvartate* "Discerning wisdom approaches for one whose mind is concentrated." Since *puruṣa* is immutable and always separate, the reality or knowledge of this is not really new. Therefore the YBh says that discerning wisdom "approaches" the person, rather than vice versa, because *prajñā* is not something that is newly created or achieved. The process involves removing obstacles in order to unveil wisdom and the true nature of reality.

[15] YS 1.21-22.

and the categories of yogins, vary. However, most important here is the recognition of individual differences among yogins, and the suggestion that different practices will work for different types of people. In recognition of this, the YS lists a number of alternative practices. Since the *sūtra* style is brief and avoids unnecessary elaboration of topics, it is quite safe to assume that the alternative practices were too important to leave out.[16] Their importance and inclusion may rest on the necessity of providing an accurate portrait of the breadth of practices in the Yoga system, or simply on the efficacy of the techniques they discuss. Thus, just as *asaṃprajñāta-samādhi* is close for those whose ardor is intense,[17] it is also close for those who occupy their minds with *Īśvara* (*Īśvara-praṇidhānād vā*).[18]

---

[16] Rukmini 1981, 217.

[17] YS 1.21.

[18] There is some disagreement among scholars regarding the significance of YS 1.23, *Īśvara-praṇidhānād vā* (or from occupying the mind with the lord) and its relation to the surrounding *sūtras*. J. W. Hauer views *sūtras* 1.23-51 as a separate section of practice all dealing with *Īśvara-praṇidhāna*, and therefore finds that the text contains four rather than three main categories of practice (Phillips 1985, 401).

Bhattacharya, although not directly addressing this topic, does view *Īśvara-praṇidhāna* as an alternative *upāya* (means) to *abhyāsa-vairāgya*, which was described in YS 1.12 (1985, 163). He supports this view by noting the importance of the word '*vā*' in the *sūtra*, which identifies it as an alternate means. As well, Bhattacharya notes that the fifth case ending of *praṇidhāna* agrees with the ablative case ending of the word expressing 'means' in YS 1.12, namely "*abhyāsa-vairāgyābhyām*" (1985, 164). Bhattacharya concludes that

> it follows that there are two means to *cittavṛttinirodha*, the first in the joint application of *abhyāsa* and *vairāgya* and the second is devotion (*praṇidhāna*) to *Īśvara*. Thus it is clear that the means known as *abhyāsa-vairāgya* is the first means and the means called...*Īśvara-praṇidhāna*...is alternative to it (1985, 165).

This does not necessarily mean, however, that *Īśvara-praṇidhāna* is completely separate from the category of *abhyāsa-vairāgya*. The *vā* may, in fact, connect 1.23 with

Īśvara is an important metaphysical concept in the YS. *Īśvara-praṇidhāna* is investing forth the mind, or occupying the mind, with this metaphysical concept. Although Feuerstein suggests that *bhakti* (loving devotion) may comprise part of *īśvara-praṇidhāna*,[19] the *sūtras* immediately following 1.23 discuss *īśvara* as a logical construct rather than as a deity requiring or

---

sūtras 1.21-22 that discuss how *samādhi* is closer to those yogins whose ardor is intense, mild or medium. In this case, like intense ardor, it is an additional factor that will decrease the time it takes to attain *samādhi* for those who practice *abhyāsa-vairāgya*.

Feuerstein takes a different perspective on the relation of 1.23 to the other *sūtras*. He maintains that *īśvara-praṇidhāna* is "at best an alternative to the five factors mentioned in 1.20 [*śraddhā, vīrya, smṛti, samādhi*, and *prajñā*]. Probably, however, the word *vā* has to be understood in the sense of 'or more specifically,' which makes *īśvara-praṇidhāna* a particular instance of *abhyāsa* ([1979]1989, 42).

While acknowledging that it is not completely clear how the *īśvara-praṇidhāna* section of the YS relates to the other three categories of Yoga practice discussed in the text, and, in particular, how it relates to YS 1.12 and following, the section does appear to be almost separate. This, however, does not mean that it is an addition to the original text. Rather, it may have been included as a second tradition. From this perspective, there may have been a more atheistic form of Yoga, which had a strong psychological and philosophical focus, and this atheistic Yoga is represented in the first part of the YS. The theistic form of Yoga, with an emphasis on focusing one's mind on a quintessential figure or concept (still not an anthropomorphic deity), was then added to the atheistic form in order to represent more fully the different perspectives found in yogic practice and belief. The theistic form and practices were then incorporated into the section of the text that examines the methods that yogins with concentrated or focused minds employ to attain *samādhi*. Thus, from this perspective, there are still three main categories of practice, with *īśvara-praṇidhāna* being a special, possibly theistic, case associated with the first category.

Gerhard Oberhammer, however, takes the opposite view, maintaining that Yoga was originally theistic, and that the YS contains "perhaps the oldest statement of the basic structure of an authentic theistic meditation" (1989, 204). Even he admits though that Patañjali did not make much use of this type of theistic meditation (1989, 205). This being the case, it seems clear that there is a preference for the atheistic methods, which are possibly earlier.

[19] [1979] 1989, 42.

deserving devotion.[20] As well, *sūtra* 1.27 associates *īśvara* with the *praṇava* and *sūtra* 1.28 reads:

> *taj-japas-tad-artha-bhāvanam*
> There is (i.e., there should be)
> repetition of it (the *praṇava*) and
> contemplation of its meaning.

Other than this, there is no mention of devotional practices.

The *praṇava*, which is the signifier for *īśvara*,[21] is associated with *oṃ*. The word comes from *pra* (forth)+√*nu* (to shout, exult). *Nu* is likely connected with the word '*nava*' 'new,' that is, what is new, at the beginning. In other words, it signifies the first creative principle. The *praṇava* is the essence of the Veda in sound form. That essential form is also thought identical with the essential or ultimate aim of Yoga, in this context, the ideal yogin, *īśvara*. Repetition of the *praṇava*, and contemplation or cultivation of it (*bhāvana*), thus provides a direct connection with this ultimate principle. From this perspective, it is likely to be a more effective means than any other because it is direct and less abstract. It is, therefore, within the mental reach of more people, provided that they can maintain an appropriate level of focused awareness. Indeed, the YBh mentions specifically that the mind of the yogin who has repeated the *praṇava* and contemplated its meaning becomes one-pointed.[22] All Yoga practices aim at this goal; however, *īśvara-praṇidhāna* and repetition of the *praṇava* may be particularly effective.

---

[20] See *sūtras* 1.24-1.27.

[21] YS 1.27.

[22] *tadasya yoginaḥ japataḥ praṇavārthaṃ ca bhāvayataḥ cittam ekāgraṃ sampadyate* (YBh 1.28)

Repetition of the *praṇava* is also significant for here the physical discipline of Yoga combines with mental discipline and metaphysics. Sound and language are associated with breath, and as breath is the easiest instrument for a yogin to carry around, it is the closest and most convenient tool for meditation. As the *sūtra* calls not only for repetition of the *praṇava* but contemplation as well, a psychological, intellectual component is introduced, along with a key metaphysical concept. The abstract nature of Yoga's first principle is thus combined with the mind-body complex by means of breath. It is justified then that this strongly holistic approach is singled out as particularly effective.

This holistic approach is not limited to the specific practice of *Īśvara-praṇidhāna.* The entire system of practices gathered under the category of *abhyāsa-vairāgya* (or gathered in the first *pāda*) reflects this approach. The five practices listed in 1.20 are also strongly holistic. *Śraddhā* (faith) has an emotional and psychological component and can incorporate the metaphysical aspect of *Īśvara-praṇidhāna* as well. *Vīrya* (energetic effort) is not simply a matter of will-power, but rather involves a basic physical and psychological strength and energy in the organism as a whole. *Smṛti* (mindfulness, attentiveness) clearly falls into the psychological realm, but, as we see in *sūtras* 1.30-32, this depends on having a healthy body.

Vairāgya, the concomitant result of *abhyāsa*, reinforces this holistic approach to such an extent that we could consider it a practice as well. For this reason, it is appropriately paired with *abhyāsa*. *Vairāgya* is the awareness, the sensing or feeling that seen and revealed objects are no longer desired.[23] According to the YBh, seen objects are mundane things such as women (and conversely, it is understood, men for women), food, drink and power. Revealed objects are both traditionally handed-down information, such as the Veda and its ancillary literature, or the beliefs associated with this information. For instance, if the scriptures promise heaven, the yogin must be disinterested in this too. *Vairāgya* therefore involves the spheres of external objects, body, mind, and belief systems.

Even superior to this type of *vairāgya*, is the indifference to the *guṇas* that comes about from having knowledge of *puruṣa*.[24] This is superior because external objects, the body, mind and belief systems, are all included under the category of the *guṇas*. This superior form of detachment transcends, or perhaps abandons, everything that exists as an evolute of *prakṛti*. In effect, the holistic approach is finally overthrown, or overcome, by ingrained dualism.

Up until that point of transcendence, *abhyāsa-vairāgya* is a thoroughly holistic set of practices that, in a broad sense, forms the two poles of any type of Yoga practice.[25] Employing a water metaphor, the YBh explains the relation between the two: *vairāgya* impedes the stream toward sense objects, while *abhyāsa* opens up or encourages the stream of *viveka* (distinctive or

---

[23] *dṛṣṭānuśravika-viṣaya-vitṛṣṇasya vaśīkāra-saṃjña vairāgyam* "The sensing/feeling of subjugation for the one without thirst of seen and revealed objects, is (felt as) detachment" (YS 1.15).

[24] *tat-paraṃ puruṣa-khyāter guṇa-vaitṛṣṇyam* "Superior to that is indifference to the *guṇas* due to knowledge of *puruṣa*" (YS 1.16).

[25] Feuerstein 1980, 78.

discerning knowledge).[26] This approach thus represents a balance between nurturing or cultivating states of mind and consciousness, and closing off or disengaging from other objects, states and beliefs. This fundamental two-fold approach can help overcome even serious distractions and obstacles that the yogin may encounter, and the YS lists some specific practices in this category that are particularly useful.

Antarāyas (Impediments), *Vikṣepas* (Distractions), and Symptoms

The repetition and contemplation of the *praṇava* results in inward-mindedness and the absence of impediments or obstacles.[27] *Sūtras* 1.30-1.40 discuss the nature of these impediments, their symptoms, and a number of methods in addition to *īśvara-praṇidhāna* that can overcome them.

The impediments, which are *citta-vikṣepas* (distractions of or for *citta*), are: *vyādhi* (sickness); *styāna* (languor); *saṃśaya* (doubt); *pramāda* (negligence, or slackness in practice); *ālasya* (sloth);

---

[26] YBh 1.12.

[27] *tataḥ pratyak-cetanādhigamo 'py antarāyābhāvaś ca* "Then there is attainment of the interior mind and also the absence of obstacles (YS 1.29). Patañjali does not explain the term *pratyak-cetanā.* There is also some debate regarding how the compound *pratyak-cetanādhigamo* should be split (Bhattacharya 1985, 76). The YBh paraphrases it as "*sva-rūpa-darśanam apy asya bhavati*" ("for him there is also the sight of his [true] self") (1.29). The YSBhV defines the term as "*yathāvat-sva-rūpa-saṃvedanam*" ("the experiencing or feeling of one's nature/self as it really is).

Pratyak-cetana' simply means "one whose thoughts (*cetana*) are turned inward" (Monier-Williams). The result of this inward-mindedness would be *pratyak-cetanā*, the consciousness of what is inside (i.e., *puruṣa*). Miller (1995, 37) and Feuerstein ([1979]1989, 45) read the compound as introspection or inward-mindedness, respectively. Arya reads the compound as *pratyak-cetanā*, inward consciousness, but maintains that, "the intent of the sūtra is simply to state that through *īśvara-praṇidhāna* the consciousness is drawn inwards by divine grace, naturally leading to the realization of the inwardly conscious self" (1986, 322).

avirati (dissipation, or non-abstention); *bhrānti-darśana* (wandering thinking about the nature of things); *alabdha-bhūmikatva* (non-attainment of stages [of yogic states]); and *anavasthitatva* (instability).[28] According to the YBh, these nine impediments arise with the *citta-vṛttis*, and in the absence of these impediments, the *citta-vṛttis* do not occur.[29] A particularly intimate and important connection thus exists between these impediments and the *citta-vṛttis.* The extinction of these impediments and their accompanying symptoms seems a crucial part of *citta-vṛtti-nirodha.*

The YBh offers an explanation of each of the impediments. *Vyādhi* is sickness that is caused by an imbalance of the *dhātus* (humors: *vāta*, wind; *pitta*, bile; *śleṣman*, phlegm); or by an imbalance of the *rasa* (blood), or by the *karaṇa* (sense organs: eye; ear; nose; tongue; skin). *Styāna*, languor, is the non-working of the *citta.* The term derives from √*styai* (be collected into a heap or mass; stiffen or grow dense). *Styāna*, then, although clearly psychological, carries an almost physical sense of thickness. *Saṃśaya*, doubt, is the type of knowledge that "touches both ends." This category, which in modern terms we call "sitting on the fence," would include concerns about whether or not one is on the right path. *Pramāda* is the non-cultivation of the means of *samādhi*, that is, non-diligence in Yoga practice. It is therefore negligence and inattentiveness. *Ālasya*, sloth, is the absence of action or exertion of the body and of the *citta* due to heaviness. *Avirati*, dissipation, is the non-stopping (i.e. continued engagement) of a *citta* whose nature is still tied to objects.

---

[28] YS 1.30.

[29] See YBh 1.30, *sahaite citta-vṛttibhir bhavanti / eteṣām abhāve na bhavanti.*

Bhrānti-darśana is contrary or perversive knowledge. It is thinking or insight based upon erroneous cognition or knowledge (*viparyaya-jñānam*). *Alabdha-bhūmikatva* is the non-attainment of any stage of *samādhi*. Here lack of success would discourage the practitioner and thus become an impediment. Finally, *anavasthitatva* is the non-fixity of the *citta* on the stage that is attained, and the consequent lack of confirmation needed for enthusiastic and diligent pursuit of practice.

As with other lists in the YS, the order of this list is not incidental. The order of items moves from the physical to the psychological, and from the external to the internal. This is obvious in the case of sickness versus the other items. However, the external to internal continuum is evident even among the psychological items. Languor, doubt, negligence in practice and sloth are internal states that can easily and fairly accurately be inferred by any careful observer. It would be more difficult, if not impossible, to infer dissipation (in the sense of having a mind still involved with objects) or erroneous conception from behaviour alone. One would usually need to speak with a person to detect their presence. Only the person practicing, a guru, or someone else thoroughly familiar with Yoga would likely be able to detect the final two items—non-attainment of any stage of *samādhi*, and instability in these stages. They are therefore even more internal than the preceding psychological items.

Since there is also a conception that the grossest stain washes out more easily than a subtle stain, the order of the list may also suggest that physical imbalances can be more easily remedied than subtle psychological imbalances. This is not to say that the former deserve less attention than the latter. The *sūtra* seems to indicate that some level of physical health is a prerequisite for mental work.

The inclusion of these impediments in the first *pāda* is interesting, for it may indicate that even fairly advanced yogins can struggle with these issues, and make progress. Finally, the list in 1.30 clearly shows an association and dependency between the body and the mind, and also illustrates the close connection between Yoga and Indian medicine.

Having noted the impediments of *citta*, YS 1.31 then lists their symptoms:

> *duḥkha-daurmanasyāṅgam ejayatva-*
> *śvāsa-praśvāsā vikṣepa-sahabhuvaḥ*
> pain, depression, tremors of limbs,
> [wrong] inhalation and exhalation,
> these are the ones that accompany
> the distractions.

The YBh again offers explanations for each of these terms. *Duḥkha* is suffering that pertains to the body and the mind (*ādhyātmika*), and is caused by living beings or supernatural agencies. The YBh list of the causes of *duḥkha* also reveals a logical order. Here the location of causes moves from internal to external and fundamental to optional: the self (body and mind); living beings; and finally those things for which the person may have no explanation (*ādhidaivika*, supernatural). The internal awareness of limitation, aggravation etc., is the fundamental *duḥkha*. In the absence of that internal awareness, the other two types of *duḥkhas* would not come across as *duḥkha*. *Duḥkha* is therefore suffering taken in its widest possible sense, with acknowledgment of the connection between internal awareness and external events. The YBh instructs that living beings afflicted with such suffering should try to ward it off. *Daurmanasya,* literally 'being in a bad condition of mind,' is the disturbance of mind that arises from the failure or non-fulfillment of desire. The YBh comment on *aṅgam-ejayatva*, the trembling of limbs, is less helpful, "*yad aṅgānyejayati kampayati tad aṅgam ejayatvam*" (that which shakes the limbs, causes them to tremble, is the unsteadiness of the limbs). This possibly refers to nervousness or unease that makes the person unable to remain calm and still. *Śvāsa* is wrong inhalation, breathing which licks up or swallows the air. This may refer to mouth-breathing, which is a common sign of nervousness. *Praśvāsa* is wrong exhalation, which could also occur during mouth-breathing. Alternatively, Vācaspati Miśra in the TV indicates that *śvāsa* and *praśvāsa* are problematic because they are forms of *anicchata prāṇa* (unintended breath, or breath lacking volitional control) and therefore are contrary to the practice of *prāṇāyāma* (breath control).[30]

This list presents the accompaniments of the impediments or distractions. These accompaniments, therefore, are symptoms or marks (*liṅga*) on the basis of which one can infer the existence of distractions in a person who displays them. They can function then as screening tools for discerning the proper attainment of stage. Fundamentally, the "association with *duḥkha* etc. is the criterion of deciding whether an acquirement is yogic or not."[31] Similarly, we may infer that the presence of equanimity, joy, steadiness and disciplined awareness of breath could indicate attainment of yogic stages. The employment of repeated practices related to some of these as a way of purifying the *citta*, confirms such a view.

---

[30] TV 1.31.

[31] Bhattacharya 1985, 160.

Practices

Having noted the impediments and their accompanying symptoms, YS 1.32 recommends *eka-tattvābhyāsaḥ*, the repeated practice (*abhyāsa*) of focusing on one thing (*tattva*, lit. "thatness," a real unit, existent, essence) in order to counter-act and get rid of them.[32] YS 1.33 provides methods for purifying the *citta*:

> *maitrī-karuṇā-muditopekṣāṇāṃ*
> *sukha-duḥkha-puṇyāpuṇya-*
> *viṣayāṇām bhāvanātaś citta-*
> *prasādanam*
> clarity of mind (*citta*) (is achieved) through the cultivation of friendliness (*maitrī*), compassion (*karuṇā*), joy (*muditā*), and equanimity (*upekṣā*) which pertain to (i.e. are to be viewed as proper responses to) pleasure, pain, virtue and vice (respectively).

The *sūtra* gives the sense that *maitrī* and the other *tattvas* are not merely feelings that one cultivates in a general way, but rather they relate to specific occasions or instances. The YBh appears to share this perspective, as it explains that one should cultivate *maitrī* with respect to all living beings who have obtained the enjoyment of pleasure.[33] That is, one should not be envious of those who have good fortune. One should also cultivate compassion in respect to those who are distressed, rejoice in virtue, and cultivate

[32] *tat-pratiṣedhārtham eka-tattvābhyāsaḥ.*

[33] YBh 1.33.

equanimity—that is, not be reproachful—with respect to those whose character is lacking in virtue.

Clarity of the *citta* (YS), as well as a *citta* that is one-pointed (*ekāgram*) and steady (YBh) arises from cultivation of these four *tattvas*. This seems psychologically plausible, for if a person has these attitudes toward other people, and if these attitudes grow out of practice and not out of superiority, then cultivation of such attitudes would lead to calm, unbiased thinking and peace of mind. A mind that is peaceful and undistracted is better able to concentrate and maintain focus, or be clear. In contrast, jealousy, callousness, sociologically negative behaviour or attitudes, and the superiority implicit in them, tend to distract and focus the mind on externals.

The order of the list reveals that cultivation of *maitrī*, *karuṇā*, *muditā*, and *upekṣā* also has strong ethical, communal and individual aspects. *Maitrī* and *karuṇā* are the most communal in orientation. *Muditā* is more internal in orientation than the previous two, and *upekṣā* is perhaps the most internal and abstract of the four in the list. That the YS shares the exact terminology of this list with the Buddhist (Pāli canon) tradition and Jain tradition indicates the strong association in all of these traditions between moral and spiritual development.[34] Indeed, Vācaspati Miśra regards the cultivation of these four attitudes as necessary practices. He considers the remainder of practices in the first *pāda* as merely optional. Furthermore, if, as the YBh does, we read the following *sūtras* as providing options for cultivating *manasaḥ*

---

[34] *Maitrī*, *karuṇā*, *muditā*, and *upekṣā* are common, non-technical terms found in Yoga, Buddhism and Jainism. Their use for individual meditation and ethical practice may well originate in the Yoga tradition, which has, it seems, always displayed some overlap or influence among Indian religions.

sthitim (steadiness of mind), then the cultivation of *maitrī* etc. is essential in order to purify or clarify the *citta*, while other practices then help to stabilize it.

YS 1.34 lists the next method for cultivating the clarity of *citta*, or steadiness of mind (*manas*)[35]

> *pracchardana-vidhāraṇābhyāṃ vā*
> *prāṇasya*
> or (clarity of *citta*) occurs through
> expulsion and retention of the breath
> (*prāṇa*).

Prāṇāyāma (breath control) is also one of the eight limbs of Yoga.[36] The YS may mention breath control under both *abhyāsa-vairāgya* and *aṣṭāṅga-yoga* sections because it is of value to those who possess focused minds as well as those who possess externally oriented, or extroverted, minds. In addition, the terms *pracchardana* and *vidhāraṇa* may include some types of breath control that are not part of the *prāṇāyāma* disciplines listed in YS 2.29.[37]

Ordinary forms of exhalation and inhalation are clearly not what YS 1.34 means by *pracchardana* and *vidhārana*. If Vācaspati Miśra is correct that there must be an element of mindfulness accompanying proper breathing, then mindful awareness of breath is a part of *pracchardana* and *vidhārana*. More specifically, according to the YBh,

---

[35] YBh 1.34.

[36] YS 2.29.

[37] Arya 1986, 347.

kauṣṭhyasya vāyoḥ nāsikā-
puṭābhyāṃ prayatna-viśeṣāt
vamanaṃ pracchardanam
pracchardana is the ejecting of the
internal air through the two nostrils
by a special kind of effort.[38]

Vidhāraṇa is nothing other than *prāṇāyāma*, control or restraint of the breath.[39] The breath control method recommended here thus seems to include full attentiveness to a slow, disciplined way of inhaling and exhaling, without allowing breath to enter or exit suddenly.[40]

While the preceding *sūtra* on achieving clarity of *citta* had a strong psychological and ethical approach, YS 1.34 on breath emphasises a physical and psychological technique. That this tradition, along with the Buddhists and Jains, was cognizant of the connection between mind and body is seen in this consideration of ethical, psychological, and physical techniques. Specifically, here the Yoga tradition recognizes some type of relationship between the mind and breath, between thought and breath. Speech shows this close connection, as does the idea that breath is a close aspect of the lifeforce or principle (*prāṇa*), a view that certainly predates the YS. In fact, *prāṇa*, even in ancient scriptures, provides a crucial link not only between mind and body, but between the individual and the cosmos as well, or the micro and macrocosm.

prāṇam āhur mātariśvānaṃ
vāto ha prāṇa ucyate,

---

[38] YBh 1.34.

[39] YBh 1.34.

[40] TV 1.34.

> *prāṇe ha bhūtaṃ bhavyaṃ ca*
> *prāṇe sarvaṃ pratiṣṭhitam*
> The air (wind) that moves in the sky [sky as the mother's womb, and air that moves therein] is called *prāṇa*. The *prāṇa* [in the living body] is called *vāta*.[41]
> In *prāṇa* [as the highest principle] reside the *bhūta* (created object with spatio-temporal dimensions) and the *bhavya* (object to be created in the future). Thus all have position in *prāṇa*.[42]

Here we observe the idea that *prāṇa* is both a functional and material basis of human life that accomodates and transcends the individual along with space and time (*bhūta-bhavya*). A number of later *Upaniṣads* support such an interpretation. For example, in the *Maitrāyaṇi* (MU) the seer speaks of an inner gate of *prāṇa*, thus relating to the individual, and outer gate of the sun, relating to the macro, field, or cosmos.[43] Similarly, Āyurveda, the Indian medical tradition, also reflects on breath as an agent that affects—we may even say links or unifies—the physical and psychological realms. Although working from a monistic metaphysical perspective rather than the dualistic view present in the YS, the *Caraka-saṃhitā* (CS) comments on breath, psyche, and body can apply equally to the *kṣetra*-realm of Sāṃkhya-yoga.

---

[41] One of the *tridoṣas* in Āyurveda.

[42] AV XI.4.15. Translation by Dr. S. N. Bhavsar; correspondence.

[43] Dr. S. N. Bhavsar. See, for example MU 5.1.

The CS states repeatedly, "*loka-saṃmitaḥ puruṣaḥ*," "the person [*puruṣa* as individual rather than soul] corresponds (is equal) to the world (universe)," and that the material elements that form the universe also form the person and vice versa.[44] Likewise, the body follows the mind or psyche, and the psyche or mind follows the body—in other words, intentionality is accomplished through physicality.[45] Breath or wind (*prāṇa*, *vāyu*) is then thought of as the mediating agent between body and mind:

vāyus tantra-yantra-dharaḥ...
niyantā prāṇetā ca manasaḥ,
sarvendriyāṇām udyojakaḥ,
sarvendriyārthānām abhivoḍhā,
sarva-śarīra-dhātu-vyūhakaraḥ,
sandhānakaraḥ śarīrasya
Vāyu is the supporter (upholder) of
the instrument (machine) that is the
bodily system...
the restrainer and leader of the mind
(*manas*),
the inciter (exciter) of all the senses
(sense organs),
the transporter (bearer) of the objects
of all the senses,

[44] *evam ayaṃ loka-saṃmitaḥ puruṣaḥ / yāvanto hi loke mūrtimanto bhāva-viśeṣāstāvantaḥ puruṣe, yāvantaḥ puruṣe tāvanto loke iti* (CS 4.4.13).

[45] *śarīraṃ hyāpi sattvam anuvidhīyate, sattvaṃ ca śarīram* (CS 4.4.36). I use "intentionality" here in its broad sense, rather than specifically philosophical sense.

the arranger of the *dhātus*[46] in the
entire body,
the uniter (the one who causes or
promotes union) of the body
(1.12.8).

Thus, although the distinctions between inner and outer, self and other, individual and field, are concepts that are normally held by most people, and reinforced by common experience, the Indian medical, philosophical and yogic traditions indicate that *prāṇa* has properties that unify or transcend such categories. In analysis and practice, these traditions found that *prāṇa* has temporal, spatial, functional and material aspects. There existed a common understanding that *prāṇa* provides a link between the physical, physiological and psychological dimensions of living beings. *Prāṇa* is a bridge between matter and mind; an activity of being that involves the material and structural elements of physique while affecting and directing the functional dimensions of our cognitive faculties.[47] Therefore the development of techniques for manipulating this relationship between breath and mind was obviously important enough for Patañjali to mention it as a separate option.

Following the section on breath, the YS begins the list of objects that can provide a support for focusing the mind (*manas*):

viṣayavatī vā pravṛttir utpannā
manasaḥ sthiti-nibandhinī

---

[46] A *dhātu* is that which supports, upholds or sustains the body. For a discussion on the relationship between *bhūtas*, *doṣas*, and *dhātus*, see Dasgupta ([1922]1975, Vol. 2, p. 317f).

[47] I am greatly indebted to Dr. S. N. Bhavsar for directing my attention to the importance of *prāṇa*, for his suggestions of the above passages, and for reflections on the significance of *prāṇa* for mind/brain-body and practice.

> A result that refers to an object,
> when arisen becomes a basis for the
> stability of the mind.[48]

In this practice, yogic activity centers on a worldly object and uses that object as the foundation for practicing stability of mind.

The YBh on this *sūtra* lists a number of bodily objects for focus: the tip of the nose; the tip of the tongue; the palate; the middle of the tongue; and the root of the tongue. Although every step has not been specified, the YBh intention is clear to this extent: even when the corresponding object is not present, at the nose tip etc., a (totally pleasing) sensation that the object would have produced arises. This generates confidence about the efficacy of the path—presumably by demonstrating the influence of the mind on material objects. Direct personal experience of one teaching can help to validate the rest of the teachings. Thereafter, the yogin will approach practice with greater faith, energetic effort, attentiveness and concentration.[49] The commentary thus provides not only suggestions for objects of focus, but also a rationale for why this type of practice is useful.

YS 1.36 reads:

> *viśoka vā jyotiṣmatī*
> or (an outcome) that is without
> sorrow and consisting of illumination

---

[48] YS 1.35. The result, or proceeding forth (*pravṛtti*) that the *sūtra* refers to is, according to the TV, *sākṣātkāra* (lit. 'making evident to the senses). It is, therefore, a type of direct evidence in the form of experience. The YSBhV indicates that this type of direct sensory result gives the yogin confidence. It gives the yogin enthusiasm or encouragement to continue the practice of Yoga, just as the rising of smoke heralds the generation of fire (thereby encouraging one's efforts) when rubbing wood together (*yogānuṣṭhānaṃ pratyutsāha-janano nirmathya-mānasyāgner iva dhūma-samudbhavaḥ*).

[49] YBh 1.35.

(when arisen becomes the basis for
the stability of *manas*).

This option for practice consists of a more inward or subtle type of reflection than that of the previous *sūtra.* The initial experiences identified in 1.35 are with respect to objects, whereas, according to the YBh, in 1.36 they are with respect to *buddhi*, and represent a type of internal illumination. Even experiences of smell, touch, etc. that occur in the absence of objects (i.e. as in YBh 1.35), still have objects as their points of reference or bases. Thus, according to the YBh, there are two sorrowless (internal) perceptions or experiences: those related to objects, and those that are merely *asmitā*—where only the sense of I-amness or basic identity exists. Only the latter consists of illumination.[50] The YSBhV further specifies that the object-related one precedes the illuminated one.

Given this interpretation of 1.36, YS 1.37 represents another progression,

vīta-rāga-viṣayaṃ vā cittam
or (an outcome) that is the mind
(*citta*) from which objects of
attachment are gone (when arisen
becomes the basis for the stability of
the mind).

In other words, the focus here is contemplation of a *citta* that is free from attachment to objects. While the illumination experience that is the focus of 1.36 is subtle and certainly doesn't have an external object, it nevertheless includes a sense of identity that is, in fact, an object (and one that usually generates strong attachment). The focus of 1.37, however, is the coming into being

[50] YBh 1.35.

of a mind that is free from attraction.[51] This *sūtra* maintains the movement toward more difficult or higher levels of practice found in the previous *sūtras*.

Continuing this movement, *sūtra* 1.38 focuses on the experience of dream sleep and dreamless sleep:

> *svapna-nidrā-jñānālambanaṃ vā*
> or (a mind) which has the support in
> the form of dream-knowledge and
> dreamless sleep-knowledge (attains
> stability).

Here, focusing the mind on the form the mind has in dreaming or non-dreaming sleep is viewed as conducive to stabilizing states of meditation. The idea is not to focus on the objects that were experienced in a dream, but rather to recognize that without the objects being physically present, there is still knowledge and experience of them. From this the yogin learns that it is possible to dissociate the experience from the object, a valuable lesson in detachment. Non-dream sleep gives the sense of a state without any experience of objects—even consciousness of identity.[52]

Sūtras 1.39 and 1.40 broaden the possibilities of focus. Anything, from the most minute thing to the largest thing, can be an object of meditation:

> *yathā'bhimata-dhyānād vā* //

---

[51] *vīta-rāga-cittālambanoparaktaṃ vā yoginaś cittaṃ sthiti-padaṃ labhata iti* "Or the mind of the yogin, coloured by the support in the form of an attachment-free mind, obtains/acquires the stage of stability" (YBh 1.37).

[52] The significance of dream and non-dream sleep has a long history in Indian philosophy (see, for example, the *Bṛhadāraṇyaka Upaniṣad* 4.3.21). The use of dream-cognition and deep or dreamless sleep-cognition here, however, is different. Continuation of the stage of concentration—of freedom from the external world and identity—is emphasized here.

> *paramāṇu-parama-mahattvānto'sya vaśīkāraḥ*
> or (the mind attains stability) due to meditation on whatever one prefers.
> His (a yogin's) mastery is (can be) from that which is most minute to that which is the greatest.

Thus stability of the mind can be attained, and maintained, whether the mind is concentrating on the smallest thing (an atom) or on something large, or whether the mind is focusing on readily apparent aspects of an object or those that are subtle.[53] In the end, it seems that anything can be a useful object of meditation if the person is able to bring a rigorous and enduring focus to it.

The category of practices found in the first *pāda* reveals several important aspects that are also generally relevant to the text as a whole. Analysis of the lists in this section on *abhyāsa-vairāgya* reveals an implicit order as well as a great deal of embedded knowledge. Items on the lists tend to move from the external to the internal, and from the physical to the abstract or subtle. Further, the lists, and indeed this entire section, display a holistic

---

[53] Bhattacharya maintains that *paramāṇu* is a synonym for *sūkṣma* (subtle). Therefore, the *sūtra* refers to the yogin's mastery over the *tanmātras*, subtle elements (Bhattacharya 1985, 121). With this interpretation, the first *pāda sūtras* on methods refer to the yogin acquiring focus on, and mastery over, all the manifestations and levels of *prakṛti*. In light of previous *sūtras*, both interpretations (small and large, subtle and gross) seem possible. A number of objects of meditation have been mentioned, which favors the first reading. The inclusion of the experiences in YBh 1.35 and deep sleep in YS 1.38 might favor the Bhattacharya's interpretation. I include both as possibilities, but, based only on the *sūtras* themselves, incline toward reading 1.40 as "from that which is most minute to that which is the greatest," particularly since 1.39 says to meditate on whatever one chooses. A subtle element seems a less likely choice than a small stone or flower for meditation. Further, mastery of mental stability toward extremely large or small objects would seem to imply simultaneous mastery of the more subtle elements that accompany each experience of an object.

approach that includes not only the mind-body, but ethical or social and religious elements as well. This approach may represent the merging of theoretical thinking with extensive observation of practice. Although the ultimate goal of this system is *kaivalya* (aloneness), the fundamental category of *prakṛti* underlies the mind, body and world. Therefore the connection between mind, body, and society that these practices illustrate is not unexpected. The presumed efficacy of the practices rests, in part, on this understanding of interconnection. In addition to this, everything except *puruṣa*, we are told, undergoes a process of transformation (*pariṇāma*) and Yoga practices, whether ethical, physical or psychological, if we even divide these conceptually, only affect the direction of this change. This is why the YBh author emphasizes, in accordance with the doctrine of *sat-kārya-vāda*, the idea that *vairāgya* only impedes the stream toward sense objects while *abhyāsa* opens up the stream toward distinctive knowledge.[54] The philosophical concepts in the YS are therefore not awkwardly grafted onto Yoga practices, as some suggest, but rather philosophy and practice constitute a well-integrated whole and represent a thoroughly holistic approach. As Arya says, "practice is cultivating and nurturing *viveka*, a view of life, of reality and of oneself and one's attitudes and works in the light of the philosophy and the experience of discernment or discriminating wisdom."[55]

Finally, in seeking to understand the purpose or results of these practices, we see throughout this section of the text an emphasis on practicing and stabilizing certain mental states. This should give us some sense that there exist, according to the YS, states of

---

[54] YBh 1.12.

[55] Arya 1986, 195.

consciousness quite apart from the *citta-vṛttis*. Whatever *citta-vṛtti-nirodhaḥ* may be, it is not the absence of *citta* entirely, but rather some enhancement, apart from the *vṛttis*, that perhaps includes (at least up to the final stages of Yoga) the perfection of aspects such as friendliness, compassion, joy, equanimity and extraordinary powers of focus.

KRIYĀ-YOGA

The *sādhana-pāda* (chapter on means, i.e. the second chapter) begins with a definition of the second category of practices, *kriyā-yoga*:

> *tapas-svādhyāyeśvara-praṇidhānāni*
> *kriyā-yoga*
> Ascetic practices, study and
> occupying the mind with *īśvara*
> comprise the Yoga of activity.[56]

According to the YBh, the purpose of this section is to show how even a *vyutthita-citta* (active, externally-oriented or extroverted, mind) can be restrained through Yoga.[57] YS 2.2 is more specific though, stating that:

> *samādhi-bhāvanārthaḥ kleśa-tanū-*
> *karaṇārthaś ca*
> The purpose (of *kriyā-yoga*) is to
> cultivate *samādhi* and to thin out the
> *kleśas*.

In this respect, *kriyā-yoga* bears some similarity to *abhyāsa-vairāgya*. Both contain positive and negative aspects, namely

---

[56] YS 2.1.

[57] YBh 2.1.

cultivation of certain states and detachment from other states or things.

The *kleśas* and their cause become the focus of the *sūtras* following 2.2 until the *aṣṭāṅga-yoga* section begins on 2.28-29. The three practices identified as *kriyā-yoga* were so well known in the Indian tradition that there was no need to provide further detail. Indeed, even the commentary on these *sūtras* is brief. In general though, all three practices of *kriyā-yoga* are special measures or techniques, in the sense that people would not do these things unless they deliberately found time for them. There is an implication here of conscious decision and initiative, which, in turn, presupposes that some philosophizing about normal, ordinary life has already been carried out by the individuals about to undertake the specific practices of *kriyā-yoga*.

Regarding each of the practices, *tapas* is, in fact, one of the oldest concepts in the Hindu tradition. In Vedic hymns, the power of heat, *tapas*, brings about creation.[58] *Tapas* is consequently identified with the sacrifice and its creative power. Over time, it appears that the idea of *tapas* became internalized until it signified not only internal, creative heat, but also the purifying practices that produce it. It is in this sense then, that *tapas* likely acquired the connotation of ascetic practices.[59]

Since *tapas* is such an old and central concept, it is not surprising that the YBh makes a strong statement regarding its importance:

nātapasvino yogaḥ siddhyati

---

[58] See, for example, Ṛg-Veda X.129 and X.190.

[59] Kaelber 1989, 144.

> Yoga cannot be
> accomplished/perfected for the one
> who does not possess *tapas*.[60]

Impurity, which arises from traits formed from karma, *kleśas*, and contact with objects, cannot be dissipated without *tapas*, and therefore it is a necessity in yogic practice. Again, this is the old and central notion of *tapas* as a set of practices—and a creative heat arising from them—that purifies.

The most common practices associated with *tapas* are fasting, prolonged sitting (or, less commonly, remaining in one position) and enduring pairs of opposites such as heat and cold.[61] Given that there is some recognition in the YS that concentration depends upon a certain level of bodily health,[62] the references to *tapas* need not necessarily imply extreme or harmful practices. Rather, *tapas* likely refers to practices that are ascetic yet beneficial.[63] The general trend in the YS is one of recommending a non-extreme and perhaps even pleasing procedure.[64]

Svādhyāya means literally 'your own study.' The YBh describes it as "repetition of the purifying *praṇava* etc., or the study of the *śastras* on liberation (*mokṣa*)."[65] This process therefore involves both study and recitation and shows a special concern with speech and meaning. This strong focus on intellect and language differentiates it from other methods.

---

[60] YBh 2.1.

[61] YSBhV 2.1.

[62] YS 1.30-31.

[63] Chatterjee 1989, 86.

[64] See, for example, YS 1.39.

[65] YBh 2.1.

The third method that comprises *kriyā-yoga* is *īśvara-praṇidhāna.* This was mentioned previously in YS 1.23 where it was associated with repetition of the *praṇava* and contemplation of its meaning. In 2.1 though, the YBh describes it as

> *īśvara-praṇidhānaṃ sarva-kriyāṇāṃ parama-gurāv arpaṇaṃ, tat-phala-saṃnyāso vā*
>
> *īśvara-praṇidhāna* is the resigning/placing of all actions on the supreme guru (god?), or the renunciation of its fruits/results.

While such surrender of actions and renunciation does have a meditative element, and agrees with the BhG reading, the emphasis of *īśvara-praṇidhāna* in 2.1 is, not surprisingly, on action and it seems to allow, or incorporate, a more actively devotional approach than the practice described in 1.23.

Together, the practices of *kriyā-yoga* cover all aspects of religious life. All of the practices are oriented toward the external; ascetic practices, study, and surrender of actions, all imply some interaction with the outside world. Therefore these practices are particularly suitable for a yogin with an extroverted mind. They help that practitioner begin to thin out negative tendencies and orient the mind toward *samādhi*.

AṢṬĀṄGA-YOGA

Aṣṭāṅga-yoga consists of: *yama* (restraints); *niyama* (observances); *āsana* (postures); *prāṇāyāma* (breath control); *pratyāhāra* (withdrawal of senses); *dhāraṇā* (concentration); *dhyāna* (meditation); and *samādhi* (literally, 'comprehensive placement,' 'fulfillment,' 'total attainment').[66] According to the YS,

> *yogāṅgānuṣṭhānād aśuddhi-kṣaye*
> *jñāna-dīptir ā viveka-khyāteḥ*
> from the performance of the limbs of
> yoga there comes about the
> dwindling of impurity (which results
> in) the light of knowledge that
> reaches to *viveka-khyāti*
> (distinguishing or distinctive
> knowledge, discerning wisdom).[67]

In this, *aṣṭāṅga-yoga* is similar to both *abhyāsa-vairāgya* and *kriyā-yoga* in its two-fold emphasis of detaching or extinguishing and cultivating.

Patañjali's *aṣṭāṅga-yoga* is probably preceded by the *ṣaḍ-aṅga-yoga* (six-limbed yoga) found in the *Maitrāyaṇi Upaniṣad.*[68] This six-limbed Yoga consists of: *prāṇāyāma* (breath control); *pratyāhāra* (withdrawal of the senses); *dhyāna* (meditation); *dhāraṇā* (concentration); *tarka* (reasoning); and *samādhi.* The YS thus can be thought of as having added *yama* (restraint) and *niyama* (observance) to this list, and having replaced *tarka* with *āsana* (posture). Dasgupta suggests that the substitution of *āsana* for *tarka* indicates an early change in the relations between the Sāṃkhya school and the Yoga school.[69] If, as seems likely, *ṣaḍ-aṅga-yoga* represents the earlier tradition, then as they grew into

---

[66] YS 2.29.

[67] YS 2.28.

[68] Feuerstein 1974, 71.

[69] Dasgupta [1930]1974, 65.

fully formed schools, Sāṃkhya increasingly came to emphasize *tarka* (reasoning), while Yoga, if we consider the three categories of practices in the YS, took a number of different approaches.

The YSBhV, however, provides a non-historical line of reasoning for the YS's inclusion of extra limbs. It states that even to qualify for, or begin Yoga, there must be the following of *yama* and *niyama*.[70] Therefore, *yama* and *niyama* are implied in earlier lists that contain only six limbs.

Beyond these lines of reasoning, the changes in the lists from six-limbed to eight-limbed Yoga represent the acceptance of a strongly holistic set of methods. *Aṣṭāṅga-yoga* includes ethics and posture, and the list as a whole suggests a fine awareness of how to control and direct the entire mind-body complex. I do not mean to suggest here that the earlier, six-limbed Yoga does not contain holistic elements or an awareness of the mind-body complex. Rather, I want to emphasize that Pātañjala Yoga *particularly* focuses on these aspects.

Regarding the *aṣṭāṅga-yoga* list as a whole, there is some question whether the eight limbs represent a sequential series of practices, in effect a stage theory, or are practices meant to be performed concurrently. The answer may be that they are both. The YSBhV does present the limbs as stages:

> *yama-niyama-yuktasyādhikṛtasya*
> *yogina āsanādy-aṅgānāṃ pūrve*
> *sthira-pada-*
> *prāptasyottarottarānuṣṭhānaṃ*
> *prāptam* | *na hi prathamaṃ sopānam*
> *anāruhyottaram ārodhum śakyam* ||

---

[70] YSBhV 2.29, *yama-niyamavator yogādhikāropapatteḥ*.

> When the yogin is rightly qualified [i.e. has mastered] restraints and observances, then there can take place (the practice of) posture etc. The performance of each subsequent limb occurs when there is firmly rooted attainment of previous limbs. For it is not possible to mount the subsequent steps without having surmounted the first.[71]

Given this, the *yamas* would certainly represent the first stage of Yoga for ordinary people who are beginning Yoga practice.[72] However, the passage does not necessarily imply that people would abandon the *yamas* as they move on to other limbs. Just as a person would not likely cultivate friendliness and compassion (YS 1.33), only to "progress" and abandon these qualities, a yogin is not likely meant to give up the practice of the *yamas* and *niyamas* when he/she moves on to other limbs. Instead, a firm and continuing foundation in the early limbs means that the yogin becomes capable of further growth and practice.

Yamas (Restraints)

> *ahiṃsā-satyāsteya-*
> *brahmacaryāparigrahā yamāḥ*
> The *yamas* are: *ahiṃsā* (non-violence); *satya* (truthfulness); *asteya* (non-stealing); *brahmacarya*

---

[71] YSBhV 2.29.

[72] Dasgupta[1920]1989, 125.

> (continence); and *aparigraha* (non-accumulation).[73]

As with the list of *kleśas* in YS 2.3, the first item is the basis for the other items on the list. Thus *ahiṃsā*, the first *yama*, is also the most fundamental. It is the root of the other *yamas* as well as the *niyamas* (observances).[74] Thus the system of *aṣṭāṅga-yoga* clearly rests, and relies, on the practice of non-violence.

The YBh offers a very broad definition of *ahiṃsā*:

> *tatrāhiṃsā sarvathā sarvadā sarva-bhūtānām anabhidrohaḥ*
>
> In this (list), *ahiṃsā* is the non-harming of all creatures by any means at all times.[75]

The word '*anabhidroha*' (non-harming) refers not only to avoidance of oppression or violence, but also to avoidance of deception—of doing anything that would be unexpected or that would not live up to the expectations of another. The notion of *ahiṃsā* here therefore seeks to eradicate the most basic root or source of violence. Since to live is to injure others, the highest form of *ahiṃsā* is to pursue an ethical-spiritual path and avoid rebirth altogether.

The YBh also has a precise, but rather intriguing, explanation of *satya* (truthfulness). *Satya* is truthfulness in speech and mind. Truthfulness corresponds to an object as it is, or to what is seen or inferred. Communication should not, of course, be deceiving, confusing or lacking in information. However, even if speech is

---

[73] YS 2.30.

[74] YBh 2.30, *uttare ca yama-niyamās tan-mūlāḥ*

[75] YBh 2.30.

truthful and correct, it should not be used to harm other creatures, for that would be evilness rather than truthfulness.[76] Since *satya* is based on *ahiṃsā*, something that is truthful cannot be violent in any way.

The explanation of *asteya* (non-stealing) is brief. Theft is unsanctioned (*aśāstra-pūrvaka*) taking of someone else's material goods and making them one's own. *Asteya* is the prohibition against such actions.[77] This prohibition is understandable and appropriate given that yogins are not to cultivate desires or to cause harm.

Brahmacarya (continence), according to the YBh, is the restraint or control of the generative organ on the part of a person who is guarding his other senses that are not (directly) meant for celibacy.[78] The YSBhV, in accordance with Upaniṣadic practices of *brahmacarya*, explains that more is required here than mere celibacy. *Brahmacarya* is not only restraint of the sex organ, but other senses as well. This restraint is therefore physical, mental and verbal.

The final *yama* is *aparigraha* (non-accumulation). Non-accumulation of objects is non-acceptance based on the understanding that acquiring, keeping or protecting, dissipation, clinging to, or abusing (*hiṃsā*), objects are all faults.[79] That is, in

---

[76] YBh 2.30.

[77] YBh 2.30.

[78] The YSBhV rightly takes *guptendriyasya* as a *bahu-vrīhi* compound: *brahmacaryaṃ guptendriyasya guptānyendriyasya puruṣasya abrahmacaryārthavāṅ-manasādi-vṛtti-śūnyasya upasthendriya-saṃyama iti* "Continence is the restraint of the sex organ, on the part of a *guptendriya* (man), i.e. on the part of one who has protected other sense organs (and) who is devoid of the state of the mind (speech etc.) that are not meant for the vow of continence (2.30).

[79] YBh 2.30.

accumulation, it is thought that a person indulges in *hiṃsā* one way or another. As well, any activities associated with accumulation would encourage the yogin to direct attention to external things, and this would detract from practice.

The *yamas* are meant to modify and restrain the yogin's relation with the external world. Many religions have such ethical practices, however the YS adds that:

> *jāti-deśa-kāla-samayānavacchinnāḥ*
> *sārva- bhaumā mahā-vratam*
> a great vow consists (in practicing
> the *yamas*) in all spheres (in respect
> to all things) regardless of birth,
> place, time and custom.[80]

This means that the practice of non-violence is extended to all living things, that truthfulness must be maintained at all times, that there must never be accumulation of objects, etc. The yogin must not allow class, custom, time, or place to modify or mitigate these restraints. From the phrasing, this applies to future lives, if rebirth occurs, as well as the present life. The great vow thus shows the strength of commitment to the yogic path.

Niyamas (Observances)

The *niyamas* are: *śauca* (purity); *saṃtoṣa* (contentment); *tapas* (ascetic practices); *svādhyāya* (study); and *īśvara-praṇidhāna* (occupying the mind with *īśvara*).[81] The last three comprise the practices of *kriyā-yoga*. However, the YBh offers slightly more information on ascetic practices in this section of the text.

---

[80] YS 2.31.

[81] YS 2.32.

Śauca (purity) has its source in the external world and the internal milieu. External purity comes from such things as the use of special type of cleansing earth (a soap substitute, but perhaps having some medical or health benefits as well), from water, and from the consumption of pure food. Internal purity is the complete washing of impurities from the *citta*.[82] There is a strong sense here that the Yogin must attain purity, it is not something that is a given, or a necessary part of the human condition. Since the list in this *sūtra* has the same structure as YS 2.30, *śauca* may well be the basis for the other *niyamas*, just as *ahiṃsā* is for the *yamas*. The YS, in these lists, seems to present the most difficult and thematically the most basic practice first and then moves to more specific practices that arise from, or depend upon, the first.

Saṃtoṣa (contentment) is the absence of desire to take additional means, that is, to be content with things that are at hand and not to seek more.[83] The difference between *samtoṣa* and *aparigraha* (non-accumulation)[84] is that *saṃtoṣa* seems more inward, directed against the impulse to take more, whereas *aparigraha* seems more external. The commentary on *aparigraha* supports this view, focusing on reasons why a yogin should not accumulate external objects. *Saṃtoṣa* may eventually grow out of a disciplined practice of *aparigraha*.

Tapas (ascetic practice) is "*dvandva-sahanam*" (the enduring of opposites).[85] By this is meant the enduring of hunger and thirst, cold and heat, standing and sitting, the complete absence of

---

[82] YBh 2.32.

[83] YBh 2.32.

[84] YS 2.30.

[85] YBh 2.32.

communication even through gesture etc., and the absence of communication through speech. Ascetic practice also includes vows such as *kṛcchra* (various forms of penance or mortifications), as well as the more specific vows of *cāndrāyaṇa* (lunar penance) and *sāṁtapana* (solar penance).[86]

The YSBhV specifies that *kṛcchra* involves three days of eating only in the morning, then three days of eating only in the evening, then three days of eating only what is offered, and finally three days without consuming anything. Lunar penance requires that the yogin begins with one mouthful of food per day and increases up to fifteen mouthfuls, as the moon increases in size, then decreases the mouthfuls of food down to one again. The solar penance also involves fasting and restrictions on what one eats. The YSBhV describes this type of fast as living on the urine of cows, a bit of cow dung, milk, sour milk, clarified butter, and a type of juice made from water and *kuśa* grass, accompanied by a complete fast for one night.[87] While these types of fasts are certainly very rigorous, nothing suggests that the yogin would or should undertake these practices to the point where health is endangered.

Svādhyāya (study) in the list of *niyamas* is the same as in the commentary on *kriyā-yoga.* It is the study of *śāstras* on *mokṣa* (liberation) and recitation of the sacred *praṇava* (sacred syllable).[88]

Īśvara-praṇidhāna (occupying the mind with *Īśvara*) is also the same as in the commentary on *kriyā-yoga.* It is the offering up of all action to the supreme guru.[89]

---

[86] YBh 2.32.

[87] YSBhV 2.32.

[88] YBh 2.32.

[89] YBh 2.32.

The *niyamas* generally have a more internal locus than the *yamas*. Despite this, they do not focus solely on the mind. *Śauca* is clearly based on the recognition that purity of the body is connected to purity of mind, and *tapas* also appears to be based on a similar recognition. In an article on pandits, Aklujkar reaches the same conclusions regarding restraint in diet, as well as the *yama brahmacarya*, "the pandits' behaviour is sending a signal of close relation between matter and mind and between matter and society."[90]

The *yamas* and *niyamas* reflect the recognition of the unity of the mind-body complex in Yoga practice. The *yamas* though display a more ethical, external orientation than the *niyamas*. As with the previous two categories of practice, the *yamas* and *niyamas* also employ the cultivation-disassociation approach. It is also interesting to note that there may not be as much separation between means and resulting states as people outside the tradition might be inclined to expect. The first two *niyamas* particularly, are both techniques that one can practice and states that result from practice, and that one cultivates for further practice.

Divergent Thoughts and the Cultivation of the Opposite Thoughts

Distractions—the mind being pulled in divergent directions—may still arise in practice even when the yogin is focusing and is practicing the *yamas* and *niyamas*. For these, as in the first *pāda*, the YS suggests the cultivation of opposites:

vitarka-bādhane pratipakṣa-
bhāvanam

---

[90] Aklujkar 1999, 57.

> When disturbance in the form of divergent thoughts exists (the yogin should practice) cultivation of the opposite position (or stance)[91]

For the types of thoughts that might be contrary to Yoga experience, the YS, not surprisingly, selects *hiṃsā* (harming, etc.):

> *vitarkā hiṃsādayaḥ kṛta-kāritānumoditā lobha-krodha-moha-pūrvakā mṛdu-madhyādhimātrā duḥkhājñānānanta-phalā iti pratipakṣa-bhāvanam*
>
> Cultivating the opposite is (realizing that) divergent thoughts such as (the thought of) violence etc., whether performed, caused to be performed, or approved of, and whether caused by greed, anger or delusion, and whether mild, moderate, or extreme (in intensity), result in endless suffering and ignorance.[92]

Ahiṃsā is the first *yama*, and is the basis upon which all other restraints and limbs of Yoga are founded. A thought of harming something would be the basis then of all other divergent or non-beneficial thoughts. By specifying "harm etc.," the YS therefore covers all possible negative thoughts and the YBh gives the ones corresponding or pertaining to the five *yamas*.

---

[91] YS 2.33. *Vitarka* here is used in a different sense than in YS 1.17. In 1.17, it means the gross grasp of an object of meditation. Here it means specific conceptualization.

[92] YS 2.34.

The categories or qualities of divergent thoughts mentioned in 2.34 are also significant. This list is comprehensive and insightful. The yogin is urged to consider not simply the results of harmful thoughts in general, but very specific and sometimes subtle types of thoughts and the motivating factors behind them. The yogin should think broadly about the thoughts or actions of harm. Harm might be active, inactive, performed under compulsion, or performed by another with the yogin's approval. The causes of such harmful thoughts or actions may be due to avarice, anger, or delusion/infatuation, causes which are mentioned in the YBh as the powerful emotional states whose actions result in the growth of the *karmāśaya* (reservoir of karma) and whose source is the *kleśas*.[93] The yogin must also keep in mind the degree of the thought or action that is harmful. Whether weak or mild, medium or strong, the yogin must strive to cut it off through cultivation of the opposite.

This practice is considered effective because the cultivation of the opposite isn't simply "the power of positive thinking," such as summoning up peaceful thoughts and emotions instead of harmful thoughts and feelings, but rather is a thorough analysis of the nature of divergent thoughts, actions and their effects. Once this takes place, the yogin can gain some distance from the thoughts and through this distance gain the ability to withstand and overcome them. *Bhāvana* implies continuous effort and improvement.[94] It is plausible that this practice would lead to deep and lasting psychological changes.

---

[93] YBh 2.12.

[94] Feuerstein [1979] 1989, 83.

Āsana (Posture)

Unlike the later form of haṭha-yoga, the YS does not provide much detail or elaboration on *āsana* (posture). YS 2.46 simply reads

> *sthira-sukham āsanam*
>
> the posture (should be) stable and comfortable.

Such a posture would not interfere with meditation practices. The YBh doesn't offer much elaboration on this *sūtra*, mentioning only eleven *āsanas*. These eleven are: *padmāsana* (lotus position); *bhadrāsana* (throne pose); *vīrāsana* (hero pose); *svastika*; *daṇḍāsana* (staff pose); *sopāśraya* (the support posture); *paryaṅka* (full cross-legged position); *krauñca-niṣadana* (the heron posture); *hasti-niṣadana* (the elephant posture); *uṣṭra-niṣadana* (the camel pose); and *sama-saṃsthāna* (the confirmed).[95] However, other than the next two *sūtras*, which briefly mention the results of posture (relaxation of tension and *samāpatti* or conjunction with the infinite, along with the ability to be unaffected by the opposites), the category of *āsana* in the YS is simple and pragmatic.[96] The primary purpose is to offer some postures that

---

[95] *tadyathā—padmāsanaṃ, bhadrāsanaṃ, vīrāsanaṃ, svastikaṃ, daṇḍāsanaṃ, sopāśrayaṃ, paryaṅkaṃ, krauñca-niṣadanaṃ, hasti-niṣadanam, uṣṭra-niṣadanam, sama-saṃsthānaṃ, sthira-sukhaṃ , yathā sukham ca ity evam ādīni.* My enumeration and translation of the postures are in accordance with those of Swāmi Hariharānanda Āraṇya ([1963] 1983, 228), Swāmī Veda Bhāratī (2001, 568), and Feuerstein (1991, 147). The YSBhV and TV add further detail regarding specific positions associated with each posture. From the inclusion of "*ādi*" (etc.) in the YBh, it is clear that other positions were known but not mentioned.

[96] There is some disagreement over the translation of YS 2.47 "*prayatna-śaithilyānantya-samāpattibhyām.*" Feuerstein translates *anantya* as "the infinite" ([1979] 1989, 91). I have also translated it as "infinite," since this seems to agree with the YSBhV reading, *anantaṃ viśvam, ananta-bhāva ānantyam.* Miller (1995, 56-57) initially translates *ananta* as the "Cosmic Serpent," but acknowledges that it may also

are useful either for preparing the body for meditation, or for sitting in meditation.

Prāṇāyāma (Breath Extension or Control)

The YS has already listed breath control as one of the techniques for attaining the clarity of *citta*.[97] As part of *aṣṭāṅga-yoga*, the yogin can practice *āyāma* (extension) of the breath (*prāṇa*) once the *āsana* has become steady. According to YS 2.49,

> *tasmin sati śvāsa-praśvāsayor gati-*
> *vicchedaḥ prāṇāyāmaḥ*
> When that (steady posture) has occurred, *prāṇāyāma* is the stopping of movement between inhalation (of a particular type) and exhalation (of a particular type).

The particular type of inhalation and exhalation is what differentiates it from normal breathing, which is often shallow or chest-based and lacking in mindful awareness. The external air is drawn in with a downward movement (*apāna*).[98] The internal air from the abdomen (*kauṣṭhya*) is exhaled in association with an upward movement.[99] Swāmī Veda Bhāratī points out that *prāṇāyāma* may include the breaking or stopping first of uncontrolled or jerky breathing, so that the breath can flow

---

refer to "the infinite" in a more abstract sense. The two translations, in the end, amount to the same thing; however, since there is little in the way of mythology in the YS, it would be odd to find a direct or intended reference to the "Cosmic Serpent" *per se* here.

[97] See YS 1.34.

[98] YSBhV 2.49.

[99] YBh 2.49.

smoothly and harmoniously before the retention of breath is practiced.[100]

YS 2.50 lists a number of divisions or aspects of breath extension or control:

> *bāhyābhyantara-stambha-vṛttir*
> *deśa-kāla-saṅkhyābhiḥ paridṛṣṭo*
> *dīrgha-sūkṣmaḥ*
> It is external, internal or pillar-like,
> delimited by place, timespan, and
> number (of exhalations and
> inhalations), (and) long and subtle.

According to the YBh, it is external when there is a pause in breath after exhalation. When there is a pause in breath after inhalation, it is internal. When, as a result of a single effort (*sakṛt prayatnāt*), there is the absence of both, this is called pillar-like (holding without break, *stambha-vṛttiḥ*). The latter is not something unhealthy or unnatural. Rather, just as when water that is dropped on a hot stone shrivels from all sides and disappears, so also the movement of the two (*śvāsa* and *praśvāsa*) disappears as part of this stretching or extension.[101]

The YBh also says that all three forms of breath can be regulated according to place, that is, each breath has a certain sphere or space. Drawing largely from Vāchaspati-Miśra's commentary, Dasgupta explains the spatial nature of breath:

> as the breathing becomes slower, the
> space that it occupies also becomes
> smaller and smaller. Space is again

[100] Bhāratī 2001, 593.

[101] YBh 2.50.

> of two kinds: internal and external. At the time of inhalation, the breath occupies internal space, which can be felt even in the soles of hand and feet just like the slight touch of an ant. To try to feel this touch along with deep inhalation, serves to lengthen the period of cessation of breathing. External space is the distance from the tip of the nose to the most remote point up to which breath can be felt by the palm of the hand, or by the movement of any light substance like cotton, etc. placed there. Just as the breathing becomes slower and slower, the distances traversed by it also become smaller and smaller.[102]

This, however, does not really explain how place relates to the third form of breath. The YSBhV suggests that the external space is when the breath that is drawn in extends from the tip of the nose to the big toe (*nāsikāgra-prabhṛty-āpādāṅguṣṭhaṃ*), and internal space is when the expelled breath extends from the big toe to the tip of the nose (*pādāṅguṣṭha-prabhṛty-ānāsikāgram*). The restrained breath, however, pervades the entire body, from the sole of the foot to the head (and vice versa) (*āmastakāpāda-talvyāptiḥ*).

It is, therefore, not precisely clear what the YS means by space. However, there is some sense of breath's place in relation to the

[102] Dasgupta [1920] 1989, 128.

body, and also the idea that this can be regulated. Further, from the YSBhV, it seems to be defined in terms of direction.

The regulation of *kāla* (time) and *saṃkhya* (number) seem much easier to understand than place. According to the YBh, time is how long each *prāṇāyāma* can be maintained or extended. Instead of time, the *prāṇāyāmas* "can also be measured by the number of normal duration breaths."[103] The breath that is regulated in such a manner becomes long and subtle.[104] Held long, it spreads further—flattens out—and becomes more difficult to notice, that is, becomes subtle. In other words, with *prāṇāyāma* there should be observable changes in the yogin's manner of breathing.

The ability to control or extend breath, a vital force, helps train the practitioner in concentration and an internal focus. This perspective on the usefulness of *prāṇāyāma* is particularly apparent in YS 2.51-53

> *bāhyābhyantara-viṣayākṣepī*
> *caturthaḥ*
> (Breath extension) that is
> transcending (literally, "being drawn
> or impelled away from") the range of
> the external and internal is (called)
> the "fourth"[105]
> *tataḥ kṣīyate prakāśāvaraṇam*

---

[103] Dasgupta [1920] 1989, 129.

[104] YS 2.50.

[105] 2.51.

> Then the covering of light (i.e. one
> that hides the light, makes it
> imperceptible) passes (wanes)[106]
> *dhāraṇāsu ca yogyatā manasaḥ*
> And there is (comes about) fitness of
> the mind (*manas*) for
> concentration[107]

Here this fourth type of breath control transcends the range (*viṣaya*) of external and internal, brings a type of illumination, and makes the mind fit for *dhāraṇā* (concentration). There are various interpretations regarding the nature of this "fourth type," but it appears to represent a further and subtler degree of control or mastery in breath expansion.

Pratyāhāra (Withdrawal of the Senses)

The control of the breath prepares the yogin to withdraw focus from the external world. *Pratyāhāra* is the final "outer limb" of Yoga, and thus marks the transition to the inner, contemplative, limbs.[108] YS 2.54's mention of the senses assuming the resemblance of *citta*, reflects this transition,

> *sva-viṣayāsaṃprayoge citta-*
> *svarūpānukāra ivendriyāṇāṃ*
> *pratyāhāraḥ*
> When there is disconnection with
> objects, withdrawal of the senses has
> the resemblance, as it were, of the

---

[106] 2.52.

[107] 2.53.

[108] YS 3.7.

own-form (i.e. nature) of the *citta*
itself.

In other words, at this point restraint is the goal of both senses and *citta.* When this occurs, there is supreme mastery of the sense organs.[109] Thus the sense organs revert or return to *citta*, just as a swarm of bees will rise with their leader and will only settle when the leader settles.[110] This bee metaphor seems particularly apt. It captures the pleasure-seeking nature of the senses, as well as their tendency to be very active. All this external activity is like a confusing buzz that veils a veridical apprehension of reality.

Withdrawal of the senses would be impossible without some training in the previous limbs of Yoga so that the mind itself is inward-oriented. The final three limbs certainly nurture such a state, but the connection between breath and mind and sense organs suggests that the limbs are not mutually exclusive, but rather inclusive. That is, each stage presupposes the earlier stage(s), and later stages serve to deepen the practice and attainments of any previous limb. Regardless of the stages' arrangements, YS 2.54 suggests that, with the proper practice of *pratyāhāra*, there is control over impulses, behaviours, and sensory focus. The task that remains is to strengthen the nature and duration of the interior focus.

Dhāraṇā (Concentration)

The inner limbs begin with *dhāraṇā* (concentration). The root of this word, '*dhṛ*' ('hold, carry, maintain') gives a sense of the energy that *dhāraṇā* requires, as does YS 3.1

---

[109] YS 2.55.

[110] YBh 2.54.

> *deśa-bandhaś cittasya dhāraṇā*
> Concentration is the binding of the *citta* to one specific spatial object [either inside or outside].

Concentration is, therefore, a process or action, although a purely cognitive one.[111]

The YBh does not offer any details regarding the actual practice or nurturing of concentration, but it does mention some points of focus for concentration. These traditional points of focus include: the navel *cakra*; the heart lotus; the light at the head (presumably the illumination that seems to be present when the eyes are shut for concentration); the tip of the nose; and the tip of the tongue. External objects may be used as well.[112]

Dhyāna (Meditation)

Dhyāna refers to the state of concentration on one object over a period of time,

> *tatra pratyayaikatānatā dhyānam*
> Meditation is the total focus of the cognitive events (or processes) on that (one place).[113]

---

[111] *cittasya vṛtti-mātreṇa bandha iti* (YBh 3.1).

[112] YBh 3.1. "In ancient times the lotus, i.e. the core of the heart, was the principal region or object for fixation of the mind....Later a system of keeping the mind steadfast on the six or twelve plexuses within the body came into vogue" (Āraṇya [1963] 1983, 250). The YBh mentions some of these traditional "plexuses" or *cakras*. According to tradition, the navel circle is a place where all vital currents of energy meet in the form of a circle. The top of the head marks the end of the main nerve or energy channel. The place of energy there is thus referred to as radiant or a light. The mind can also be held on other places.

[113] YS 3.2.

In *dhyāna* there is a focus that is not interrupted by other experiences. There is also maintenance or evenness of the same standard or quality of focus. For these reasons, *dhyāna* is a higher state than *dhāraṇā*. In *dhāraṇā*, the *citta* might focus on one thing, but other cognitive events about that one thing could present themselves. In *dhyāna*, however, there is no such interruption and the quality or uniform nature of the experience is maintained.

Samādhi

Samādhi is one of the terms in the YS that is, perhaps, best left untranslated.[114] *Sam-ā-√dhā* means to place or put things together. It carries a sense of completion, restoration, of putting things right. *Samādhi* is therefore a state and process when all the various activities of *citta* are collected together to form some type of intense and harmonious union.

The YS defines this final limb of Yoga as,

> *tad evārtha-mātra-nirbhāsaṃ*
> *svarūpa-śūnyam iva samādhi*
> *Samādhi* is that same [meditation]
> when only the object is reflected in it
> and when the own-nature (of the
> meditator or *citta*) is absent.[115]

---

[114] Arya leaves *samādhi* untranslated, as do Dasgupta and Leggett. Feuerstein follows Eliade's translation of the term as "enstasy" since it is "a condition of great stillness and focusedness in which we 'stand in' (*en stasis*) our true nature" (Feuerstein 1991, 108). Miller translates *samādhi* as "pure contemplation." This, however, may not be as meaningful for those unfamiliar with mystical traditions. Preference for leaving the term untranslated is given further support by Woods' translation of *samādhi* as "concentration" (he translates *dhāraṇā* as "fixed-attention"). Hence translating the term can confuse rather than clarify.

[115] YS 3.3.

In *samādhi*, there is the experience of the object, but not of the experiencer, regardless of whether the latter is Self, or *buddhi*, or *citta*. The meditator is thus completely absorbed by the nature of the object of meditation to such an extent that it seems as if the meditator no longer has any idea of his/her own nature or identity.[116]

In the end then, the practices of *aṣṭāṅga-yoga* blend all spheres or worlds of experience of the yogin. The fundamental *yamas* and *niyamas*, particularly *ahiṃsā*, change the yogin's relation with the external—including social—world, and undoubtedly, change the way in which others perceive and relate to the yogin. From there, a long process of internalization and focus, utilizing both body and mind, leads, as with the other categories of Yoga practice, to less involvement with identity and self.

---

[116] *tad-eva dhyānaṃ dhyeyākāra-nirbhāsaṃ pratyayātmakena svarūpeṇa śūnyam iva yadā bhavati dhyeya-svabhāvāveśāt, tadā samādhir ity ucyate* (YBh 3.3).

Five

The Plot Thickens

An Analysis of the Effects of Yoga Practice

To study Yoga from the perspective of the cognitive sciences is to bring practice onto the world stage. We have already established that, in their different ways, both Yoga and the cognitive sciences strive to explain mind in terms of matter. A scientific analysis of Yoga practices can help us to understand the processes that underlie some of the techniques that the YS includes in the practice sections. Yoga's purpose is to bring about changes in the mind and body of the practitioner. Therefore, by understanding the nature of these changes, we deepen our understanding of Yoga. Maintaining, so far as we can, a practical and scientific approach can also aid us in our attempts to comprehend the goals, or results of Yoga. In other words, metaphysics and faith aside, it is useful to remember that Pātañjala Yoga, either in its entirety or in part, was and is practiced by human beings. Therefore, although precise and accurate studies of this form of Yoga are few, psychology and neuroscience can still help to explain, in a general way, how practices work and what effects they may have, if any, on the mind-body. In turn, this close study of the practices of Pātañjala Yoga from the perspective of the health and cognitive sciences can also suggest further avenues of research. It can thicken the plot, so to speak, as we explore Yoga and the nature of mind, identity, and consciousness.

We see repeatedly in the YS the presence of two poles of practice: cultivation and detachment or disassociation. In other words, one trains oneself and repeatedly practices certain states or behaviours, while restraining oneself from repeating other unwanted states or behaviours. The recognition in YS 1.14 that these practices need to be undertaken "assiduously for a long time, uninterruptedly, and with reverence," gives a realistic sense of how difficult it is to change. Unlike some other Indian belief systems, there is no god who will effect these changes. Indeed, although some extraordinary powers (*siddhis*) may be acquired from birth, herbs, *mantras* or the practice of austerities (as well as *samādhi*),[1] no shortcuts to the ultimate, divine or otherwise, are possible on this path. There is no "hocus pocus" surrounding the practices of Pātañjala Yoga. The final goals of Yoga are perhaps, in the end, outside the realm of science, but until that point, the practices themselves are systematic and should be largely amenable to analysis or study.

Unfortunately, however, trying to gain direct and accurate understanding of the effects of Yoga practice from scientific studies is problematic. In modern times, there are many different forms of Yoga. Lack of adequate recognition of this fact can lead to contradictory results, or at the very least, make verification of findings and comparisons between studies difficult. A study reporting the effects of "yoga meditation" may in fact be referring to Transcendental Meditation (TM), Kuṇḍalinī Yoga, Tantric Yoga, Haṭha Yoga, or (in very rare cases) meditative techniques

---

[1] YS 4.1.

that are part of Pātañjala Yoga. Greater specificity of subject matter is often required, particularly as yoga practice can occur within the Hindu, Buddhist, or Jain traditions, or as part of a modern, completely secular context.

To complicate matters further, researchers use different instruments to measure the effects of Yoga practice. They also study the effects of Yoga on different parts of the body, or on different brain functions. Currently the majority of studies are focusing on the efficacy of Yoga practice for relief from asthma and carpal tunnel syndrome. These topics may concern urban dwelling office workers; however, they are far removed from the goals of Pātañjala Yoga. There also seems to be less research done today on the effects of Yoga practice on the brain than there was in the 1960s and 1970s. This is particularly unfortunate given the technological advances in brain scanning.[2]

Finally, results from studies are difficult to correlate because the amount of experience that subjects have in Yoga practice varies greatly. Subjects in these studies may be considered as "experienced" after only one to five years of practice. The results

---

[2] With the support of the Dalai Lama, and works such as James H. Austin's Zen and the Brain, researchers who study forms of Buddhist meditation are making better progress in understanding its effects on the brain. Nonetheless, Hans Lou and his co-researchers at John F. Kennedy Institute (University of Copenhagen, Denmark) are contributing some valuable studies on yogic meditation. Lou is employing PET scans and EEGs in order to understand the neural basis of different states and aspects of consciousness (Lou et. al. 1999). His particular focus is Yoga-nidrā guided meditation (Lou et. al. 1999). Lou's work has appeared recently in the neuroscience journal Human Brain Mapping (1999, vol. 7:98-105) and has been noted in the Lancet (Morris 1998, 1038). One can only hope that this marks renewed interest in studying Yoga practices and their effects on the brain. Unfortunately though, Lou's study uses very few subjects (nine in total), who practiced different forms of Yoga (Kriyā, Nidrā, "and other Yoga techniques") (Lou et. al. 1999, 99).

for these practitioners will likely bear little resemblance to the results obtained from studying a truly proficient yogin.[3]

In other words, good studies of advanced Yoga practitioners are rare and not easily replicable. We can, and should, however, examine some studies and theories that relate, either directly or indirectly, to Yoga practices in order to keep these practices within the realm of matter (according to tradition) and to explore how, and to what extent, such practices may change body, mind and identity.

PLASTICITY

There are, in the West, two commonly repeated myths in folk psychology. The first is that a massive die-off of neurons begins around age forty. This ushers in an irrevocable downhill slide in cognitive capacities until death. Such a view is, perhaps, the neural equivalent of the old adage "don't trust anyone over thirty." Neural loss or pruning does take place and is, at least in healthy adults, likely an adaptive process. However the loss of neurons and corresponding decline of cognitive abilities is not as dire as the first view presents. The second view is the optimistic opposite of the neural die-off perspective. It is the often-repeated idea that we only use ten percent of our brains. People who espouse such a view are also likely to suggest that if we could harness the powers of the latent ninety percent, we would have psychic powers. It is difficult to determine the original source of this idea. Brain imaging studies though demonstrate clearly that it is a myth. The

---

[3] Most studies are done with subjects who receive instruction on some form of Yoga for the purposes of that study. Studies utilizing experienced practitioners—see Telles and Desiraju 1992, or Kothari et. al. 1973, for example—are rare.

brain is, in fact, a highly competitive environment, one in which growth and loss is common. Practices in Yoga, as with all human learning in general, ultimately rely on these processes and capabilities for change, for plasticity, in the brain.

Plasticity refers to the "ability of the brain to undergo adaptive change, especially in response to environmental input and to loss of function due to damage."[4] Plasticity is a useful term, for it allows us to correlate behavioural and psychological changes with neural changes. In other words, we can relate changes in behaviour, mood, learning, etc. with neuronal changes. Here environment, behaviour, experiences and brain become intimately related. The challenge then is to understand how culture, behaviour, and psychology affect the brain.

Change or plasticity is not the sudden accessing of a latent mass or area of brain tissue. Rather it can refer to a number of changes in the brain including the formation of new synapses, the loss of existing synapses or neurons, and even the genesis of new neurons.

The factors that influence the brain's ability to change are manifold and currently the subject of numerous studies. There are at least 360 genes that are turned on by brain activity, some of which seem to relate to structural change. These genes either build more contact points between cells or use proteases, enzymes that can degrade protein molecules, to make room for other growth.[5] Age is certainly a factor, and there do seem to be critical or sensitive periods of development, especially for hearing, vision and language.[6] Another factor that influences plasticity is the area of

---

[4] Rains 2002, 494.

[5] Halber 2000, 2.

[6] Steven and Blakemore 2004, 1251.

the brain involved. Different areas of the brain display different degrees of plasticity.[7] Here, rather than the unrelenting neural die-off, we now know that even the adult brain is capable of change and reorganization. Specifically, the motor cortex, somatosensory cortex (which processes information about a specific part of the body), visual, auditory and olfactory cortices are all capable of plasticity throughout adulthood.[8] The olfactory bulb and the dentate gyrus of the hippocampus are even capable of producing new neurons. This is particularly interesting considering the role of the hippocampus in the formation and stabilization of new memories and learning.[9] Research on this topic is intriguing, but is still in its early stages.

Other than region, one of the key factors in determining the degree of plasticity in the adult brain is use. Plasticity does vary among individuals, but a number of studies do indicate the veracity of the old adage "use it or lose it."[10] In some ways, a type of neural Darwinism exists. Activity helps to form new synapses and axon branches, and to stabilize or strengthen existing connections.[11] Within this environment, the strength of certain "competitors" will also affect the degree of plasticity. As Pavlovian conditioning first indicated, repetition, behavioural importance, attention, and expectation all are important factors in learning. They also, not surprisingly, tend to strengthen or

---

[7] Afifi and Bergman 1998, 35.

[8] Steven and Blakemore 2004.

[9] Gould 2004, 145.

[10] See, for example, Hundert 1989 and Greenfield 1997.

[11] LeDoux 1996.

enhance plasticity in parts of the brain.[12] To the extent that we see these same factors present in the categories of practice in Yoga, we can expect that plasticity, or change in brain structure or function is, or may, be enhanced.

ABHYĀSA AND *VAIRĀGYA*

Abhyāsa (repeated practice) and *vairāgya* (detachment) are the primary ways to bring about the goal of Yoga, the control or cessation of the five *vṛttis*. The yogin does not set out to directly suppress, through will, these *vṛttis*. It might be possible, through will, to suppress, at least to some extent, mental construction, sleep and memory; but it would be difficult, if not impossible, to practice cutting off valid cognition, such as direct perception, and erroneous cognition. In addition to this, active thought suppression may not only be ineffective, but counter-productive.[13]

Abhyāsa is the repeated practice to remain in the *state* of *citta-vṛtti-nirodha*.[14] If the goal of Yoga is solely the extinction of the five *vṛttis*, with nothing else replacing these, then a hammer to the head would work as well as any other technique, and be much quicker. However, in an effort to achieve and maintain this state, the YS mentions a number of techniques and states that the yogin must practice these diligently for a long time.[15] The text indicates that *vairāgya* and wisdom develop as one engages in practice. What we have then, rather than the cognitive effects of a blow to the head, is a long, slow process of learning new behaviours and

---

[12] Stein et. al. 1995, 131-132; Merzenich and deCharms 1996, 62-63; 69-71.

[13] Wenzlaff and Wegner, 2000.

[14] YS 1.13.

[15] YS 1.14.

cognitive states, and repeating these, while unlearning formerly habitual or normal behaviours and cognitive states. We will likely understand more about the final results of Yoga practice if we pay attention to the actual practices and what changes that they might effect.

The five *upāyas* (means) that are the first list of practices under *abhyāsa-vairāgya*, are: *śraddhā* (faith); *vīrya* (energetic effort); *smṛti* (mindfulness, attentiveness); *samādhi*; and *prajñā* (wisdom). Leaving aside the last two items until we examine the final stages or results of Yoga, we can see that the first three *upāyas* provide us with a good example of the types of mental qualities and techniques that the yogin repeatedly practices.

Although belief in a god or deities is not necessary in Pātañjala Yoga practice, reverence and faith are important practices and qualities. YS 1.14 mentions that *abhyāsa* must be undertaken with *satkāra*, reverence, or an awareness of Yoga's importance and value. The commentary connects this reverence with the demonstration of faith (*śraddhā*), and YS 1.20 places faith first on the list of *upāyas*. Faith is certainly necessary to whole-heartedly pursue such a path of practice. Many studies show connections between faith and health;[16] however given that the faith is often deity-oriented, and that the results may also reflect healthier life-styles of religious adherents, these types of studies may not be as relevant to this form of *śraddhā* in the YS.

Alternatively, the well-known, and until fairly recently much maligned, placebo effect reflects a type of faith, specifically the faith on the part of the subject that the intervention is going to have a positive or negative outcome. I am not suggesting here that

[16] See, for example, Hafen et. al. 1996.

Yoga practice is merely a sugar pill, only that a strong correlation exists between expectation and result. In a review of literature regarding psychosocial interventions and immunity, researchers mention "strong belief on the part of the subject" as one of the key factors in bring about a therapeutic effect in a variety of disorders (depression, anxiety, cancer) for approximately 35% of people receiving them.[17] The YS seems to assume or cultivate a certain level of health on the part of the practitioner, yet we may view the results of Yoga as holding some therapeutic effect, or value, for the practitioner. This link between expectation and result is strongest when a person actively learns, takes part in, or receives some change in treatment rather than is merely informed of the efficacy of treatment.[18] Repeated practices, study of texts that reinforce the goals of Yoga, affirmation by the surrounding culture, and the modeling of behaviours and attitudes by a guru or advanced yogin may all increase *śraddhā* on the part of the practitioner, leading to increased confidence, perhaps even perceived (or actual) positive experiences resulting from practice. Studies on yoga that utilize subjective reports, may, in part, be reflecting these types of expectations.

The YBh likens *śraddhā* to a protective parent.[19] If *śraddhā* protects the yogin from doubts and encourages persistence in yogic practices such as mantra meditation, breathing practices, performance of *āsanas*, etc. then there may result both subjective and objectively measurable decreases in stress and correlated increases in energy (*vīrya*). Even with the difficulties in drawing

---

[17] Hall and O'Grady 1991, 1076.

[18] Petrovic et. al., 2005.

[19] YBh 1.20.

results from studies on Yoga, there appears to be evidence for such effects. For example, studies often report that Yoga reduces stress and increases health and a sense of well-being.[20]

The functioning of the hypothalamic-pituitary-adrenal axis (HPA) may provide some explanation for the link between Yoga practice and reduced stress. Connections or pathways between the brain and the immune system are of two basic types: electrical and chemical. Electrical pathways use nerves that connect the tissues of the immune system to the autonomic nervous system (ANS), which, in turn, is mediated by the central nervous system (CNS) and in particular by the hypothalamus.[21]

Chemical pathways between the brain and immune system use hormones, neuropeptides (intercellular messengers) and other chemical messenger molecules.[22] Most importantly here, the hypothalamus orchestrates the activity of the pituitary gland, which is responsible for the production of hormones involved in growth,

---

[20] See Collins 1998; Udupa et. al. 1972; Criswell 1989. For an excellent review of studies on religion and health, including good analysis of the limitations of such studies, see Lee and Newberg 2005.

[21] Some parts of the body that contain immune tissue include the spleen, bone marrow, lymph nodes, thymus (positioned high behind the breastbone), tonsils and gut (Martin 1995, 76). Cells that are destined to become lymphocytes, the white cells that carry out the bulk of the immune system's activities, are originally produced in the bone marrow. Some of these cells migrate to the thymus where they multiply and mature into lymphocytes (Hafen et. al. 1996, 31-32). These cells that develop in the thymus are called T cells. Lymphocytes that develop in areas outside the thymus, for example in the bone marrow, are called B cells. T cells can help trigger B cells or other T cells to turn on or off. B cells secrete antibodies (Hafen et. al. 1996, 31-32).

The thymus, spleen and lymph nodes contain beds of lymphocytes and are also interlaced with many different types of nerves that form different types of nerve pathways. Through these pathways, the sympathetic nervous system (part of the ANS) regulates the development of immune responses (Sternberg 2000, 106-107).

[22] Martin 1995, 76; Hafen et. al. 1996, 30.

metabolism, behaviour and defense processes.[23] When a stimulus is stressful, the amygdala activates a portion of the hypothalamus, which then releases corticotropin releasing hormone (CRH) (also sometimes referred to as corticotropin releasing factor, or CRF). This causes one of the pituitary gland's lobes, the adenohypophysis, to begin secreting adrenocorticotropic hormone (ACTH) into the bloodstream. ACTH then stimulates the adrenal cortex, which releases cortisol.

The HPA-axis is significant as elevated CRH is associated with depression. Further, cortisol and other stress-activated secretions bind with the receptors on the lymphocytes, thereby altering immune function.[24] Since the nervous system responds more quickly than the immune system can, a short-term stressful situation should not impair immune functioning too badly. However, if stress becomes chronic, the immune cells have no time to return to normal functioning, and the immune system is impaired.[25] Beyond this, the chemical changes due to stress have profound effects on thinking and memory processes. While a certain amount of stress may focus a person's attention, too much stress will impair it. Arousal that is accompanied by the emotional state of fear or stress takes up a significant amount of the body's energy resources, leaving the person unable to accurately apprehend the environment or to think clearly.[26] Here then we see how the external world, the person's reaction to it, the response of

---

[23] Buckingham et. al. 1997, 10.

[24] Hafen et. al. 1996, 37.

[25] Sternberg 2000, 111-112.

[26] Gazzariga 1988, 203.

the person's nervous system and immune system, and the emotional states of the person are linked.

If the necessary quality of *śraddhā* acts like a reassuring parent, and encourages practice, the above could explain, or provide a theory, for some of the health benefits and decreased stress levels that are ascribed to yoga. For example, in a study of ten men who underwent a holistic type of yoga practice for three months, results showed a significant decrease in heart rate and blood pressure.[27] The results are what one would expect if Yoga reduces stress. Interestingly enough, there were also increases in the activity level of acetylcholinesterase (AChE) and in monoamine oxidase (MAO).[28]

MAO is an enzyme that helps to "maintain neuron firing rates throughout the body within homeostatic limits."[29] AChE is a chemical that controls the amount and concentration of the neurotransmitter acetylcholine. Without the inhibiting action of AChE, there is continuous signaling of cells, resulting in over-stimulation and physiological response. Therefore, these increases in MAO and AChE indicate an altered autonomic balance.

---

[27] Joseph et. al. 1981. For three months, ten soldiers underwent daily Yoga practice consisting of prayer (a possible *śraddhā* component to this study), *āsanas* (postures), *prāṇāyāma* (breath control), and meditation. Although the variety of practices means that we cannot judge the effects of one practice versus another, this is a comprehensive program for a scientific study of Yoga and therefore it can give some sense of the effects that Pātañjala Yoga practice, taken as a whole, might have.

Results showed: a decrease in heart rate from a mean of 64 (plus or minus 1.90 SE) beats per minute to 59 (plus or minus 2.30) (P<0.001); reduction in blood pressure from 117/80 (plus or minus 1.60/1.30 SE) to 114/73 (plus or minus 1.80/1.60) (P<0.01); an increase in monoamine oxidase (MAO) (P<0.01); and an increase in the activity level of acetylcholinesterase (Joseph et. al. 1981, 121-123).

[28] Joseph et. al. 1981.

[29] Richardson 1993, 75.

Specifically, the results indicate that a holistic type of yogic practice likely leads to "a predominance of the parasympathetic system."[30] In other words, the effect of yogic practice is a quieting of the activities of the sympathetic division of the ANS—the opposite of a stress reaction.

These results, combined with the findings of other studies showing a decrease in catecholamines after yogic practice, and significant decreases in cortisol for long-term practitioners of meditation, indicate that comprehensive yogic practice could result in a sense of decreased stress and increased wellbeing.[31] This may occur through stimulation of the parasympathetic system and decrease in the reactivity of the sympathetic nervous system as well as, in some way, moderation of the HPA-axis, as decreases in cortisol may suggest.

Although this is a complex topic, and much more study is needed, from the above we can see a link between *śraddhā*—especially as it might decrease doubts and encourage practice, leading to a decrease in stress and its physiological effects—and an increase in *vīrya*, energy that is accessible for further effort in practice. Having additional energy and less stress are important for the functioning of *smṛti* (mindfulness, attentiveness). As with *śraddhā* and *vīrya*, *smṛti* is essential for Yoga practice. The discipline and focus required for meditation depend on the prior practice and development of some level of mindfulness, or the ability to focus attention. From a cognitive perspective, attention serves to promote learning and to induce cortical plasticity.[32]

---

[30] Joseph et. al. 1981, 123.

[31] See, for example, Joseph et. al. 1981, 123; and Jevning et. al. 1978, 54-60.

[32] Merzenich and deCharms 1996, 71.

Whatever changes are happening in the brain and behaviour of a yogin are likely enhanced, or encouraged, by such attentiveness. Synaptic changes in the cortex also appear to weaken when practiced behaviours are not accompanied by attention.[33] Sustained *smṛti* may thus play a key role in encouraging new behaviours and states that the yogin is learning, while aiding in the diminution of unwanted behaviours and cognitive states. We may not yet be able to study the final two *upāyas*, *samādhi* and *prajñā* (wisdom), using this perspective; however, we can see that *śraddhā*, *vīrya*, and *smṛti* likely would play important functional roles in the progression of practice. These qualities and practices, coupled with intense internal motivation or ardor (*saṃvega*), then represent the ideal learning state for a yogin.

Īśvara-praṇidhāna and the Effects of Meditation

Īśvara-praṇidhāna, and more specifically the repetition and contemplation (*bhāvana*) of *oṃ*, is one of a number of alternative practices listed under the category of *abhyāsa-vairāgya.*[34] Recitation and contemplation of *oṃ* are said to lead to inward-mindedness and the overcoming of *antarāyas* (impediments) and *vikṣepas* (distractions).[35] As Feuerstein observes, the *sūtra's* emphasis on recitation *and* contemplation implies that mere repetition is not enough.[36] The combination of contemplation and *smṛti* is significant, for it (at least ideally) discourages *īśvara-praṇidhāna* from becoming habit, or unattended ritual, despite its

---

[33] Merzenich and deCharms 1996, 72.

[34] YS 1.23, 1.27-29.

[35] YS 1.28-29.

[36] Feuerstein 1979[1989], 44.

repetitive nature. This may distinguish it from other ritual practices and their effects. To remain in a state of calm and present focus, where the object of meditation remains fresh, is one of the challenges of mantra meditation.

There are many forms of meditation, and the YS includes an impressive array of meditative techniques. Early studies on meditation often display contrary results, partly for the reasons outlined above, but also because they study different types of meditation, and different phenomena associated with these types. More recent studies tend to distinguish between two main forms of meditation: concentrative and mindfulness-based.

Concentrative meditation focuses awareness on an object, such as a sound, image, or breath. In mindfulness meditation, awareness is not focused on any one object. Instead there is a wide and present awareness for any stimulation. Mantra meditation is an example of a concentrative form of meditation, and most of the techniques in the YS belong to this category. Sōtō Zazen and Vipassanā, both in the Buddhist tradition, are examples of mindfulness meditation. *Smṛti*, in YS 1.20 as mindfulness may represent this second category of meditation rather than the first. According to the order of *sūtras* then, mindfulness may precede practices such as mantra meditation. Alternatively, the text could be suggesting that both techniques might be useful or necessary in the advanced practice of Yoga. Either reading suggests some recognition of a difference between mantra and mindfulness meditation, and recent studies show support of this distinction, along with the distinction between states arising from these practices and relaxation.

Relaxation has long been associated with meditation, both in scientific literature and in anecdotal reports. While meditative practices may generate relaxation, this relaxation response is not the only result of meditation, as careful EEG testing of the three practices or states reveals.[37] Delta and theta, large slow waves, are common during deep sleep and drowsiness respectively. Theta can also appear during some mental tasks. In relaxation, for example sitting comfortably and quietly with one's eyes closed, alpha waves tend to dominate. Beyond this, alpha also increases in persistent attention and nonvisual thinking.[38] Visual attention paid to an object, or mental activity is associated with beta activity. These are general descriptions though, and the states or activities associated with these frequencies do vary according to age and area of the brain. Nevertheless, in a study comparing EEGs of short term meditators practicing relaxation, concentration, or mindfulness meditation, significant differences in EEG readings were found. Relaxation produced greater amplitude in delta and theta bands than either concentrative or mindfulness-based meditation. Mindfulness meditation correlated with more delta, theta, alpha and beta 1 (13-25 Hz) activity than concentrative meditation. In other words, when compared to concentration meditation, mindfulness meditation produced more slow (delta and theta) *and* fast (alpha and beta 1) activity. A possible explanation for the last finding is that the brain is both quiet (delta and theta) as well as actively aware of objects, internal or external, as they occur.[39] What the findings represent for concentrative meditation is not as clear, particularly whether it is an intermediate state between relaxation and mindfulness—a state somewhat more quiescent than mindfulness.

---

[37] Dunn et. al. 1999, 148.

[38] Austin 1999, 84.

[39] See Dunn et. al. 1999.

In a recent review of meditation studies that focus primarily (but not exclusively) on concentrative forms, Newberg and Iverson find evidence of increased activity in the prefrontal cortex (PFC), especially in the right hemisphere, and the cingulate gyrus. These areas have roles in focusing attention, which is a necessity in any type of meditation.[40] Although the findings are still preliminary, thalamic activation proportional to the increase in PFC activity during meditation may indicate decreasing sensory input into the posterior superior parietal lobe (PSPL), a decrease that other studies have also found.[41] This area analyzes and integrates visual, auditory and somatosensory information. It also helps to give us a sense of a three-dimensional body in space and to distinguish between objects. Decreasing input may then lead to a loss of the sense of difference between subject and object.[42] In addition, many studies report reductions in heart rate, respiratory rate and blood pressure during or after meditation.[43] These findings suggest that parasympathetic activity of the ANS is predominant during meditation. Another study has found that meditation activates areas or structures involved with attention and control of the ANS.[44] Lastly, a number of studies have found higher levels of melatonin in experienced meditators.[45] In mammals, the pineal gland, regulated by the anterior hypothalamus, produces and

---

[40] Newberg and Iverson 2003, 284.

[41] See, for example, Herzog et. al. 1990-91.

[42] Newberg and Iverson 2003, 285.

[43] These were among the early findings in studies on meditation. See for example, Wallace and Benson 1972; Woolfolk 1975; Jevning 1992.

[44] Lazar et al. 2000.

[45] Tooley et. al. 2000; Solberg et. al. 2004.

releases melatonin, which appears to be a potent antioxidant.[46] This may be a link between meditation and reports of better health. Melatonin also depresses the CNS and reduces pain sensitivity.

Given these findings, we can conclude, even with the limits of meditation studies, that meditation is different than relaxation. Most importantly, we can see that meditation initiates a host of changes to the body and brain. While having quiescent aspects, meditation, whether concentrative or mindfulness-based, depends on the *activity* of a great number of structures and systems. We could then expect that long-term meditation may change a person's capacity for attention, tolerance of pain, level of health, and experience of emotion or sensation. Particularly striking is the presence of both concentrative and mindfulness-based forms of meditation in the YS. These forms, done assiduously, for a long time and in combination with a variety of other yogic practices, would likely be effective agents of change.

Finally, on a psychological level, we can view meditation as a tool for cognitive restructuring.[47] The intention, repeatedly practiced, to ignore external and/or distracting stimuli (including thoughts, emotions, memories, etc.), not only begins and sustains meditation, but aims to change habitual ways of responding to such stimuli. Part of this restructuring involves dissociating from thoughts as well as emotional and physical responses that tend to arise in the wake of the stimuli.[48] This cognitive restructuring is further enhanced by repeated focus on friendliness, compassion,

---

[46] Tooley et. al. 2000.

[47] Deepak 2002.

[48] Deepak 2002.

joy and equanimity as a way of overcoming the impediments (*antarāyas*) and distractions (*vikṣepas*).[49]

Therapeutic Strategies

There are a number of ways the YS suggests to overcome the impediments (*antarāyas*) (sickness, languor, doubt, negligence, sloth, dissipation, wandering thinking, non-attainment of yogic stages and instability) and their symptoms, the distractions (*vikṣepas*) (pain, depression, tremors of limbs, wrong inhalation and exhalation). In these lists we see clear connection between body and mind, or between physical health and psychological states. Modern western science of course offers a different account of the origins of disease. Research on the HPA-axis, for example, helps us understand how stress affects the immune system and the relation between disturbances such as sickness, and the experiences of languor and sloth or heaviness. The other items on the list, however, relate more to progress in Yoga.

We can also use the scientific perspective to see some links between the *vikṣepas*. Pain or suffering, for instance, tends to bring about a state of stress. States of pain, suffering and stress are frequently linked to depression.[50] It is well established now that depression is also correlated with alterations in the immune system. Further, as noted above, stress leads to the release of catecholamines. Chronic stress can cause high catecholamine levels, the effects of which include tics and muscle tremors.[51] These perhaps are analogous to the *aṅgamejayatva* mentioned in

---

[49] YS 1.33.

[50] Gazzaniga 1988; Kiecolt-Glaser and Glaser 1991.

[51] Hafen et. al. 1996.

the list of *vikṣepas*, or at least offer a possible explanation of some of the physiological processes that underlie such unsteadiness. Finally, the effects of stress on the cardiovascular system are well documented. Wrong inhalation and exhalation, even if we read the *sūtra* as indicating unmindful inhalation or exhalation, are normal occurrences in times of stress.

Therefore, repetition of *praṇava*, that is, mantra-style or some other form of meditation, may be helpful in remedying some of the *antarāyas* and *vikṣepas*, at least in terms of providing relief from stress and over-activation of the sympathetic nervous system. The YS also provides a list of things to repeatedly focus upon (*eka-tattvābhyāsa*) in order to counteract impediments and distractions and to bring about clarity of *citta*. Focus on positive emotions or states such as friendliness (*maitrī*), compassion (*karuṇā*), joy (*muditā*) and equanimity (*upekṣā*)[52] can provide the person with objects of meditation (concentrative form) and can also aid in cognitive restructuring. In other words, focus on the qualities of friendliness and the others could decrease stress by consistently discouraging competitiveness and other negative attitudes both in times of meditation and in one's daily behaviour. The replacement of negative behaviours and attitudes through repetition or practice of friendliness, compassion, joy and equanimity could, in the long-term, result in changes in the way a yogin perceives the world and other people. The perception of an event as stressful or not is a key factor in whether or not an event triggers the fight or flight response.[53] People respond differently to stressful events—one person's thrill may be another's nightmare. By decreasing the

---

[52] YS 1.33.

[53] Hafen et. al. 1996.

tendency to take a "dog-eat-dog" approach to life, while modulating the way a yogin responds to stimuli, the practice of *maitrī* etc. could decrease the likelihood that the yogin would perceive events as stressful, or react to them as such.

Research indicates that suppression and enhancement of negative emotions through cognitive reappraisal is possible.[54] The research so far on enhancement of positive emotions is scarce or not as clear, but studies at the University of Wisconsin-Madison Laboratory for Affective Neuroscience are beginning to add to our knowledge. Although focusing on Tibetan Buddhists, one particular form of meditation in which loving-kindness and compassion pervade the meditator's mind, thereby becoming the content of the meditative experience, bears similarity to the practice of *maitrī* and other qualities in the YS. The University of Wisconsin study found changes in EEG gamma-band activity (25-42 Hz). Most intriguingly, the study also found significant differences in the EEG profiles between long-term Tibetan Buddhists and a healthy student volunteer group. The reasons for these differences are likely multi-faceted, but seem to indicate, at least in part, that even the resting state of the brain may be altered by long-term meditative practices such as those that focus on pure compassion or loving-kindness.[55]

The next method of therapeutic strategy mentioned in the YS is the expulsion and retention of breath, or *prāṇāyāma*.[56] It is not entirely clear what this practice consists of, although mindfulness of breath is likely part of the practice. The YBh mentions that the

---

[54] Jackson et. al. 2000; Ochsner et. al. 2002.

[55] Lutz et. al. 2004.

[56] YS 1.34.

practice consists of ejecting the internal air through the two nostrils by a special type of effort. Studies on yogic breathing indicate greater lung capacity and lowered respiratory rate as results of this practice.[57] One specific type of breathing exercise, alternate nostril breathing, may influence cerebral hemisphere dominance.[58] Normally humans go through a nasal cycle ranging from 25 to 200 minutes or longer, when breathing is more predominant in one nostril rather than the other.[59] This predominance, whether natural or forced, correlates with dominant EEG activity in the opposite cerebral hemisphere.[60] Later studies indicate that this nasal cycle is also linked with changes in a variety of areas including the ANS, cardiovascular system, levels of plasma catecholamines, cognition, pituitary hormones and insulin.[61] Studies on yogic breathing also indicate that it may increase hand grip strength[62] and spatial memory.[63] Given the possible effects of breath control, some of which may have been experienced or sensed by yogins, it is not surprising to find *prāṇāyāmā* in both the *abhyāsa-vairāgya* and *aṣṭāṅga-yoga* categories of practices.

Sūtras 1:35-40 offer a variety of objects that can provide support for focusing the mind on one thing. These objects may be concrete or abstract, large or small. The "focusing" in these instances does not seem to require intense physical action. Therefore the general

---

[57] Gopal et. al. 1973, 274-276.

[58] Morris 1998, 1039.

[59] Werntz et. al. 1983, 39.

[60] Werntz et. al. 1983, 39.

[61] Shannahoff-Khalsa et. al. 1997.

[62] Raghuraj et. al. 1997, 129-33.

[63] Naveen et. al. 1997, 555-561.

results of the studies on concentrative and mindfulness-based meditation would also apply here. An additional study is also relevant. A study on cerebral blood flow (CBF) during guided meditation revealed that the pattern of CBF changed according to meditative content:

> Meditation on sensations of weight of limbs and other body parts, presumably related to "motor attention" (i.e., the supplementary motor area)...was supported mainly by parietal and superior frontal activity; abstract sensation of joy by left hemisphere parietal and superior temporal (Wernicke area) activity; and visual imagery by strong activation of the occipital lobe with sparing of the V1 region, and the parietal lobe. Meditation on symbolic representation of the self was supported by bilateral parietal activity. Common to most meditative situations was a strong bilateral hippocampus activation.[64]

In other words, while the results are still preliminary, it is likely that the different objects that the YS mentions as supports for focusing the mind would correlate with different patterns of activity in the brain. Indeed, research on the neural foundations of imagery suggests that this is the case. Auditory and motor imagery

---

[64] Lou et al. 1999, 100-101.

draw on neural structures involved in hearing or movement, which may indicate a reason why mental rehearsal is effective in improving performance.[65] Visual imagery even correlates with activity in the early visual cortex (area 17), as if the person is actually seeing an external object. Such findings reveal the effects that imagery or focus on internal objects can have on a person. Furthermore, since the somatosensory system can be affected from the "top down," that is, from internally generated images and objects, this can offer an explanation of how beliefs and expectations, at least in some cases, could alter or modulate what we see during perception.[66] Meditation on parts of the body and meditation on objects that are not present, can aid, perhaps, in rehearsing new strategies of focus and equanimity, new patterns of response to self and objects. The more abstract topics of focus, such as the mind consisting only of illumination and/or identity, would be difficult to explain or measure in operational terms; however, the aspect of repetition remains the same. These subtle foci for meditation are physical and psychological rehearsals of new or valued states of consciousness and being.

The practices that comprise the category of *abhyāsa-vairāgya* were likely meant for accomplished yogins. Even while acknowledging the current limitations of studies and knowledge, we can at least see that these practices are holistic, not only in some general sense that they involve body and mind, but also in that they likely influence functioning of the CNS, ANS, immune system and endocrine system. These findings, coupled with the studies that show changed patterns of brain activity during certain

---

[65] Kosslyn et. al. 2001.

[66] Kosslyn et. al. 2001.

practices, may indicate that with repetition of these disciplines over a long time span significant and comprehensive changes could occur in the brain, and of course the body, of the yogin. In short, the belief that these practices could or would result in gradual but dramatic changes in consciousness and the perception of self and world appears to be supported not only by Yoga metaphysics and practice, but by some modern scientific studies as well.

KRIYĀ-YOGA

Not all practices in the YS were meant only for accomplished yogins. *Kriyā-yoga*, the yoga of activity, was meant to help those with active or extrovertive minds cultivate *samādhi* and thin out the *kleśas* of ignorance, sense of identity or I-amness, attachment, aversion and clinging to life.[67] *Kriyā-yoga*, as its name suggests, therefore offers some practices that would be somewhat more amenable to those who need or desire an active rather than more strictly meditative approach.

Kriyā-yoga consists of *tapas* (ascetic practices), *svādhyāya* (study) and *īśvara-praṇidhāna* (occupying the mind with *īśvara*). Of these, *īśvara-praṇidhāna* and the impact of faith has been discussed above. In addition to this, the *īśvara-praṇidhāna* of *kriyā-yoga* includes practices that are more devotional, rather than abstract, in nature, as here it involves placing all actions on the supreme guru (that is, surrendering oneself and one's actions) and the renunciation of the fruits or results of action.[68] This is a religious and devotional approach to life. What it shares with the practices mentioned in the previous section though, is the rehearsal

---

[67] YBh 2.1-2.

[68] YBh 2.1.

of behaviours and emotional states that are not self-centered. There is the possibility then of behaving "as if" one possesses equanimity and repeatedly generating emotions in consonance with this. What may then appear as mere faith, is ideally part of a comprehensive practice to change behaviour and psychology.

Of the remaining two *kriyā-yoga* practices, little can be said of *tapas.* It is unfortunately not clear in the YS what specific ascetic practices are meant. However, it is interesting that in the tradition *tapas* is always associated with heat. The hypothalamus is involved in body temperature regulation and a variety of other functions that include water balance, feeding behaviour, wakefulness and sleep.[69] It is a key instrument then of homeostasis. Ascetic practices often target these very functions, regulating fluid intake, food intake, and sleeping. It might be that such practices are useful in allowing us to modify our responses to hunger, thirst and need for sleep, so that we are not dominated as much by these needs. We could also hypothesize that ascetic practices alter the functioning of areas involved in homeostasis. Herbert Benson and others have studied advanced Tibetan yogins and found that these practitioners can increase the temperature of their fingers and toes at will by as much as 8.3 degrees.[70]

The ability to control or change body temperature may have an interesting connection to the idea or experience of self. Neuroscientist Antonio Damasio maintains that a type of foundational consciousness, which he terms "core consciousness," relies on regions of the brain that provide a view of the state of the

---

[69] Afifi and Bergman 1998.

[70] Benson et. al. 1982.

organism.[71] Although Damasio does not restrict the basis for core consciousness only to the brainstem and hypothalamus, these areas are necessary to generate what he calls the "proto-self," a "coherent collection of neural patterns which map, moment by moment, the state of the physical structure of the organism in its many dimensions."[72] The areas responsible for generating the proto-self or core consciousness can help to explain why we normally have the experience of one body, one mind, one self, despite the fact that our bodies and minds are undergo constant activity. Damasio's research on links between homeostasis, core consciousness and proto-self is interesting given the widely employment of ascetic practices in yogic traditions. It is certainly not the case that the Yoga tradition shared a similar idea of homeostasis and core consciousness, but we may be safe in assuming that practices targeting hunger, thirst, sleep, heat and cold were thought useful in the development of a yogin.

Finally, the practice of *svādhyāya*, one's own study, includes repetition of the *praṇava* (a meditative element), or the study of treatises on liberation.[73] The *praṇava*'s inclusion is not surprising given that it is traditionally thought to contain all the wisdom of the Veda. When important scriptures or treatises were studied, they would be memorized, recited and discussed. The inclusion of this type of active study seems especially significant given our current understanding of factors that encourage neuroplasticity. On a psychological level, study of the treatises would be used to clarify and reinforce goals, values, and other behavioural standards

[71] Damasio 1999, 140.

[72] 1999, 154-156.

[73] YBh 2.1.

important in the tradition. Memorization and recitation of these could eventually serve as a type of internal model for the yogin. Again, rather than having a series of practices that are strictly quiescent, we see in *svādhyaya* and the other *kriyā-yoga* practices, a potential for contributing to active changes in the yogin's behaviour, emotions, and perhaps, eventually, even fundamental sense of self. Thus in yogic terms, study could counteract clinging to life by offering options other than normal worldly life and it might also set standards of equanimity rather than attachment and aversion. *Īśvara-praṇidhāna* might do the same. *Tapas* could help mitigate responses to attachment and aversion. As these states relate especially to basic human needs such as hunger, thirst, etc. *tapas* might also help to shift the basis for experience of self and self in the world. All of them together, perhaps, could bring about significant change. Whether they would also bring about *samādhi* or the abolition of *avidyā*, is likely a matter more for tradition at this point than science.

AṢṬĀṄGA-YOGA

The YS includes many practices from the *ābhyāsa-vairāgya* and *kriyā-yoga* categories in the list of *āṣṭāṅga-yoga* practices and these will not be discussed individually here again. *Āṣṭāṅga-yoga* is composed of: *yama* (restraints); *niyama* (observances); *āsana* (postures); *prāṇāyāma* (breath control); *pratyāhāra* (withdrawal of the senses); *dhāraṇā* (concentration); *dhyāna* (meditation); and *samādhi*. Of these, the *niyamas* along with breath control and various stages and kinds of concentration and meditation are largely shared with the previous two categories of practice. Other means, such as those that comprise the *yamas*, contain some elements that are difficult to measure or define in objective terms.

The comprehensiveness of *aṣṭāṅga-yoga* poses a challenge for study, but is also an indication of its potential to effect change.

Yama is restraint, and the *yamas* include societal, physical and psychological levels of restraint. The *yamas* are *ahiṃsā* (non-violence), *satya* (truthfulness), *asteya* (non-stealing), *brahmacarya* (continence), and *aparigraha* (non-accumulation). These change the yogin's relationship with the external, including social, world. Out of the items on the list, *ahiṃsā*, the first item, is the most significant. The development of the rest of the *yamas*, and indeed all the other limbs of *aṣṭāṅga-yoga*, depends upon the practice of *ahiṃsā*. The YBh's definition of *ahiṃsā* as the "non-harming of all creatures by any means at all times,"[74] indicates that *ahiṃsā* is not just the absence of aggression. *Ahiṃsā* demands control over emotions, and likely necessitates training not merely in the suppression of anger, but in the cultivation of positive psychological qualities such as friendliness, compassion, sympathetic joy and equanimity. Beyond these psychological qualities, the yogin must then match internal standards or qualities with external behaviours or practices. This changes how the yogin relates to the world, and likely how many view the yogin. In effect, there is a tremendous shift in perspective and identity (both externally and internally) even with this first *yama*. The remaining *yamas* reinforce this orientation and help ensure that the yogin will gradually become less likely to be involved in an externally oriented, acquisitive and active life.

The *niyamas* are *śauca* (purity), *saṃtoṣa* (contentment), *tapas* (ascetic practices), *svādhyāya* (study), and *īśvara-praṇidhāna* (occupying the mind with *īśvara*). Of these, the last three items

---

[74] YBh 2.30.

are the same as *kriyā-yoga*. Purity and contentment likely add a stronger psychological component to the practices of *kriyā-yoga*. The observances of external and internal purity regulate physical and psychological behaviour. The practice of contentment would discourage an attitude or feeling of desire or want, and thereby could help in decreasing the inclination to inflict harm on others, or other things, merely to satisfy desire or need. In this manner, the *yamas* and *niyamas* reinforce each other.

Apart from such considerations, YS 2.35 to 2.45 details a number of results stemming from the practice of the *yamas* and *niyamas*. Most of these results are natural consequences of practice and therefore, while perhaps unusual or extraordinary, they do not fall under the category of *siddhis*. For example, a yogin who is practicing *ahiṃsā* is not likely to have enemies. Even if enemies did exist, the yogin's refusal to perceive them as enemies would mean that enemies would not exist *for that yogin*, or according to that yogin's experience. Finally, dedication to *ahiṃsā* could help to defuse any potentially harmful situation—thus, as the *sūtra* states, enmity would be abandoned in his presence.[75] Employing such analysis, the results of practicing the *yamas* and *niyamas* appear reasonable, although most likely rare.

The limbs following the *yamas* and *niyamas* reflect a technique that begins with learning control over voluntary musculature, then a measure of control over the ANS (*prāṇāyāma*) and finally control over attentional and thought processes.[76] While some measure of mastery over one limb might be necessary to proceed

---

[75] YS 2.35.

[76] Vahia et. al. 1973, 558.

to the next, the limbs are unlikely to represent purely linear stages and their effects likely overlap.

India has a long and well-developed tradition of what we might term postural psychology. Other schools or forms of yoga made *āsana* a sole or at least primary focus. In classical Yoga, *āsanas* receive comparatively little emphasis. The category is undoubtedly important in preparing a person for meditation, and particularly in developing the capacity to maintain a stable posture during meditation. *Āsana* practice is also a type of restraint and therefore marks a transition point between the *yamas* and *niyamas* and the latter limbs. Our bodies move constantly due to internal and external factors. Some of these movements are under willed control and others are not. While practicing *āsanas*, a person learns a measure of control over body movements that are reactive to external (noise and other distractions) as well internal (itch, discomfort, etc.) events. From this perspective, *āsana* practice complements any type of cultivation-detachment practice. In this case, a posture that is held with steadiness and ease cultivates a silence or restraint in the body, while it simultaneously promotes detachment from nervous, habitual and externally directed movements.

Along with restraint and detachment, *āsanas* appear to modulate changes in the nervous system, introducing quiescent-active poles on the physical level. A study of oxygen consumption, heart rate, rate of respiration, blood pressure and body temperature of men performing *vīrāsana* and *śavāsana* showed that *vīrāsana* induces a temporarily hypermetabolic state in which the activity of the sympathetic nervous system is enhanced.[77] This hypermetabolic

[77] *Vīrāsana* is included in YBh 2.46.

state contrasts significantly with the relaxed, lower metabolic state seen in *śavāsana.*[78] Current research on *āsana* focuses almost exclusively on potential therapeutic benefits, but if, as studies suggest, repeated use results in a fairly rapid reorganization in the somatosensory cortex, it would be interesting to know what types of changes occur during repeated, slow and attentive *āsana* practice, and to compare physiological and psychological states occurring during and after the performance of various *āsanas.*

Since *prāṇāyāma* was previously included under *abhyāsa-vairāgya*, the next limb to consider is *pratyāhāra.* Withdrawal from an external orientation is necessary in order to undertake practice of the inner limbs. The first five limbs all encourage, in various ways, this internal orientation. According to the YS, when withdrawal from objects occurs, there is supreme mastery of the sense organs.[79] Some early studies suggest that this withdrawal may allow a proficient yogin to be unaffected in meditation when external stimuli are present.[80] Along with this, the YS also mentions that when there is the disconnection from objects, *pratyāhāra* "has the resemblance of *citta* itself."[81] In an article assessing psychological research on yoga, Fraser Watts notes that

> *changes* in the sensory field...keeps our attention focused. Constant physical movement keeps us aware of what we are doing with our bodies; constant changes in the

---

[78] Rai and Ram 1993.

[79] YS 2.55.

[80] Woolfolk 1975, 1327; Corby et. al. 1978, 576.

[81] YS 2.54-55.

> content of our visual fields keeps us focused on what we can see. It is only when stability is achieved that the normal links between peripheral and central cognitive processes are severed. This leaves our central cognitive processes free to move more independently in a way that is different from normal.[82]

In the case of *pratyāhāra*, the goal is not to leave cognitive processes free to move, but to partially induce restraint in cognitive processes through decreases in sensory input. *Pratyāhāra* may be one way of dissociating from the streams of information that all seem to bind together into pictures or experience of objects that a witnessing self receives and acts upon.

Dhāraṇā, *dhyāna* and *samādhi* are the last three, inner, limbs of *aṣṭāṅga-yoga*. Concentration and meditation are practices found in the *abhyāsa-vairāgya* section of the YS and their processes and effects have already been discussed. It is worth noting though the careful distinction in *aṣṭāṅga-yoga* between *dhāraṇā* and *dhyāna*. In *dhāraṇā*, the yogin binds the *citta* to one thing, while *dhyāna* takes place only when there is total focus on that thing.[83] Here the two are part of a continuum, as well as separate practices. It is likely that all but experienced meditators encounter moments of concentration as well as meditation during a meditation session, and this may also account for differences in the results of "meditation studies." Even experienced meditators tend to go

---

[82] 2000, 78.

[83] YS 3.1-2.

through a quick sequence of withdrawing from the senses, forming the intention to concentrate, concentration and then meditation. All of these rely on a certain comfort in posture and breath control. The tradition also adds the *yamas* and *niyamas* as requirements. In the end we have "inner" psycho-physiological practices that depend on, and are not separate from, ethical behaviour.

When we take into account then the entire system of *aṣṭāṅga-yoga*, the process of change involves every aspect of human life. The *yamas*, particularly the fundamental practice of *ahiṃsā*, change the behaviour of the yogin in society. This change would likely be recognized, even reinforced—through donations of food, through respect, etc.—by people around the yogin. With the *yamas*, social identity changes. But perhaps "social" is too narrow a term for this change, as it normally applies to human society. In the yogin's case, the relationship with all creatures, even things, changes as the yogin replaces want and desire with non-violence and the other *yamas* as the basis for encountering people, living creatures and objects. The *niyamas* cultivate psychological qualities such as contentment and, through modification of diet and physical responses to bodily needs, likely change a host of psycho-physiological processes. Postures, breath control and finally the more internal practices all cultivate control over normal physical and psychological responses and, as meditation studies indicate, may give the yogin experiences that are both psychologically and physiologically novel. Here lack of external stimulation as well as a certain fixity of attention could result in alteration of the regular experience of self and object. The final limb of *aṣṭāṅga-yoga*, *samādhi*, occurs "when the own-nature (of the meditator or *citta*) is absent."[84] It therefore represents an experience, and ideally a repeated sequence of experiences, in which it is no longer feasible, according to the tradition, to speak of the meditator's normal identity. Although some researchers appear confident that they have measured this state, we are still in the early stages of examining identity, attention, concentration and meditation using objective measures, and all of these are likely involved.[85] *Samādhi* may represent a state that combines all of these functions in a novel way. Furthermore, *aṣṭāṅga-yoga*—a set of practices that is presented as a system that includes metaphysics, ethics, religion, health practices, psychological theories and techniques, and the practice of subtle focused states—needs to be studied as a single

---

[84] YS 3.3.

[85] According to some researchers, objective measures correlate with subjective reports of changes from concentration and meditation to *samādhi*. Respiratory rate and heart rate seem to increase for some experienced practitioners during certain stages of *dhāraṇā* and *dhyāna* (Telles and Desiraju 1992, 293; Corby et. al. 1978, 574). This is particularly the case right before the transition to near-*samādhi* states (Telles and Desiraju 1992, 293; Corby et. al. 1978, 574). Corby et. al. also reported a dramatic decrease in skin resistance prior to the near-*samādhi* event (1978, 574).

An earlier study of Yogi Satyamurti, who remained in a small underground pit for eight days while ECG measurements were taken, showed a pattern of physiological change similar, although more dramatic, to those reported by Telles and Desiraju and Corby et. al. Yogi Satyamurti displayed marked tachycardia for approximately 29 hours (Kothari et. al. 1973, 1647). After that point, the ECG presented a straight-line reading. Although this would suggest problems with the equipment, the researchers maintained that there was no sign of electrical disturbance of the ECG leads. The experimenters decided that the Yogi must be dead and wanted to discontinue the experiment; however, the Yogi's attendants insisted that the experiment continue. On the eighth day, approximately half an hour before the pit was opened, ECG activity returned. After the experiment, the researchers reported that they tried all kinds of manipulations to the leads to mimic the yogi's ECG readings, but were unable to do so (Kothari et. al. 1973, 1647-1648). The researchers, while stopping just short of reporting that the Yogi was able to voluntarily stop (and presumably start) his heartbeat at will, did admit that they "still could offer no satisfactory explanation for the ECG record" (Kothari et. al. 1973, 1649). The researchers also reported that the yogi's oral temperature was extremely low, 34. 8 degrees celsius—representing a state of hypothermia—when the pit was opened. So far as I know, this study was never replicated.

system, yet is largely impossible to study, at least at the moment, as a system. In other words, in this tradition *samādhi* does not occur merely as a result of meditation, but also as a result of non-violence and the other practices of Yoga. If we study it only as a psychological or physiological phenomenon, we risk missing much of its nature.

Six

Lights Up

Extraordinary Results of Yoga

According to the Yoga tradition, there comes a time after long practice and deep insight when, metaphorically speaking, the show that *prakṛti* performs ends, the lights come up, and *puruṣa*, the seer, is known as separate, untouched by the dramas of the material world.

The final results of Yoga challenge standard methods of analysis. The YS presents results in a blend of metaphor, philosophy, psychology and faith. We thus encounter both psychological or real-world results and philosophico-religious possibilities. An interdisciplinary approach is necessary in order to gain the broadest possible understanding of the nature of these results. Any one approach alone, such as philosophical, will skew the reading and translation of the YS on these final topics. To the extent that it is applicable, cognitive science is a useful aid in suggesting what a person might be like who has followed the path of Yoga. It gives us a view of the yogin based on body and practice, but we cannot stop there. In the end, this system steps outside the realm of language, concepts, and measurable experience.

SIDDHIS

The *siddhis* are perfections or accomplishments that can occur as a result of yogic practice or other methods. *Siddhis* sometimes pose a problem for Western scholars who seem to regard their more fantastic elements as irrational, superstition-based, or an artifact of the tradition. The topic is often ignored completely in more philosophically based studies and, in general, scholars seem reluctant to study the topic. Feuerstein has also noticed such reluctance and believes that scholars find the topic of the *siddhis* "discordant with Patañjali's rational approach and his philosophical objectives."[1] The relative lack of attention to this topic is unfortunate, given the prominent place of extraordinary powers in the third *pāda* of the YS.

According to the YS,

> *janmauṣadhi-mantra-tapaḥ-*
> *samādhijāḥ siddhayaḥ*
> The *siddhis* are produced due to
> birth, herbs, mantras, *tapas*, or
> *samādhi*.[2]

Birth may refer to some type of natural aptitude, which could be explained through reference to karma or attainments in a previous life. There is a long tradition of *mantras*, ritually powerful sounds or speech acts, affecting the physical body as well as external things. This inclusion of *mantra*, along with *tapas*, which has a similarly long history of association with extraordinary power, bears witness to that tradition. Since Yoga utilizes, at least in some

[1] 1980, 101.

[2] YS 4.1.

cases, the recitation of *mantra* and/or the practice of *tapas*, the presence of these two items on the list merges tradition and experience. Finally, extraordinary powers may also arise due to the experience of *samādhi*, and this relates most directly to the powers listed in the third *pāda*.

The third *pāda* of the YS lists a number of extraordinary powers that are the result of *saṃyama*, a complete restraint or control involving a special type of focus on one thing. This focus incorporates *dhāraṇā*, *dhyāna* and *samādhi*.[3] According to the YS, this powerful way of focusing, when trained on different objects, results in a number of extraordinary abilities. YS 3.16-3.52 provides a list of these, including: knowledge of past and future, including previous births (3.16, 3.18); invisibility (3.21); knowledge of objects in the world, such as the stars and their movements (3.26-28); power over the body, such as cessation of thirst (3.29-31); mastery over all material elements (3.44-48); and finally, a type of insight that leads to *kaivalya*, alone-ness or liberation, the final goal of practice.

We might, at this point, launch into a study of the paranormal to account for these *siddhis*, but this I believe, is a poor choice. Many studies of the paranormal are methodologically suspect, and too much work in this field seems to degenerate into bickering between skeptics and believers.

It is worth noting, however, that training can lead to a level of perception that may appear extraordinary to those who are untrained. For example, just as a jeweler, through years of experience, can see aspects of a jewel that untrained people cannot, so it may be possible for a yogin as a result of many years of the

[3] YS 3.4.

comprehensive type of training we have explored in the previous chapters, to have some types of mastery, control or knowledge that seem extraordinary or unnatural.[4] In this way, complete focus or *saṃyama* on certain parts of the body may indeed still one enough, and produce enough equanimity, that hunger and thirst can be subdued, or an extraordinary stillness or fixity (*sthairyam*) might result.[5] Similarly, a careful and thorough focus on language, or changes that objects undergo, might result in extraordinary knowledge of these topics.

Perhaps more important than this type of explanation, or even the acknowledgement of the influence of tradition on the YS, is the recognition that the *siddhis* are an integral part of the YS, for they exist as *logical possibilities* within this system of thought. Since everything other than *puruṣa* is only a transformation of *prakṛti*—

---

[4] It is not only accomplished yogins who demonstrate extraordinary abilities. As the jeweler example indicates, experts in many fields have powers of perception that untrained people do not possess. Neuroplasticity may be the process that underlies these powers, as they have a neural basis. For instance, with respect to listening to music, there is a neural difference according to training:

> With the allocation of specific functions to each hemisphere, the question has arisen as to which hemisphere is specialized for music. In this context, one should separate musical perception from musical execution by the naive, casual listener and the music professional. Whereas a naive listener perceives music in its overall melodic contour, the professional perceives music as a relation between musical elements and symbols (language). With this type of analysis, it is conceivable that the naive listener perceives music in the right hemisphere, whereas the professional perceives music in the left hemisphere. Musical execution (singing), on the other hand, seems to be a function of the right hemisphere irrespective of musical knowledge and training (Afifi and Bergman 1998, 377).

[5] YS 3.30-31.

with differences in quality, temporal characteristics and states due to the activities of the *guṇas*—a thorough insight into the nature of *prakṛti* at least philosophically would lead to knowledge of and a theoretical mastery over everything that is a transformation of *prakṛti*. The YBh's discussion on such transformations at this point in the text supports such a reading. Rukmani, in an article on the *siddhis*, also notes that "there seems to be a logical connection between *saṃyama* on a particular object and the resulting *siddhi*."[6] This connection, according to Yoga metaphysics, exists as a correspondence between the five elements (*bhūtas*), the five sense organs (*buddhīndriyas*), and the five subtle elements (*tanmātras*). Thorough focus on these correspondences can then, at least philosophically, allow for knowledge that transcends the specific and a mastery that transcends what is normally or practically realistic.

Therefore, rather than being a scholarly embarrassment, a mere mythical or religious artifact, or an insignificant topic in the YS, the *siddhis* form an important category of phenomena that are in some cases experiential and in all cases logical according to this system of thought. In effect, the *siddhis* are important because, at least potentially, they combine philosophy and practice. And since the Yoga system combines theory and practice in other *pādas*, it is reasonable to surmise that the *siddhis* are included not because they were a part of tradition, folk thinking or superstition, but because they are logically, and perhaps experientially, implied by the system, and because this system was not constrained by our current dichotomies and preferences.

---

[6] 1993, 221.

FINAL RESULTS OF YOGA PRACTICE: *SAMĀDHI, NIRODHA, KAIVALYA*

The *siddhis* are not the goal of yogic practice. Rather, through mastery of *saṃyama*, there occurs a gradual increase in *prajñāloka* (transcendent wisdom).[7] This wisdom reveals the distinction between *puruṣa* and *prakṛti*, and even between *puruṣa* and *sattva*—that aspect of *prakṛti* that is most similar to *puruṣa*.[8] The process of this gradual revelation, which takes place entirely within the realm of *prakṛti*, consists of developing *samāpatti* and reinforcing the experiences of *samādhi* and *nirodha*.

Samāpatti, literally "stepping toward collectively," occurs for the yogin when the *vṛttis* (fluctuations) have dwindled or ceased.[9] The term here is "*kṣīṇa-vṛtter*" and it can be translated as either "dwindled" or "ceased." This can be a crucial distinction given the definition of yoga as "*citta-vṛtti-nirodha*,"[10] for *nirodha* can be translated as "suppression" (i.e. "control") or "destruction." In both cases we have the *process* of *citta-vṛttis* dwindling or being suppressed, or the end *result* of the *citta-vṛttis* having ceased. Given this parallel structure, I maintain that the only suitable translation, and way of conceptualizing either *samāpatti* or *nirodha*, is to understand "*kṣīṇa*" and "*nirodha*" as referring to *both the process and the result*, in other words, both suppression or dwindling and cessation. On the topic of *samāpatti*, the YBh supports this interpretation, as it provides the gloss for "*kṣīṇa-*

---

[7] YS 3.5-6.

[8] YS 3.49; YSBhV 1.41.

[9] YS 1.41.

[10] YS 1.2.

vṛtter" as "*pratyastamita-pratyayasya*," "one for whom the *pratyayas* (cognitive events) have gone down (or ceased)."[11] The word "*astamita*" contains a sense of the way a sun sets, or goes down. When a sun sets, there is both the process of diminishing light, and the arrival, in the end, of something else, the night, which is the absence of light. While the sun does not cease to exist, that particular day does. Again, these verbs in this section of the text suggest a sense of gradual process and radical end or change.

Accordingly then, we can conclude that the definition of Yoga is the process of suppressing or restricting the fluctuations of *citta* and the cessation of the fluctuations of *citta*.[12] We must be careful here though, for the YS is not suggesting that the *citta* of the yogin dwindles, then ceases to exist. Rather, there is a process during which the yogin learns to control and restrain the five *vṛttis*, which are the normal processes of *citta*. Eventually, these five *vṛttis* no longer have any influence. Does this then represent a state of unconsciousness or even death? Since the text continues to speak of stages of meditation and their results, we can assume this is not the case. Instead, there seems to be a very different type of cognitive process that operates. This type of process is not included within the category of the five *vṛttis*.

At this point in the yogin's practice, although there is no longer any personal or normal involvement with external things, there may still be some sense of conventional ways of categorizing and knowing the world. The yogin may still retain the basic and conventional categories of word, object and knowledge. This is

[11] YBh 1.41.

[12] YS 1.2.

termed *savitarkā samāpatti.*[13] Once even the memory of such categories disappears, there is *nirvitarkā samāpatti*, a special unified focus without the gross or basic categories of the object of meditation.[14]

From here the yogin's focus moves to more subtle levels. According to Sāṃkhya-Yoga, existents are not just composed of gross matter (e.g. clay), but also subtle elements, the evolutes of *prakṛti* that range from the *tanmatras* to *aliṅga.*[15] A unified focus on the subtle elements of an object is called *savicārā samāpatti.*[16] When the focus moves from the subtle elements of a particular object to a special focus on a subtle element that is universal—such as "being"—this is *nirvicārā samāpatti.*[17]

Since these forms of focus still have some reference to external things, since they contain (even in the case of *nirvicārā samāpatti*) subtle traces or seeds of the external or objective world, the states that result from them are termed *sabīja samādhi* (*samādhi* with seed)[18] or *saṃprajñāta samādhi* (a *samādhi* that still involves some type of knowledge relationship with the object/external world).[19] *Nirvicārā samādhi*, the highest form of this category of *saṃprajñāta samādhi*, is likened to autumn—when the rivers flow

---

[13] YS 1.42.

[14] YS 1.43.

[15] YS 1.45. See chapter two.

[16] YS 1.44.

[17] YBh 1.44.

[18] YS 1.46.

[19] YS 1.17.

clean and the skies are clear.[20] This type of cleansing experience imparts inner clarity and a wisdom that has arisen from truth.[21]

As with other experiences, *nirvicārā samādhi* and the wisdom that arises from it leaves *saṃskāras*, impressions, behind. These *saṃskāras*, though, oppose the formation of any externally-oriented *saṃskāras*.[22] Here the YS is clearly detailing a *process*. Within this process, there may occur experiences of *nirvicārā samādhi*, and then, perhaps, experiences outside of this, such as eating, drinking, walking or teaching. In these experiences or activities however, the changes brought about by yogic practice—including the repeated experiences of this type of *samādhi*—would ensure that the yogin did not succumb to *avidyā* (ignorance) again.

At last, when even the seeds of the most subtle experiences disappear, the yogin moves into the final stages of Yoga:

> *tasyāpi nirodhe sarva-nirodhān*
> *nirbījaḥ samādhir iti*
> When there is the
> suppression/cessation of even this
> [*saṃskāra* born of *samādhi*], there is
> *samādhi* without seed, due to the
> suppression/cessation of
> everything.[23]

This is also termed *asaṃprajñāta samādhi*, a *samādhi* without object or support, and hence without seed. At this point, the yogin

---

[20] YS 1.47.

[21] *Nirvicāra-vaiśāradye'dhyātma-prasādaḥ* "When there is the clearness of *nirvicāra*, then there is clarity of the inner self (*adhyātma*) (YS 1.47). *Ṛtaṃ-bharā tatra prajñā* "In this, *prajñā* is filled with truth" (YS 1.48).

[22] YS 1.50.

[23] YS 1.51.

has moved beyond even the personal experience or insight into the distinction between *puruṣa* and *prakṛti*, for that too can be expressed in words, would be based upon conventional categories, and would form *saṃskāras*.[24] All that remains is the final residue of *nirvicārā samādhi saṃskāras*.[25]

When the remaining *saṃskāras* are finally gone, the *citta* alone, released from ignorance, is drawn towards *kaivalya*, aloneness, liberation.[26] There may be times, after this has occurred, when the yogin experiences the lower forms of *samādhi*. This, according to some, accounts for the yogin's continued existence. However, when even the intermittent *saṃskāras* are washed away by an even subtler *samādhi*, the *dharma-megha samādhi* (rain-cloud *samādhi*), then the yogin truly attains *kaivalya*. The final *sūtra* in the text offers a description of this end:

> *puruṣārtha-śūnyānāṃ guṇānāṃ*
> *pratiprasavaḥ kaivalyaṃ sva-rūpa-*
> *pratiṣṭhā vā citi-śaktir iti*
> The involution of the *guṇas*, which
> [at this point] no longer serve any
> purpose of *puruṣa*, is *kaivalya*, or
> pure awareness established in its
> own form.[27]

The YS delineates these final stages of Yoga clearly, although relying heavily on metaphorical language. The question though is what do these final stages represent? Is the yogin dead or alive,

---

[24] YS 3.55.

[25] YS 1.18.

[26] *tadā viveka-nimnaṃ kaivalya-prāgbhāraṃ cittam* (YS 4.26).

[27] YS 4.34.

comatose or aware?[28] To some extent, we are limited here by our very questions and categories.

If we review the types of Yoga practices found in the preceding chapters, we find nothing there that would induce states of coma or death. The practices presented in the YS certainly rely on dissociation from habitual or normal ways that the person thinks, feels and behaves. If the entire practice of Yoga was based upon this dissociation, with nothing else replacing it, then we might conclude that the final stages of Yoga are completely quiescent and perhaps even death-like. Instead, a number of new values, behaviours, and cognitive practices replace the old. These can include non-violence, friendliness, compassion, joy, equanimity, purity, study, mindfulness of breath, control of senses, and various forms of concentrative and meditative focus. The idea of a residue

---

[28] There is disagreement among scholars regarding these final states. Feuerstein maintains that the ultimate end of Yoga, *kaivalya*, is a state of catalepsy ([1979] 1989, 142). Whicher, in the end, refuses to "foist" the "radical dualistic perspective" of Sāṃkhya onto Yoga (1998, 289). Instead, he suggests that

> in *kaivalya* the liberated identity of *puruṣa* can incorporate an integration of spirit and matter—including our psychophysical being and nature—such that *purusa* may be seen to contain every potential experience, in fact everything within itself. Or, one could say that following the complete purification or sattvification of the mind, *puruṣa* knows itself to be everything. At this level of realization, one is no longer held captive to any sense of duality. One beholds *puruṣa*—one's true identity or Self—in the entire cosmos, and the entire cosmos, which is also one's Self, in *puruṣa* (1998, 205).

Larson (1999b) and Burley (2004) strongly disagree with Whicher's interpretation. Finally, Ghosh recognizes that from a normal perspective, the last stages of Yoga seem "little less than slow suicide" (1977, 266). Although the final state, according to Ghosh, is "complete inactivity," he does stress that there is something left—a consciousness that has nothing to do with the individual (1977, 265-266).

of *saṃskāras* can account, according to this tradition, for the yogin's continued functioning as a living being. We could think of the *saṃskāras* as representing a residual individual, that is, some traits, experiences and memories, of the yogin's former life. The YS, particularly with metaphors of clearness, indicates that any personal identity based upon these weakens, while the strongest aspects of the yogin's psychology become greater and greater abilities of focus, concentration and awareness. Again, if we set aside the *siddhis* as representing logical outcomes but not, in all cases, psychological outcomes, the increased abilities such as focus, seem a reasonable training effect or outcome.

The YS, however, moves beyond this and here the tradition steps well out of the realm of cognitive science or most current discussions of mind, consciousness and identity. It is not that we could not or should not move in the direction of understanding, as much as possible, from a scientific perspective, the stages of Yoga. Rather, once we reach this point, there are not even general parallels that we can make between neuroscience and Yoga because the tradition, according to its metaphysics, shifts the topic beyond language and individuality.

In his book *Kinds of Minds*,[29] the philosopher Daniel Dennett reflects on the connections between language, consciousness and minds. Language provides us with the abilities to not only have a concept, but to reflect *upon* that concept, to think about what it is *like* to have that concept, to replace that concept with another one, and a host of other mental activities that are essential, even defining, aspects of the human mind and consciousness.[30] I may

---

[29] Dennett 1996.

[30] Dennett 1996, 159-161.

never be able to fully describe to you what it is like to be me (and thankfully, since adolescence has long passed, I won't even attempt to do so), but most of the time, except during sleep—especially dreamless sleep—and complete focus on certain activities, there is *something* that it is like to be me. According to Dennett, language plays an enormous role in the ability to experience and reflect upon this something-ness and me-ness, even to the extent that it may be a defining factor in the nature of mind: "perhaps language is not so peripheral to minds after all. Perhaps the kind of mind you get when you add language to it is so different from the kind of mind you can have without language that calling them both minds is a mistake."[31] Dennett is primarily considering animals here, but from the perspective of Yoga, we might come to a similar conclusion. With the disappearance of even the residue of *nirvicārā samādhi saṃskāras*, and the cessation of the five *citta-vṛttis*, then the attainment of *kaivalya* (and even "attainment" here is misleading, as it implies that there is someone who attains something) any type of thing we mean by using the term "mind" is gone, along with identity and the sense of what it is like to be something.

For this reason, I do not believe it is possible to make any type of statement about *kaivalya*, other than that it is the final stage or goal of Pātañjala Yoga. What we have had from the beginning with this text is a blending of metaphysics and psychology, of philosophy and practice. As with science, practice takes us a long way in understanding this system of Yoga, and in correcting misperceptions about what the effects or results of Yoga might *really* be. At the same time, however, metaphysics and tradition

---

[31] Dennett 1996, 17.

provide a rationale for practice, and we must acknowledge this. According to the classical Yoga tradition, to speak of body, mind, identity, most aspects of consciousness, or even life and death, is merely to speak of *prakṛti*. In the YS, *kaivalya* represents something separate from all of this. Something about which nothing can actually be said.

References

DICTIONARIES

Apte, V. S. (1912/1989). *The Practical Sanskrit-English Dictionary.* 2nd ed. reprint. Delhi: Sri Satguru Publications

Monier-Williams, M. (1899/1995). *A Sanskrit English Dictionary.* New ed. Delhi: Motilal Banarsidass.

SANSKRIT SOURCES

Pātañjala-Yogasūtra-Bhāṣya-Vivaraṇam [*Pātañjalayogaśāstravivaraṇa*] *of Śaṅkara-Bhagavat-Pāda* (1952). Critically edited with introduction by S. Rama Sastri and R. Krishnamurthi Sastri. Madras Government Oriental Series, 94. Madras: Government Oriental Manuscripts Library.

PRIMARY SOURCES/TRANSLATIONS

Āraṇya, Swāmi Hariharānanda (1963/1983). *Yoga Philosophy of Patañjali.* P. N. Mukerji tr. Rev. ed. Albany: State University of New York Press.

Arya, Pandit Usharbudh (1986). *The Yoga-Sūtras Of Patañjali With The Exposition Of Vyāsa: A Translation and Commentary.* Honesdale: Himalayan Institute of Yoga Science and Philosophy.

Baba, Bangali (1976/1990). *Yogasūtra Of Patañjali With The Commentary Of Vyāsa: Translated from Sanskrit into English with Copious Notes.* Delhi: Motilal Banarsidass.

Bhāratī, Swāmī Veda (2001). *Yoga Sūtras of Patañjali: with the Exposition of Vyāsa; A Translation and Commentary.* Delhi: Motilal Banarsidass.

Deshpande, P. Y. (1978). *The Authentic Yoga: A fresh look at Patañjali's Yoga Sutras with a new translation, notes and comments*. London: Rider and Company.

Feuerstein, Georg (1979/1989). *The Yoga-Sūtra Of Patañjali: A New Translation and Commentary*. American ed. reprint. Rochester: Inner Traditions.

Leggett, Trevor (1990). *The Complete Commentary by Śaṅkara on the Yoga-Sūtra-s: A Full Translation of the Newly Discovered Text*. London: Kegan Paul International.

Maurer, Walter H. (1986). *Pinnacles Of India's Past: Selections From The Ṛgveda*. Philadelphia: John Benjamins Publishing.

Miller, Barbara Stoler (1995). *Yoga: Discipline of Freedom—The YogaSutra Attributed to Patanjali*. Berkeley: University of California Press.

Rukmani, T. S. (2001). *Yogasūtrabhāṣyavivaraṇa of Śaṅkara*. New Delhi: Munshiram Manoharlal.

Sarasvati, Svami Satya Prakash (1992). *Atharva-Veda Saṃhitā*. Vol. 4 Kāṇḍa XI-XV. New Delhi: Veda Pratishthana.

Sharma, Priyavrat (1981/2004). *Caraka-Saṃhitā: Agniveśas treatise refined and annotated by Caraka and redacted by Dṛḍhabala*. Ninth edition. Volume 1 (Sūtrasthāna to Indriyasthāna). Jaikrishnadas Ayurveda Series #36. Varanasi: Chaukhambha Orientalia.

Woods, J. H. (1914/1988). *The Yoga-System Of Patañjali: Or The Ancient Hindu Doctrine of Concentration of Mind*. Reprint. Delhi: Motilal Banarsidass.

SECONDARY SOURCES

Ader, Robert, David L. Fenton, and Nicholas Cohen eds. (1991). *Psychoneuroimmunology*. 2nd ed. New York: Academic Press (Harcourt Brace Jovanovich).

Afifi, Adel K. and Ronald A. Bergman (1998). *Functional Neuroanatomy: Text and Atlas*. New York: McGraw-Hill.

Aklujkar, Ashok (2001). "The Pandits from a Piṇḍa-brahmāṇḍa Point of View." In *The Pandit: Traditional Sanskrit Scholarship in India. Festschrift Parameshvara*

Aithal. pp. 19-42. Axel Michaels, ed. New Delhi: Manohar. South Asian Studies Series.

--- (forthcoming). "Vindhyavāsa, author of the Yoga-bhāṣya." In *Excursions into Pre-Bhartṛhari Thought*. Pune: Bhandarkar Oriental Research Institute.

Alper, Harvey P. ed. (1989). *Mantra*. Albany: State University of New York Press.

Austin, James H. (1998/1999/2000). *Zen and the Brain*. Fifth printing of 1999 paperback ed. Cambridge: MIT Press.

Baars, Bernard J., William P. Banks, and James B. Newman ed.s (2003). *Essential Sources in the Scientific Study of Consciousness*. Cambridge: MIT Press.

Bannerjee, M. K. (1982). "General Systems Philosophy and Sāṃkhya-Yoga: Some Remarks." *Philosophy East and West*. Vol. 32, no. 1.

Benson, Herbert (1977). "The Relaxation Response: Therapeutic Effect." Letter. *Science*. Vol. 278, no. 5344. Dec. 5.

Benson, Herbert, John W. Lehmann, M. S. Malhotra, Ralph F. Goldman, Jeffrey Hopkins and Mark D. Epstein (1982). "Body temperature changes during the practice of g Tum-mo yoga." *Nature*. (*Letters*) 295, 234-236.

Bhattacharya, Ram Shankar (1985) *An Introduction To The Yogasūtra*. Delhi: Bharatiya Vidya Prakasana.

Bijlani, R. L. (2004). "Influence of Yoga On Brain And Behaviour: Facts And Speculations." Guest Editorial. *Indian Journal of Physiology and Pharmacology*. Vol. 48, no. 1.

Blackmore, Susan (2004). *Consciousness: An Introduction*. Oxford: Oxford University Press.

Blalslev, Anindita N. (1991). "The Notion Of Kleśa And Its Bearing On The Yoga Analysis Of Mind." *Philosophy East and West*. Vol. 41, no. 1.

Bower, James M. and Lawrence M. Parsons (2003). "Rethinking the "Lesser Brain." *Scientific American* 289 (2):50-57.

Buckingham, Julia C., Glenda E. Gillies, and Anne-Marie Cowell eds. (1997). *Stress, Stress Hormones and the Immune System.* Chichester: John Wiley & Sons.

Buckner, Randy L. and Mark E. Wheeler (2001). "The Cognitive Neuroscience of Remembering." *Nature Reviews Neuroscience.* (2): 624-634.

Burley, Mikel (2004). "'Aloneness' and the Problem of Realism in Classical Sāṃkhya and Yoga." *Asian Philosophy.* Vol. 14, no. 3: 223-238.

Carpenter, R. H. S. (1996). *Neurophysiology.* 3rd ed. New York: Oxford University Press.

Carrier, Martin, and Jürgen Mittelstrass (1991). *Mind, Brain, Behaviour: The Mind-Body Problem and the Philosophy of Psychology.* Translation of *Geist, Gehirn, Verhalten.* Revised and expanded English edition. Berlin: Walter de Gruyter.

Chalmers, David (1995). "The Puzzle of Conscious Experience." *Scientific American.* Dec.

Chapple, Christopher (1981/1983). "Citta-vṛtti and Reality in the Yoga-Sūtra." *Proceedings of the Institute for Advanced Studies of World Religions Conference, 1981.* Stony Brook, New York: IASWR.

--- (1994). "Reading Patañjali Without Vyāsa: A Critique of Four *YogaSūtra* Passages." *Journal of the American Academy of Religion.* Vol. 62, no. 1.

Chatterjee, Asoke (1989). *Upaniṣadyoga And Pātañjalayoga: A Comparative Approach.* Calcutta: Calcutta University Press.

Churchland, Patricia Smith (1986). *Neurophilosophy: Toward a Unified Science of the Mind/Brain.* Cambridge: MIT Press.

--- (2002). *Brain-wise: Studies in Neurophilosophy.* Cambridge: MIT Press.

Churchland, Paul M. (1988/1993). *Matter and Consciousness: A Contemporary Introduction to the Philosophy of Mind.* Rev. ed., new material. Fifth printing. Cambridge: MIT Press.

--- (1994/1998) "Betty Crocker's theory of consciousness: A review of John Searle's *The Rediscovery of the Mind.*" Orig. pub. in *London Review of Books.* In *On the Contrary: Critical Essays, 1987-1997.* See Churchland and Churchland 1998.

--- (1995/1996). *The Engine of Reason, the Seat of the Soul.* First MIT Press paperback ed. Cambridge: MIT Press.

---(1996). "The Future of Psychology, Folk and Scientific." In *The Churchlands and their Critics.* See McCauley 1996.

Churchland, Paul M., and Patricia S. Churchland (1996a). "The Future of Psychology, Folk and Scientific." In *The Churchlands and their Critics.* See McCauley 1996.

---(1996b). "McCauley's Demand for a Co-level Competitor." In *The Churchlands and their Critics.* See McCauley 1996.

---(1997/1998). "Recent Work on Consciousness: Philosophical, Theoretical, and Empirical." Reprint from *Seminars in Neurology.* In *On the Contrary: Critical Essays, 1987-1997.* See Churchland and Churchland 1998.

---(1998). *On the Contrary: Critical Essays, 1987-1997.* Cambridge: MIT Press.

Collins, Clare (1998). "Yoga: Intuition, Preventive Medicine, and Treatment." *Journal of Obstetric, Gynecologic, and Neo-Natal Nursing.* Sept./Oct.

Conger, George P. (1953). "A Naturalistic Approach to Sāṃkhya-Yoga." *Philosophy East and West.* Vol. 3, no. 3.

Conze, Edward (1967). *Buddhist Thought In India.* Ann Arbor: University of Michigan Press.

Corby, James C., Walton T. Roth, Vincent P. Zarcone Jr., Bert S. Kopell (1978). "Psychophysiological Correlates of the Practice of Tantric Yoga Meditation." *Archives of General Psychiatry.* Vol. 35, May.

Cornwell, John ed. (1998). *Consciousness and Human Identity.* Oxford: Oxford University Press.

Coward, Harold G. (1983). "Psychology and karma." *Philosophy East and West.* Vol. 33, no. 1

Crick, Francis (1994). *The Astonishing Hypothesis: The Scientific Search for the Soul.* New York: Charles Scribner's Sons.

Crick, Francis and Christof Koch (1995). "Why Neuroscience May Be Able to Explain Consciousness." *Scientific American*. Dec.

Criswell, Eleanor (1989). *How Yoga Works: An Introduction to Somatic Yoga*. Novato, CA: Freeperson Press.

Damasio, Antonio R. (1994/1995). *Descartes' Error: Emotion, Reason, and the Human Brain*. Orig. ed. New York: G. P. Putnam's Sons. First Avon Books Trade Printing. New York: Avon Books.

--- (1999). *The Feeling of What Happens: Body and Emotion in the Making of Consciousness*. New York: Harcourt Brace and Company.

Damasio, Antonio R., Thomas J. Grabowski, Antoine Bechara, Hanna Damasio, Laura L. B. Ponto, Josef Parvizi, and Richard D. Hichwa (2000). "Subcortical and cortical brain activity during the feeling of self-generated emotions." *Nature Neuroscience*. Vol. 3, no. 10. Oct.

Danielou, Alain (1964/1991). *The Myths And Gods Of India*. Princeton Bollingen Series. Rochester: Inner Traditions International.

Danos, Peter, Steve Guich, Lennart Abel, and Monte S. Buchsbaum (2001). "EEG Alpha Rhythm and Glucose Metabolic Rate in the Thalamus in Schizophrenia." *Neuropsychobiology*. Vol. 43, no. 4: 265-272.

d'Aquili, Eugene G., and Andrew B. Newberg (1993). "Religious And Mystical States: A Neuropsychological Model." *Zygon*. Vol. 28, no. 2. June.

Dasgupta, Surendranath (1930/1974). *Yoga Philosophy In Relation To Other Systems Of Indian Thought*. Delhi: Motilal Banarsidass.

---(1922/1975). *A History Of Indian Philosophy*. Delhi: Motilal Banarsidass. Vol. 1 and 2.

---(1924/1987). *Yoga As Philosophy And Religion*. Delhi: Motilal Banarsidass.

---(1920/1989). *A Study of Patañjali*. Second ed. Delhi: Motilal Banarsidass.

Davidson, Richard J. (2000). "Affective Style, Psychopathology, and Resilience: Brain Mechanisms and Plasticity." *American Psychologist*. Vol. 55, no. 11. Nov.

Deepak, K. K. (2002). "Neurophysiological Mechanisms Of Induction Of Meditation: A Hypothetico-Deductive Approach." Review Article. *Indian Journal of Physiology and Pharmacology*. Vol. 46, no. 2.

Dennett, Daniel C. (1991). *Consciousness Explained.* First Paperback ed. Boston: Little, Brown And Company.

---(1996). *Kinds Of Minds: Toward an Understanding of Consciousness.* New York: Basic Books.

Dunn, Bruce R., Judith A. Hartigan, and William L. Mikulas (1999). "Concentration and Mindfulness Meditations: Unique Forms of Consciousness?" *Applied Psychophysiology and Biofeedback.* Vol. 24, no. 3.

Eliot, T. S. (1963/1983). "Little Gidding." *Collected Poems 1909-1962.* Reprint. London: Faber and Faber.

Engel, Andreas K., Pascal Fries, Pieter R. Roelfsema, Peter Konig, Michael Brecht, and Wolf Singer (2003). "Temporal Binding, Binocular Rivalry, And Consciousness." In *Essential Sources.* See Baars, 2003.

Feuerstein, Georg (1974). *The Essence of Yoga: A Contribution To The Psychohistory Of Indian Civilisation.* New York: Grove Press.

---(1979) *The Yoga-Sūtra Of Patañjali: An Exercise in the Methodology of Textual Analysis.* New Delhi: Arnold-Heinemann.

---(1980) *The Philosophy of Classical Yoga.* Manchester: Manchester University Press.

---(1991). *Sacred Paths: Essays on Wisdom, Love and Mystical Realization.* Burdett, NY: Larson Publications.

Feuerstein, Georg and Jeanine Miller (1971/1972). *Yoga And Beyond: Essays In Indian Philosophy.* Orig. published in Great Britain as *A Reappraisal of Yoga.* New York: Schocken.

Filliozat, J. (1949/1964). *The Classical Doctrine Of Indian Medicine: Its origins and its Greek Parallels.* Dev Raj Chanana tr. Delhi: Munshiram Manoharlal.

Flanagan, Owen (1995). "Behaviourism" and "Mind, History of the Philosophy of." In *The Oxford Companion To Philosophy.* See Honderich 1995.

Franco, Eli and Karin Preisendanz (1997). *Beyond Orientalism: The Work of Wilhelm Halbfass and its Impact on Indian and Cross-Cultural Studies*. Poznań Studies in the Philosophy of the Sciences and the Humanities. Vol. 59. Amsterdam: Rodopi.

Frauwallner, Erich (1953). *Geschichte der indischen Philosophie*. Salzburg: Otto Müller. Vol. 1.

---(1973/1993). *History Of Indian Philosophy*. V. M. Bedekar tr. Delhi: Motilal Banarsidass. Vol. 1.

Gazzaniga, Michael S. (1988). *Mind Matters: How Mind and Brain Interact to Create Our Conscious Lives*. Boston: Houghton Mifflin Co.

---(2000). "Cerebral Specialization and interhemispheric communication: Does the corpus callosum enable the human condition?" *Brain* 123: 1293-1326.

--- (2004). *The Cognitive Neurosciences III*. editor-in-chief. Cambridge: MIT Press.

Ghosh, Jajneswar (1977). *A Study Of Yoga*. 2nd rev. ed. Delhi: Motilal Banarsidass.

Gleitman, Henry (1981). *Psychology*. New York: W. W. Norton & Co.

Goldstein, Murray (1995). "Forward." In *Brain Repair*. See Stein et. al., 1995.

Gopal, K. S., O. P. Bhatnagar, N. Subramanian, and S. D. Nishith (1973). "Effect Of Yogasanas And Pranayamas On Blood Pressure, Pulse Rate And Some Respiratory Functions." *Indian Journal of Physiology and Pharmacology*. Vol. 17, no. 3. Jul.

Greenfield, Susan (1998). "How Might the Brain Generate Consciousness?" In *From Brains to Consciousness?* See Rose 1998.

Grinshpon, Yohanan (1997). "Experience And Observation In Traditional And Modern Pātañjala Yoga." In *Beyond Orientalism*. See Franco and Preisendanz 1997.

Hafen, Brent Q., Keith J. Karren, Kathryn J. Frandsen, and N. Lee Smith (1996). *Mind/Body Health: The Effects of Attitudes, Emotions, and Relationships*. Boston: Allyn and Bacon.

Halbfass, Wilhelm (1988). *India and Europe: An Essay in Understanding*. Albany: State University of New York Press.

---(1991). *Tradition and Reflection: Explorations in Indian Thought*. Albany: State University of New York Press.

Halber, Deborah (2000). "Nedivi studies the importance of ongoing neural connections." From *MIT News Office*. May 31, 2000. http://web.mit.edu/newsoffice/2000/nedivi-0531.html

Hall, Nicholas R. S., and Maureen P. O'Grady (1991). "Psychosocial Interventions and Immune Function." In *Psychoneuroimmunology*. See Ader et. al. 1991.

Hartshone, Charles (1988). "Śaṅkara, Nāgārjuna, and Fa Tsang, with some Western Analogues." In *Interpreting Across Boundaries: New Essays in Comparative Philosophy*. See Larson and Deutsch 1988.

Herzog, Hans, Vikram R. Lele, Torsten Kuwert, Karl-Josef Langen, Elena Rota Kops, and Ludwig E. Feinendegen (1990-91). "Changed Pattern of Regional Glucose Metabolism during Yoga Meditative Relaxation." *Biological Psychology/Pharmacopsychology*. Vol 23.

Hickmott, P. W. and M. Constantine-Paton (1996). "Neurotransmitter Receptor Regulation and Its Role in Synaptic Plasticity and Stabilization." In *The Mind Brain Continuum*. See Llinás and Churchland 1996.

Hofstadter, Douglas R. and Daniel C. Dennett eds. (1981). *The Mind's I: Fantasies And Reflections On Self And Soul*. New York: Bantam Books.

Honderich, Ted, ed. (1995). *The Oxford Companion To Philosophy*. Oxford: Oxford University Press.

Hopkins, Thomas J. (1971). *The Hindu Religious Tradition*. Belmont, CA: Wadsworth Publishing.

Hornsby, Jennifer (1995). "Folk Psychology." In *The Oxford Companion To Philosophy*. See Honderich, 1995.

Hundert, Edward M. (1989). *Philosophy, Psychiatry And Neuroscience: Three Approaches To The Mind; A Synthetic Analysis of the Varieties of Human Experience*. Oxford: Clarendon Press.

Ingle, D. J., M. A. Goodale, and R. J. W. Mansfield ed.s (1982). *Analysis of Visual Behaviour*. Cambridge: MIT Press.

Jacobsen, Knut A. (1993). "Ordinary Nature: *Pakati* in the Pāli Scripture." *Asian Philosophy*. Vol 3, no. 2.

---(1999/2002). *Prakṛti in Sāṃkhya-Yoga: Material Principle, Religious Experience, Ethical Implications*. Delhi: Motilal Banarsidass.

Jasper, H. H., L. Descarries, V. F. Castelluci, and S. Rossignol, ed.s (1998). *Consciousness: At the Frontiers of Neuroscience, Advances in Neurology*. Philadelphia: Lippincott-Raven. Vol. 77.

Jevning, R., R. K. Wallace, and M. Beidebach (1992). "The Physiology of Meditation: A Review. A Wakeful Hypometabolic Response." *Neuroscience and Biobehavioural Reviews*. Vol. 16.

Joseph, Rhawn (1996). *Neuropsychiatry, Neuropsychology, and Clinical Neuroscience: Emotion, Evolution, Cognition, Language, Memory, Brain Damage, and Abnormal Behaviour*. Second ed. Baltimore: Williams & Wilkins.

Joseph, Santha, K. Sridharan, S. K. B. Patil, M. L. Kumaria, W. Selvamurthy, N. T. Joseph, and H. S. Nayar (1981). "Study of some physiological and biochemical parameters in subjects undergoing yogic training." *Indian Journal of Medical Research*. Vol. 74, Jul.

Joshi, K. S. (1965). "On the Meaning of Yoga." *Philosophy East and West*. Vol. 15, no. 1.

---(1968). "On the Possibility of Yogic Powers." *International Philosophical Quarterly*. Vol. 8.

Kaelber, Walter O. (1989). *Tapta Mārga: Asceticism And Initiation In Vedic India*. Albany: State University of New York Press.

Katz, Steven T. (1978). *Mysticism and Philosophical Analysis*. New York: Oxford University Press.

Kaul, H. Kumar (1989). *Yoga in Hindu Scriptures*. Delhi: Surjeet Publications.

Kiecolt-Glaser, Janice K., and Ronald Glaser (1991). "Stress and Immune Function in Humans." In *Psychoneuroimmunology*. See Ader et. al. 1991.

Kosslyn, Stephen M., Giorgio Ganis, and William L. Thompson (2001). "Neural Foundations Of Imagery." *Nature Reviews Neuroscience*. Vol. 2. Sept.

Kothari, L. K., A. Bordia, and O. P. Gupta (1973). "Studies on a Yogi During an Eight-day Confinement in a Sealed Underground Pit." *Indian Journal of Medical Research*. Vol. 61, no. 11. Nov.

Krishna, Daya (1988). "Comparative Philosophy: What It Is and What It Ought to Be." In *Interpreting Across Boundaries: New Essays in Comparative Philosophy*. See Larson and Deutsch 1988.

Kumar, Shiv (1984). *Sāṃkhya-Yoga Epistemology*. Delhi: Eastern Book Linkers.

Kuppuswamy, B. (1985/1990). *Elements of Ancient Indian Psychology*. Delhi: Konark Publishers Pvt. Ltd.

Lahuis, B., C. Kemner, and H. Van Engeland (2003). "Magnetic resonance imaging studies on autism and childhood-onset schizophrenia in children and adolscents---a review." *Acta Neuropsychiatrica*. Vol. 15, no. 3.

Larson, Gerald James (1979). *Classical Sāṃkhya: An Interpretation of its History and Meaning*. Delhi: Motilal Banarsidass.

---(1983). "An eccentric ghost in the machine: Formal and quantitative aspects of the Sāṃkhya-Yoga dualism." *Philosophy East and West*. Vol. 33, no. 3. Jul.

---(1988). "Introduction: The 'Age-Old Distinction Between the Same and the Other.'" In *Interpreting Across Boundaries: New Essays in Comparative Philosophy*. See Larson and Deutsch 1988.

---(1995). "Classical Yoga Philosophy And Some Issues In The Philosophy Of Mind." *Religious Studies and Theology*. Vol. 13-14. Apr.

---(1999). "Classical Yoga as Neo-Sāṃkhya: A Chapter In The History Of Indian Philosophy." *Asiatische Studien*. Vol. LIII, no. 3.

---(1999b). "On the Integrity of the Yoga Darsana: A Review." *International Journal of Hindu Studies*. Vol 3, no. 2.

Larson, Gerald James, and Ram Shankar Bhattacharya, ed. (1987). *Sāṃkhya: A Dualist Tradition in Indian Philosophy: Encyclopedia of Indian Philosophies*. Vol. 4.

Larson, Gerald James and Eliot Deutsch, ed. (1988). *Interpreting Across Boundaries: New Essays in Comparative Philosophy*. Princeton: Princeton University Press.

Lazar, Sara W., George Bush, Randy L. Gollub, Gregory L. Fricchione, Gurucharan Khalsa, and Herbert Benson (2000). "Functional Brain Mapping of the relaxation response and meditation." *NeuroReport*. 11(7):1581-1585. May 15, 2000.

Lecours, André Roch (1998). "Language Contrivance on Consciousness (and Vice Versa)." In *Consciousness: At the Frontiers of Neuroscience*. See Jasper et. al., 1998.

Ledoux, Joseph (1996/1998). *The Emotional Brain: The Mysterious Underpinnings of Emotional Life*. First Touchstone Edition. New York: Touchstone.

Lee, Bruce Y. and Andrew B. Newberg (2005). "Religion and Health: A Review And Critical Analysis." *Zygon*. Vol. 40, no. 2. June.

Llinás, Rodolfo and Patricia S. Churchland, ed. (1996). *The Mind-Brain Continuum: Sensory Processes*. Cambridge: MIT Press.

Lipton, Peter (1998). "Binding the Mind." In *Consciousness and Human Identity*. See Cornwell 1998.

Lou, Hans C., Troels W. Kjaer, Lars Friberg, Gordon Wildschiodtz, Soren Holm, and Markus Nowak (1999). "A O-H_2O PET Study of Meditation and the Resting State of Normal Consciousness." In *Human Brain Mapping*. Vol. 7.

Lutz, Antoine, Lawrence L. Greischar, Nancy B. Rawlings, Matthieu Ricard, and Richard J. Davidson (2004). "Long-term meditators self-induce high-amplitude gamma synchrony during mental practice." PNAS (*Proceedings of the National Academy of Sciences of the USA*). Vol. 101, no. 46. 16369-16373.

Lyons, William ed. (1995). "Introduction." In *Modern Philosophy of Mind*. Lyons ed. London: Orion.

Martin, A., C.L. Wiggs, L.G. Ungerleider, and J.V. Haxby (1996). "Neural correlates of category-specific knowledge." *Nature*. 379:649-652.

Martin, G. Neil (2003). *Essential Biological Psychology*. New York: Oxford University Press.

Martin, Paul (1997/1998). *The Sickening Mind: Brain, Behaviour, Immunity and Disease*. London: Flamingo.

McCauley, Robert N., ed. (1996). *The Churchlands and their Critics*. Cambridge: Blackwell Publishers.

---(1996). "Explanatory Pluralism and The Co-evolution of Theories in Science." In *The Churchlands and their Critics*. Cambridge: Blackwell Publishers.

Merzenich, M. M., and R. C. deCharms (1996). "Neural Representations, Experience, and Change." In *The Mind-Brain Continuum*. See Llinás and Churchland, 1996.

Midgley, Mary. "One World, but a Big One." In *From Brains to Consciousness? Essays On The New Sciences Of The Mind*. See Rose 1998.

Miller, Jeanine (1971/1972). "Forerunners of Yoga: The Keśin Hymn (X.136)." In *Yoga And Beyond: Essays In Indian Philosophy*. See Feuerstein and Miller 1971/1972.

Mishra, Satyendra Prasad (1989). *Yoga And Āyurveda: Their Alliedness and Scope as Positive Health Sciences*. Varanasi: Chaukhambha Sanskrit Sansthan.

Mohan, Madan, D. P. Thombre, Bharathi Balakumar, T. K. Nambinarayanan, Sachin Thakur, N. Krishnamurthy, and A. Chandrabose (1992). "Effect of Yoga Training On Reaction Time, Respiratory Endurance And Muscle Strength." *Indian Journal of Physiology and Pharmacology*. Vol. 36, no. 4.

Morris, Kelly (1998). "Meditating on Yogic Science: A News Feature." In *The Lancet*. Vol 351 (9108), Apr. 4.

Müller, Max (1919/1971). *The Six Systems Of Indian Philosophy*. 4th ed. Varanasi: The Chowkhamba Sanskrit Series Office.

Naveen, K. V., R. Nagarathna, H. R. Nagendra, Shirley Telles (1997). "Yoga Breathing Through a Particular Nostril Increases Spatial Memory Scores Without Lateralized Effects " *Psychological Reports*. Vol. 81, no. 2. Oct.

Newberg, A. B., and J. Iverson (2003). "The neural basis of the complex mental task of meditation: neurotransmitter and neurochemical considerations." *Medical Hypotheses*. Vol. 61, no. 2.

Newberg, Andrew, Abass Alavi, Michael Baime, Michael Pourdehnad, Jill Santanna, Eugene d'Aquili (2001). "The measurement of regional cerebral blood flow during the complex cognitive task of meditation: a preliminary SPECT study." *Psychiatry Research: Neuroimmaging Section*. Vol. 106.

Norra, Christine, Till Dino Waberski, Wolfram Kawohl, Hanns Jürgen Kunert, Dorothee Hock, René Gobbelé, Helmut Buchner, and Paul Hoff (2004). "High-Frequency Somatosensory Thalamocortical Oscillations and Psychopathology in Schizophrenia." *Neuropsychobiology* Vol. 49, no. 2: 71-81.

Oberhammer, Gerhard (1989). "The Use of Mantra in Yogic Meditation: The Testimony of the *Pāśupata*." In *Mantra*. See Alper 1989.

Ochsner, Kevin N., Silvia A. Bunge, James J. Gross, and John D. E. Gabrieli (2002). "Rethinking Feelings: An fMRI Study of the Cognitive Regulation of Emotion." *Journal of Cognitive Neuroscience*. Vol. 14, no. 8.

Ogata, Akira and Taihei Miyakawa (1998). "Religious experiences in epileptic patients with a focus on ictus-related episodes." *Psychiatry and Clinical Neurosciences* Vol. 52:321-325.

Panikkar, Raimundo (1988). "What Is Comparative Philosophy Comparing?" In *Interpreting Across Boundaries: New Essays in Comparative Philosophy*. See Larson and Deutsch 1988.

Parvizi, Josef, and Antonio Damasio (2001). "Consciousness and the brainstem." *Cognition*. Vol. 79.

Persinger, Michael (1987). *Neuropsychological Bases of God Beliefs*. New York: Praeger.

Phillips, Stephen H. (1985). "The Conflict Of Voluntarism And Dualism In The *Yogasūtra: (Or How to Get 'Mukti' from Metaphysics). Journal of Indian Philosophy*. Vol. 13.

Place, U. T. (1956/1995). "Is Consciousness A Brain Process?" orig. pub. *British Journal of Psychology*. Vol. 47. In *Modern Philosophy Of Mind*. See Lyons, 1995.

Puligandla, R. (1970). "Phenomenological reduction and yogic meditation." *Philosophy East and West*. Vol. 20, no. 1.

Purves, Dale, George J. Augustine, David Fitzpatrick, Lawrence C. Katz, Anthony-Samuel LaMantia, James O. McNamara, and S. Mark Williams, ed.s (2001). *Neuroscience*. Sunderland: Sinauer Associates.

Raghuraj, P., R. Nagarathna, H. R. Nagendra, and S. Telles (1997). "Pranayama Increases Grip Strength Without Lateralized Effects." *Indian Journal of Physiology and Pharmacology*. Vol. 41, no. 2. Apr.

Rai, L., and K. Ram (1993). "Energy Expenditure And Ventilatory Responses During Virasana – A Yogic Standing Posture." *Indian Journal of Physiology and Pharmacology*. Vol. 37, no. 1.

Rains, G. Dennis (2002). *Principles of Human Neuropsychology*. Boston: McGraw Hill.

Raju, P. T. (1985). *Structural Depths of Indian Thought* Albany: State University of New York Press.

Ramachandran, V. S. and Sandra Blakeslee (1998). *Phantoms in the Brain: Probing the Mysteries of the Human Mind*. New York: William Morrow.

Rensink, Ronald A., J. Kevin O'Regan, and James J. Clark (2003). "To See Or Not To See: The Need For Attention To Perceive Changes In Scenes." In *Essential Sources*. See Baars, 2003.

Restak, Richard (1991). *The Brain Has A Mind Of Its Own: Insights From A Practicing Neurologist*. New York: Harmony Books.

---(1995). *Brainscapes: An Introduction to What Neuroscience Has Learned about the Structure, Function, and Abilities of the Brain*. New York: Hyperion.

Richardson, J. S. (1993). "On the Functions of Monoamine Oxidase, the Emotions, and Adaptation to Stress." *International Journal of Neuroscience*. Vol. 70, no. 1-2. May.

Robertson, Lynn C. (2003). "Binding, Spatial Attention And Perceptual Awareness." *Nature Reviews Neuroscience* 4 (Feb.):93-102.

Rose, Steven ed. (1998). *From Brains to Consciousness? Essays On The New Sciences Of The Mind*. Princeton: Princeton University Press.

Rosemont, Henry, Jr. (1988). "Against Relativism." In *Interpreting Across Boundaries: New Essays in Comparative Philosophy*. See Larson and Deutsch 1988.

Rukmani, T. S. (1981). "The Identity Of The Self (An analytical approach based on early Sanskrit texts)." *Indian Philosophical Quarterly*. Vol. 8, no. 4. Jul.

---(1993). "Siddhi-s In The Bhāgavata Purāṇa And In The Yogasūtra-s Of Patañjali—A Comparison." *Buddhist Philosophical Researches*. Delhi: Motilal Banarsidass.

Rukmini [sic.], T. S. (1981). "Patañjali's Yogaūstras [sic.]—A Synthesis Of Many Yogic Traditions." *ABORI*. LXII.

Sacks, Oliver (1995/1996). *An Anthropologist On Mars: Seven Paradoxical Tales*. Vintage Canada ed. Toronto: Vintage Canada.

Scharfstein, Ben-Ami (1988). "The Contextual Fallacy." In *Interpreting Across Boundaries: New Essays in Comparative Philosophy*. See Larson and Deutsch 1988.

Schweizer, Paul (1993). "Mind/Consciousness Dualism in Sāṅkhya-Yoga Philosophy." *Philosophy and Phenomenological Research*. Vol. 53, no. 4. Dec.

Searle, John R. (1981). "Minds, Brains, and Programs." In *The Mind's I*. See Hofstadter and Dennett.

Sen Gupta, Anima (1981/1982) *Classical Sāṁkhya: A Critical Study*. 2nd rev. ed. New Delhi: Munshiram Manoharlal.

Sinari, Rakmant (1965). "The Method of Phenomenological Reduction and Yoga." *Philosophy East and West*. Vol. 15, no. 3-4.

Singer, Wolf (1998). "Consciousness from a Neurobiological Perspective." In *From Brains to Consciousness?* See Rose 1998.

Smith, David (1998). "Ageing of the Brain: Is Mental Decline Inevitable?" In *From Brains to Consciousness*? See Rose 1998.

Smith, Edward E. and John Jonides (1999). "Storage and Executive Processes in the Frontal Lobes." *Science*. (283) no. 5408: 1657-1661.

Solberg, Erik E., Are Holen, Oivind Ekeberg, Bjarne Osterud, Ragnhild Halvorsen, and Leiv Sandvik (2004). "The effects of long meditation on plasma melatonin and blood serotonin." *Med Sci Monitor*. Vol. 10, no. 3.

Sporns, Olaf (1998). "Biological Variability and Brain Function." In *Consciousness and Human Identity*. See Cornwell 1998.

Squire, Larry R. (1998). "Memory and Brain Systems." In *From Brains to Consciousness?* See Rose 1998.

Stein, Donald G., Simon Brailowsky, and Bruno Will (1995). *Brain Repair*. Oxford: Oxford University Press.

Sternberg, Esther M. (2000). *The Balance Within: The Science Connecting Health And Emotions*. New York: W. H. Freeman and Company.

Telles, Shirley, and T. Desiraju (1992). "Heart Rate and Respiratory Changes Accompanying Yogic Conditions Of Single Thought And Thoughtless States." Letter. *Indian Journal of Physiology and Pharmacology*. Vol. 36, no. 4.

Tola, Fernando, and Carmen Dragonetti (1991-1992). "On The Yogasūtras Of Patañjali." *ABORI*. Vol. 72-73.

Tononi, Giulio, and Gerald M. Edelman (1998). "Consciousness and the Integration of Information in the Brain." In *Consciousness: At The Frontiers of Neuroscience*. See Jasper et. al. 1998.

Tulving, Endel (2002). "Episodic Memory: From Mind to Brain." *Annual Review of Psychology*. 53:1-25.

Turk, David J., Todd F. Heatherton, William M. Kelly, Margaret G. Funnell, Michael S. Gazzaniga, and C. Neil Macrae (2002). "Mike or me? Self-recognition in a split-brain patient." *Nature Neuroscience* 5 (9): 841-842.

Udupa, K. N., and R. H. Singh (1972). "The Scientific Basis of Yoga." *Journal of the American Medical Association (JAMA)*. Letter. Vol. 220, no. 10. June 5.

Ungerleider, L. G. and M. Mishkin (1982). "Two cortical visual systems." In *Analysis of Visual Behaviour*. See Ingle et. al., 549-586.

Vahia, N. S., D. R. Doongaji, D. V. Jeste, S. Ravindranath, S. N. Kapoor, and I. Ardhapurkar (1973). "Psychophysiologic Therapy Based on the Concepts of Patañjali." *American Journal of Psychotherapy*. Vol. 27, no. 4. Oct.

Vellucci, Sandra V. (1997). "The Autonomic and Behavioural Responses to Stress." In *Stress, Stress Hormones and the Immune System*. See Buckingham et. al. 1997.

Wallace, Robert Keith, and Herbert Benson (1972). "The Physiology of Meditation." *Scientific American*. Feb.

Watts, Fraser. "Psychological research questions about yoga." *Mental Health, Religion & Culture*. Vol. 3, no. 1.

Werner, Karel (1975). "Religious Practice And Yoga In The Time Of The Vedas, Upaniṣads and Early Buddhism." *ABORI*. Vol. 56.

---(1977). *Yoga And Indian Philosophy*. Delhi: Motilal Banarsidass.

---(1996). "Indian Conceptions of Human Personality." *Asian Philosophy*. 6, no. 2.

Werntz, Deborah A., R. G. Bickford, F. E. Bloom, and D. S. Shannahoff-Khalsa (1983). "Alternating cerebral hemispheric activity and the lateralization of autonomic nervous function." *Human Neurobiology*. Vol. 2.

Wezler, A. (1984). "On the Quadruple Division of the Yogaśāstra, the Caturvyūhatva of the Cikisāśāstra and the 'Four Noble Truths' of the Buddha." *Indologica Taurinensia*. 12.

Whicher, Ian (1995). "Cessation and Integration in Classical Yoga." *Asian Philosophy*. Vol. 5, no. 1.

---(1998). *The Integrity of the Yoga Darśana: A Reconsideration of Classical Yoga*. Albany: State University of New York Press.

---(1998b). "The Final Stages of Purification in Classical Yoga." *Asian Philosophy*. Vol. 8, no. 2.

Wiggs, C.L., J. Weisberg, and A. Martin. (1999). "Neural Correlates of Semantic and Episodic Memory Retrieval." *Neuropsychologia*. Vol. 37, no. 1: 103-118.

Wilson, Edward O. (1998). *Consilience: The Unity of Knowledge*. New York: Alfred A. Knopf.

Woolfolk, Robert L. (1975). "Psychophysiological Correlates of Meditation." *Archives of General Psychiatry*. Vol. 32. Oct.

Yardi, M. R. (1987). "Sāṅkhya and Yoga In The *Mokṣadharma* And The *Bhagavadgītā*." *ABORI*. 68.

Young, G. Bryan, and Susan E. Pigott (1999). "Neurobiological Basis of Consciousness." Neurological Review. *Archives of Neurology*. Vol. 56. Feb.

Zelazo, Philip R. and Philip D. Zelazo (1998). "The Emergence of Consciousness." In *Consciousness: At the Frontiers of Neuroscience*. See Jasper et. al., 1998.

Index

abhiniveśa (see also *kleśas*), 58, 62–65
abhyāsa (repeated practice), 124, 126–134, 140, 151, 184
abhyāsa-vairāgya (repeated practice and detachment), 5, 18, 123–152, 156, 183–201, 208–209
āgama, 51, 103
ahiṃsā, 60, 158–162, 176, 205–206, 210, 223
Aklujkar, Ashok, 21, 164
aliṅga, 37, 39, 220
amygdala, 100, 110–112, 187
anātman, 61
anger (see also *krodha*), 13, 70, 74, 165–166, 205
ANS, 86, 100, 186, 189, 193, 198, 200, 206
antar-aṅga (internal limbs), 20, 173–176
antarāyas, 135–139, 190, 195–196
anumāna, 51
arousal state (see also ANS), 86–88
Arya, Pandit Usharbudh (see also Bhāratī, Swāmi Veda), 17, 43–44, 51, 54, 110, 129, 135, 142, 151, 175
āsana (postures), 155–156, 167–168, 204, 207–208
asmitā (see also *kleśas*), 27, 39–40, 58, 62–63, 72, 76, 148
association areas (see also cortex), 91, 94–95
aṣṭāṅga-yoga (eightfold yoga), 5, 19, 123–125, 142, 153, 155–176, 198, 204–212
Atharva-veda, 9, 11, 144
attention, 3, 24, 87–89, 94–96, 105–108, 117–118, 121, 137, 146, 161, 182, 184, 187, 189, 192–194, 199, 204–212, 214
Austin, James H., 99–100, 108, 112, 179, 192
avidyā (see also *kleśas*), 12, 58–63, 70, 72, 76, 81, 125, 166, 201, 204, 221–222
aviśeṣa, 37, 40
axon, 85, 182
axons, 85, 88, 90, 105
Āyurveda, 144

bahir-aṅga (external limbs), 20, 158–173
behaviour, 14, 84–85, 89, 94, 99–100, 111–112, 137, 141, 164, 181, 187, 190, 196, 202, 204, 206, 210
Bhagavad-Gītā, 12–14, 104, 126, 155
Bhāratī, Swāmi Veda (see also Arya, Pandit Usharbudh), 167–169
Bhattacharya, Ram Shankar, 15–17, 20, 130, 135, 139, 150
bhāvana, 132, 190
Bhavsar, S. N., 27, 44, 144–146
bhūtas (elements), 37, 40, 146, 217

binding problem (see also perception), 106–108, 174
brahmacarya, 127, 158, 160, 164, 205
brainstem, 86–89, 91, 99, 111, 115, 203
breath (see also *prāṇa*), 11–12, 51, 87–88, 114, 133, 138, 139, 142–146, 155–156, 168–173, 185, 188, 191, 195–197, 204, 207, 210, 223
buddhi, 28, 34, 43–48, 51, 63, 72, 74, 78, 101, 148, 176
buddhīndriyas (sense organs), 38, 40, 217
Buddhism, 7, 14, 16–17, 34, 61, 129, 141, 179, 191

Caraka-saṃhitā, 144–145
categories of practice, 123–126
cerebellum, 86–87, 91
Chapple, Christopher, 64
Churchland, Patricia S., 97, 101–102
citi, 45, 78, 222
citta (mind-field), 30, 34, 43–81, 101, 103, 124, 135–136, 138–143, 148, 152, 162, 168, 172–176, 196, 208–210, 219, 222
citta-bhūmis, 50
citta-vṛtti-nirodha (see also *nirodha*), 68, 126–127, 136, 183, 218
citta-vṛttis, 65
CNS, 86, 186, 194, 200
commentarial sources on YS, 20–22
compassion (see also *karuṇā*), 16, 140, 152, 158, 194, 196–197, 205, 223
concentration (see also *dhāraṇā*), 8, 10, 20, 124, 147, 149, 154–156, 171–175, 188, 192, 204, 209, 211, 224
contemplation (see also *bhāvana*), 125, 132–133, 135, 148, 155, 175, 190
corpus callosum, 92, 99
cortex, 87, 90–91, 93–95, 97–99, 105–107, 110, 115, 117–118, 120, 182, 187, 190–200, 208

Damasio, Antonio, 89, 202–203
Dasgupta, Surendranath, 15–16, 36, 38, 124, 128, 146, 156, 158, 170–171, 175
death, 64–65, 87, 89, 180, 219, 223, 226
dendrites, 85
Dennett, Daniel, 224–225
Deshpande, P. Y., 124
desire (see also *kāma*), 70, 72, 74, 139, 162, 201, 206, 210
dhāraṇā (concentration), 8, 19, 155–156, 172–174, 204, 209, 211, 215
dhyāna (see also meditation), 20, 155–156, 174–175, 204, 209, 211, 215
diencephalon (see also forebrain), 90, 98
draṣṭṛ (the Seer, see also *puruṣa*), 17, 25–28, 34, 63, 78, 144, 213
dreams (see also sleep), 53, 66, 86, 93, 113–115, 149
dṛśya (the seen, see also *prakṛti*), 28, 34–35, 42, 52
duḥkha, 12, 29, 41, 60, 61, 63–64, 68, 138–139, 166, 195
dvandvas, 100
dveṣa (see also *kleśas*), 58, 62, 64, 69–70, 112

emotion (see also specific emotions), 4, 41, 42, 64, 66, 70, 84, 89, 94, 97, 99–101, 110–111, 113, 127, 133, 166, 187, 194, 196–197, 202, 204–205
empathy, 94

equanimity (see also *upekṣā*), 16, 139–141, 152, 195–196, 200, 202, 204–205, 216, 223
evolutes (of *prakṛti*), 37, 40–42, 47, 72, 220

faith (*śraddhā*), 32, 80, 127–128, 131, 133–134, 147, 177–178, 184–185, 188–189, 201, 213
fear, 13, 65, 97, 111–112, 187, 196
Feuerstein, Georg (George), 8, 17, 21, 24–25, 29, 43–44, 46, 64, 124–126, 131, 134–135, 156, 167–168, 175, 190, 214, 223
forebrain, 87–90, 98
Frauwallner, Erich, 11, 13–15
frontal lobes, 94, 117

Gage, Phineas, 84–85, 94–95
Gazzaniga, Michael S., 92–93, 104, 117–119, 187, 195
god module, 96
guṇas, 12, 13, 15–16, 29, 35–37, 39–42, 47, 50–51, 57, 60, 134, 217, 222

H.M, 95–96, 118–120
hearing, 88, 95, 116, 119, 182, 193
hindbrain, 87–88, 90
hippocampus, 91, 95, 100–101, 118, 182, 199
homeostasis, 100, 202–203
hunger, 97, 100, 162, 202–204, 216
hypothalamic-pituitary-adrenal axis (HPA), 186–187, 189, 195
hypothalamus, 98–100, 111, 115, 186, 193, 202–203

identity, 1–8, 23, 27, 30, 41, 54, 62–65, 75–76, 79, 81, 83, 85, 87–88, 94–96, 98, 103, 108, 121, 123, 148–149, 176, 178, 180, 200–201, 205, 210, 223–226
imagination, 101
impediments (see also *antarāyas*), 135–136, 138–140, 190, 195–196
Indus Valley, 10
inference (see also *anumāna*), 51, 65, 103
Īśvara (lord), 32–33, 124, 130–132, 152, 161, 163, 201, 205
īśvara-praṇidhāna, 130–133, 135, 155, 161, 190, 201, 205

Jainism, 7, 14, 16, 34, 141
Joshi, K. S., 9
joy (see also *muditā*), 16, 97, 139–140, 152, 195–196, 199, 205, 223

kaivalya (liberation), 2–3, 8, 18, 65–66, 102–103, 151, 215, 222–225
kaivalya-pāda, 19
kāma, 70
karma, 58, 66, 69–70, 72, 154, 166, 214
karmāśaya, 66, 69–70, 166
karmendriyas, 38, 40
karuṇā (compassion), 16, 140–141, 196
Kaṭha Upaniṣad, 9, 12, 25
Keśin Hymn, 11
kevala, 30
kleśas, 48, 56–66, 69, 70–72, 101, 112, 152–154, 159, 166, 201
kriyā-yoga (yoga of activity), 5, 19, 32, 123–125, 152–155, 161, 163, 201–204, 206
krodha, 70, 74
kṣetra (the field, see also *prakṛti*), 35, 58

language (see also speech), 5, 11, 18, 23, 27, 53, 79, 84, 91, 95, 112–113, 121–122, 133, 154, 181, 213, 216, 222–224
Larson, Gerald James, 11–13, 15, 25, 44, 223
lateralization, 92–93
learning, 119, 181–183, 189, 206
LeDoux, Joseph, 86, 111, 182
left hemisphere, 91–93, 97, 199, 216
liberation (see also *kaivalya*), 2–3, 8, 14, 18, 20, 31–32, 41–42, 52, 54, 72, 75–76, 80, 102, 113, 124, 154, 163, 203, 215, 222
limbic system, 98–100, 111
liṅga, 139
lists (organisation of), 8, 17, 56, 58, 88, 130, 135, 137–138, 142, 147, 150, 157, 162, 195, 215
lobha, 70

Mahābhārata, 7, 12–13, 21, 24
mahat, 39–40
maitrī (friendliness), 16, 140–141, 196–197
manas, 9, 38, 40, 43–44, 46–48, 72–73, 142, 145–146, 148, 172
mantra, 17, 24, 178, 185, 191, 214
meditation (see also *dhyāna*), 8, 10, 12–14, 20, 42, 99, 104, 108, 124, 131, 133, 140–151, 155–156, 165, 167, 174–175, 178–179, 185, 188–189, 191, 193-204, 207–211, 219–220, 223
medulla, 87, 89, 115
memory (see also *smṛti*), 5, 44–45, 51, 54–55, 66–69, 78, 84, 93–97, 100–101, 114–121, 129, 182–183, 187, 194, 198, 220, 224
midbrain, 87–88, 115
Miller, Barbara Stoler, 8, 17, 43, 125, 135, 168, 175
mindfulness (see also *smṛti*), 128–129, 133, 142, 184, 189, 191–192, 197, 223
misperception (see also *viparyaya*), 52, 84, 110–111
moha, 41, 70
mokṣa (see also *kaivalya*, liberation), 154, 163
movement, 7, 38, 40, 64, 87—89, 91–92, 94, 98–99, 104, 119–120, 149, 182, 199, 207–208, 215
muditā (joy), 16, 140–141, 196
myelin, 90

neuroanatomy, 84–101
neurons, 85–88, 91, 106, 115, 180–182, 188
neuroplasticity, 5, 180–183, 189, 203
neurotransmitters, 85, 188
Newberg, A., 186, 193, 232, 238
nidrā (sleep), 51, 53, 55, 101, 113
nirodha, 2, 19, 102, 124, 218
niyamas, 125, 161–167, 176, 204–207, 210

occipital lobe, 91, 97, 105, 117, 119, 199
oṃ, 132, 190

pain, 94, 99, 138, 140, 194–195
parietal lobes, 91, 94, 105, 107, 116–117, 193, 199
pariṇāma (see also *prakṛti*), 37, 40–41, 151
Patañjali, 15–16
perception (see also *pratyakṣa*), 5, 29, 42, 51, 54–55, 65, 69, 84–85, 94–97,

103–105, 107–108, 110, 112, 116, 120–121, 183, 196, 200–201, 215–216
Persinger, Michael, 96, 240
personality, 25, 63, 79, 84, 94–95, 128
pituitary gland, 100, 186
plasticity (see also neuroplasticity), 180–183
PNS, 86
pradhāna, 34, 39
prajñā (wisdom), 128–129, 131, 184, 190, 218, 221
prakṛti, 1, 3, 4, 13, 24, 34–43, 48, 55, 61, 63–65, 71–72, 76, 78–83, 108, 134, 150–151, 213, 216, 218, 220, 222, 226
pramāṇa (valid cognition), 51, 55, 62, 101, 103, 109
praṇava, 132–133, 135, 154–155, 163, 196, 203
prāṇāyāma (see also *prāṇa*, breath), 139, 142–143, 155–156, 168–172, 188, 197, 204, 206, 208
pratyāhāra, 155–156, 172–174, 204, 208–209
pratyakṣa (see also *pramāṇa*), 51, 103
pratyaya, 46, 54, 56–57, 67, 75, 219
prefrontal cortex, 94, 100, 111, 117, 193
projections, 88, 91, 100, 111
proto-Śiva seal, 10
puruṣa, 1, 12–13, 24–34, 41–42, 45–47, 52–53, 58, 61, 63–65, 71–72, 75–81, 102–103, 113, 129, 134–135, 145, 151, 213, 216, 218, 222–223

rāga (see also *kleśas*), 58, 62, 64–65, 69–70, 112, 148, 201, 204
rajas, 34–36, 41, 50
Ramachandran, V. S., 95–96
reticular formation, 87–89, 115
Ṛg-veda, 9, 11, 24–25
right hemisphere, 91–93, 117, 193, 216
RV 10.90 (*puruṣa* hymn), 24

ṣaḍ-aṅga-yoga (six-limbed yoga), 156–157
sādhana-pāda, 19, 152
samādhi, 8, 18–20, 67, 124, 128–131, 136–137, 152, 155–156, 175–176, 178, 184, 190, 201, 204, 209–211, 214–215, 218, 220–222, 225
samādhi-pāda, 18
samāpatti, 29, 168, 218, 220
Sāṃkhya, 1, 11, 13, 17, 21, 25, 30–31, 34, 36–37, 47, 58, 64, 156, 223
Sāṃkhya-kārikā, 25, 30, 32, 36, 45, 47, 64–65
Sāṃkhya-Yoga, 13–15, 25, 30, 220
saṃskāras, 19, 48, 54, 60, 65–72, 101, 128, 221, 222, 224–225
saṃyama (complete control), 20, 215–218
saṃyoga, 28, 34, 50, 62, 72–81, 102–103, 123
Śaṅkara, 21
sannyāsin, 94
sat-kārya-vāda, 36, 151
sattva, 34–36, 41, 47, 50, 218
ātman (soul), 12, 13, 61
kṣetrajñā (field-knower, soul), 13
sensation, 9, 12, 14, 44, 87–89, 91, 94–95, 97–101, 105, 110–111, 116, 122, 145, 147, 155–156, 160, 172–173, 193–194, 197, 199, 204, 208–210, 223
sense organs (see also *buddhīndriyas*), 34–35, 38–40, 51, 73, 86, 103, 136, 145, 160, 173, 208, 217
sickness, 135–137, 195

siddhis (extraordinary powers), 20, 26, 42, 178, 206, 214–217, 224
Śiva, 10
sleep (see also *nidrā*), 5, 13, 44, 51, 53, 55, 84, 87, 89, 99–101, 113–115, 149–150, 183, 192, 202–203, 225
smṛti (memory), 51, 54–55, 68–69, 96, 101, 128–129, 131, 184, 189–190
speech, 92, 120, 154, 159–160, 163, 214
sphoṭa, 15
split-brain patients, 92
śraddhā, 127–128, 131, 184–185, 188–189
śruti, 59
stress, 185–189, 195–196, 223
svābhāsa, 42, 46, 50, 73–74, 78
svādhyāya, 161, 201, 203, 205
synapse, 86, 99

tamas, 34–36, 41, 50, 54
tanmātras, 38–40, 150, 217
tapas, 124, 127, 153–154, 161, 164, 201–202, 204–205, 214
tattvas (existents), 12–13, 38, 140–141
Tattva-vaiśāradi, 21, 125, 139, 143, 147, 167
telencephalon (see also forebrain), 90, 98
temperature, 94, 99–100, 202, 207, 211
temporal lobes, 95–96, 111, 118
thalamus, 91, 98–99, 105, 110, 115
thirst, 30, 97, 100, 134, 162, 202–204, 215–216

Upaniṣad, 7, 9–12, 24–25, 134, 144, 149, 156, 213
uparāga (colouration), 50, 77–79, 103
upāyas, 128, 184, 190
upāyas (see also *abhyāsa-vairāgya*), 128, 184, 190
upekṣā (equanimity), 16, 140–141, 196

Vācaspati Miśra, 21, 54, 139, 141–142
vairāgya (detachment), 30, 124, 126, 128, 130, 134, 151, 183
Vaiśeṣika, 9
vāsanās, 46, 66, 69–70, 75, 84, 101
Vedānta, 21
vibhūti-pāda, 19
vibhūtis (extraordinary powers), 20, 26
vidyā, 127
vikalpa (mental/intellectual construction), 51, 53, 55, 101, 112–113
violence, 60, 159, 165
viparyaya (erroneous cognition), 51, 55–57, 65, 101, 109–110
vīrya, 128–129, 131, 184–185, 189
viśeṣas, 37–38, 40
vision, 11, 26–30, 52, 59, 62–63, 75, 88, 91–92, 95, 97, 99, 104–111, 119, 135, 181, 193, 199–200, 209
viveka (see also *prajñā*, wisdom), 68, 134, 151
vṛttis (see also *citta-vṛttis*), 29, 48, 51–58, 65–67, 72, 75–77, 79, 96, 102–103, 109, 124–126, 152, 183, 218–219
Vyākaraṇa-mahābhāṣya, 15
Vyāsa, 21
vyutthita-citta (distracted mind), 19, 125, 152

wakefulness, 54, 89, 100, 113, 115, 202
Werner, Karel, 11, 25
Whicher, Ian, 223
Woods, J. H., 8, 43, 175

yamas, 158–161, 176, 204–207, 210
Yoga (history of), 7–22
yogaś citta-vṛtti-nirodhaḥ, 2, 7, 51, 55–56, 124, 218–226
Yoga-sūtra (nature of), 16–20
Yoga-sūtra-bhāṣya-vivaraṇa, 2, 21, 56–59, 125, 135, 147–148, 154, 157–158, 160, 163, 167–171, 218